*Christen Mattix*

# Skein

**skein / skān /** n.

1.      a length of thread or yarn, loosely coiled and knotted

2.      a tangled or complicated arrangement, state, or situation

3.      a flock of wild geese or swans in flight

Probably from Latin *scamnum* bench, stool.

Cover Design – Judy Ko and Christen Mattix
Cover Photo – Vanessa Osage
Editing – Miles Mattix
Proofreading – Samuel Mattix and Miles Mattix

Mattix, Christen J., 1977-
Skein: the Heartbreaks and Triumphs of a Long Distance Knitter
Library of Congress 2017909562


ISBN 978-0-6929-0150-2


www.christenmattix.com

# CONTENTS

## PART FIVE. CONNECTIONS MADE VISIBLE

# AUTHOR'S NOTE

I used my personal journals to write Part One of this book, and blog posts to write Parts Two and Three, which accounts for a difference in writing style that I have chosen to retain. For photos of this project, please visit christenmattix.com. Whenever I missed my hour of knitting at the bench, I made a note of it in these pages. I have omitted many journal entries, people and conversations that, though important to me, were too numerous to include. I have also changed identifying details and names to protect the privacy of several people, particularly neighbors that I interacted with on a regular basis. Direct quotations of conversations with people at the bench are pieced together from memory, and are not verbatim. None of the characters or events are composites; at times I grouped descriptions (such as character development) from several entries into one. I have included my misperceptions and revisions to my thoughts as evidence that this story unfolded in real time. I have told the truth to the best of my knowledge, except when to share it would harm someone else.

*This book is dedicated with my deepest gratitude to the people I met at the bench.*

# For Longing (Cyanotype Blue)
*by Christen Mattix*

I sit still
in hopes of running
into you. All night
and all day
I never stop calling
your name, hovering
like incense caught
in my hair.

Your absence fills the sky
like contrails, stretches out
as a shadow at sundown.
...the stupid distractions,
like tire tracks cut
into my internal landscape...

I touch catkins,
measure the sky
between each leaf,
watch the swallow scissor
its way from roof
to lawn, leaving
an invisible line, decipher
silence.

# PART ONE

# WAITING FOR THE BUS

# 1

# The Bench

Here's how I decided to knit a half-mile blue line from a bench down to Bellingham Bay. After commuting two quarters from Seattle to Bellingham to teach, my Seattle boyfriend and I broke up, so I decided to move to Bellingham for good, settling into my new home that looked out on the ultramarine waters of the bay. I loved that view like it was family, like it was my religion. I used to sit on a crooked bench up the street from my house, losing myself in the blue water that glinted from afar through a gap in the trees. And I loved that rickety bench with a mixture of ferocity and nostalgia. It was a vestige from the past, a former stop for a bus line that no longer ran. As someone whose car had stalled for good in an intersection moments after I arrived in town, I often wished that the bus still ran, and that I could take it to the top of the massive sledding hill where I lived—instead of breathlessly schlepping my groceries uphill on foot.

I am an artist, and as such, I feel drawn to the overlooked, things that no longer serve the purpose intended for them. One day, while sitting on the bench and absorbing the blueness of the

7

water into every cell of my body, an idea popped into my mind. What if I knit a blue line down to Bellingham Bay to connect myself to the ocean? I smiled at the crazy thought, then shelved it as another waste product of my overactive imagination. But the idea kept pestering me, like a dog scratching at the door to go out. I even awoke thinking about it.

In the meantime, my newfound teaching job took an unexpected turn. When it came time to renew my adjunct teaching contract in the winter of 2012, I was not offered any classes except a summer lecture class. I was given no explanation, and as an adjunct, I wasn't owed one. A deadly silence swallowed up my polite email inquiries to my Chair. (After she stepped down from her position, I got invited to teach again in 2015 but that didn't help me in 2012). So I sat on the bench and stared at the water and wondered how I would survive, how I could cough up my monthly rent on a year lease that I had so hopefully signed a few months earlier as I began my new life in Bellingham.

In an act of faith, I cut out the words "I HAVE ENOUGH" from black paper and stuck them to my wall. I started praying like never before, scribbling in my journal to find a way forward. I had never felt so lost. I cobbled together a series of part-time jobs; in desperation, I took anything I could find—babysitting for $10 per hour, and other temp work that was unreliable at best.

Suddenly, I could identify with the abandoned bench covered in lichen and mold that no longer had a job to perform. The idea of knitting the line to the bay had grown more insistent, and since I didn't have anything better to do, I gave in. I was scared of venturing out of the privacy of my home, afraid of the unknown. I was sure my neighbors would think I was crazy. I didn't even know if it was art I'd be making or just some eccentric bit of knitting like yarnbombing gone awry.

However, once I said yes to the idea, I started preparing for it with gusto. All the details had to be considered—the color and type of yarn, the look and feel of the needles, the daily structure. I went to JoAnn Fabrics and paced up and down the yarn aisles, stopping to look at all the shades of blue: peacock, navy, baby, robin's egg. I held the color of the water in my mind's eye, wanting to match my memory of it perfectly. Then I saw it. A brilliant, deep blue with the slightest hint of green, the color of the sky in a Giotto fresco. I scanned the label: Carron Eco Soft Yarn. Hue: Ocean. That cinched it for me. The fiber was spun from bamboo fibers and recycled plastic drinking bottles. I loved knowing that I would be knitting plastic water bottles, alluding to both thirst and recycling. I found a vintage pair of size 10 steel knitting needles at the Goodwill after digging through a pile of ugly, plastic needles of various shapes and sizes. The pair I chose looked like two huge nails, long enough to have a strong visual impact. They also had a nice weight in my hand unlike the new, ultralight chrome needles.

Now I was ready. I just needed to pick a start date. I chose May 1st, the first day of the growing season, a day I hoped would prove warm enough to knit outside. It is also Mary's Day, and I liked the pun on Mary and *mer*, the French word for sea, just as the color of the bay echoed the blue of Mary's mantle. Ironically, though I didn't know it at the time, May 1st is also International Worker's Day. I was blissfully unaware that I was about to set out on my most laborious project to date, one that would stretch the limits of my endurance beyond what I ever thought was possible.

**2**

# May Day

May 1, 2012

At 7:55 a.m., I put yarn and knitting needles in a basket, stepped outside and wound my way up the trail that led around my house, crossing the street to the bench as nonchalantly as possible—though my heart was pounding and my whole body was thrumming with excitement and nerves. With my eyes focused on the knitting, I became intensely aware of sounds—car receding in the distance, boys hollering as they ran down the hill, a crow's silky wings making the sound of a zipper. I overheard snippets of family gossip. "Don't you think it's strange that my sister is thinking about moving back to the Midwest and buying a house after Mom is gone?" I realized that my work on the bench would be less about seeing, and more about listening.

And that it was about time and patience *vis a vis* my impatience. Slowing down, tackling a huge dream one stitch at a time. Not multitasking, talking on the phone or checking messages. I was doing something completely countercultural—I half expected someone to chew me out for not being "busy" enough. One boy had to wait while a truck drove by before he crossed the road. "That truck wasted my time," he said.

It was only my first day knitting, and I already felt impatient. My mind jumped ahead trying to calculate how many hours the darn thing was going to take and whether I could finish it in one month. Somehow, I know that is not what this project is about. I purposely didn't put myself on a schedule with a fixed number of feet per day to complete. It will be done when it is done.

One lady said, "You must be waiting for something."

"Yup," I said. Waiting for Godot, I thought, pleased that my existential quandary was visible to others.

As I knit, I realized this work was also about naked presence…A quiet invitation to be. The only way I could be more present would be to sit and do nothing. There was space on the bench for someone to join me. So it was also about my loneliness, a longing for companionship. So much of the piece is still unknown to me. I only know my instructions: knit to the sea. I do not know how often to knit each day or whether it's okay to skip a day or knit at different times. I chose 8-9 a.m. as my baseline, allowing myself the freedom to knit at other times too if I so desired.

I sat on the bench like a sculpture, moving only my hands and needles. There was something pleasing about being stationary amidst the movement swirling around me—I was a rock in a stream of cars, joggers and walkers. It heightened my role as an artist, a seer, a listener. An observer of culture. What a funny job.

By the time the hour ended, my hands were numb and I was glad to retreat into my warm house. Not one person had spoken to me the entire hour.

May 2, 2012

My hour of knitting started out sunny, but ended with tiny raindrops freckling my pants. It felt like 45 degrees sitting on the bench and I was grateful for my long underwear. If you want to learn how to slow time down, knitting a half-mile is one way to do it! The hour yawned, feeling as if it would never end. Mornings are not a social time; people are headed to work or school. I recently decided to add some afternoon sessions. A dark-eyed neighbor said she liked seeing me there knitting, and then she got into her car. She looked interesting and creative in her flowing dress and long hair. I videoed the sky until the battery died on my camera.

## May 3, 2012

I sat solitary as a crow on the bench in my black coat while real crows cawed at me. One flew with a string to her nest. The knitting has begun to take on greater significance now as I knit in the rain and the line begins to spill down the bench onto the pavement.

Today I thought about my need for ritual; knitting as a ritual practice. And knots. Tying and untying knots and the wide range of connotations conjured. Positive knots–interwoven–versus negative knots–bondage. The line as blue tears. Cry me a river. Rivulet to the ocean. The artist as lunatic to be avoided and ignored. The nonplace of contemporary art in the public sphere. Who is my audience? God. And anyone else who cares to pay attention. Who cares? One person did, said she appreciated the poetry of it. "You look like a perfect snapshot of life in the Northwest, waiting at a bus stop, knitting in the rain," she said.

## May 4, 2012

Rushing out the door but today was a breakthrough! The knitting has gotten too long to ignore. One lady tried to "help" move it off the road. Two walkers, Rachel and Grace, introduced themselves and shared their sighting of starfish mating on the dock. The bench is becoming a safe place, a hub. Several more people lingered and talked. We are so in need of public meeting space in this country that's neutral and inviting. I like to think of the role of the artist as connector, community builder. Knitting as time made visible. Art as an extension of the body. Warm, touchable art. Body as extension of the earth, water, and sky. Art and artist embedded in the community.

I was troubled by my use of the word "shift" in talking to someone about my hour of knitting. *Shift* belongs to the language of labor rather than poetry or prayer.

After spending the past four days listening intently, I am now able to distinguish the footfalls of a woman, a man, a child, or an elderly person.

# 3

# Lunacy

May 5, 2012

Today a slight man with glasses came up and said in a low, gravelly voice, "So you've been sitting here knitting for several days now. There must be a tale to tell."

When I told him I was knitting a line to the ocean, he threw back his head and laughed for the sheer joy and lunacy of it.

He said, "I live in the house across from yours. How strange that I've never seen you."

"That's why I need to do this project—to meet my neighbors," I said. He divulged his dog's name, B.J., but didn't tell me his name. Then a lady with a dog greeted him, "Hi Art!" A lot of the dog owners know each other. Dogs are a good, safe talking point, a way for humans to connect.

After Art left, I felt a thrill of electricity and shivered with joy. I knew that the art was its own reward, the experience of doing this project, priceless.

That was it for interaction although I notice cars are slowing down in order to avoid driving over the knit line. The knitting is going to get a lot of wear and tear when it becomes necessary for cars to drive over it. I really need to pick up the pace and knit more. Ideally I'd like to be done by the end of May. It was very cold today and as usual, the going was comfortable for the first half hour, and painful and dreary for the second. It occurs to me that we Americans move too fast. Go, go, go. We're crazy but we don't realize it. My piece is about slow, slow, slow.

I thought about lunatics and lunacy today when a woman walked by calling to her Sheltie dog, "Come on, Luna."

The full moon is coming up now as I write.

## May 6, 2012

Beautiful, clear day. As usual my hands got very cold towards the end of the knitting. Two people, actually three, came up. One man took a picture of me and said I looked like Whistler's mother sitting so straight and tall in my black coat. This is a well-educated, cultured bunch. A woman with long hair named Mollie told me they do a neighborhood block party in July and she'll be sure to give me a flyer.

She asked, "Will there be publicity, a press release, about your knitting installation?"

"No. I am getting the word out one person at a time," I said. This personal aspect is becoming an important part of the piece–I am making the work in and for a particular community, not "the general public." There is something special about an event that is not broadcast in the impersonal mass media. "The real will be rare," I remember my professor saying in reference to Paul Cezanne. In addition, it's subversive in these days of tight deadlines to create a project that has a clear goal but an unknown completion date.

I told one woman that I was knitting to the sea, and she smiled and said she could see it in her mind. Is an event as "real" if it is caught on camera, planned and executed as something that just happens? I don't think so. Today I didn't videotape myself knitting and I'm thinking of getting rid of the camera altogether. I have no idea what I'll do with all the video I'm collecting anyway. The camera is intimidating and off-putting to passersby, and it frames the work as "art" or "film" or "performance." I want the naked act itself.

May 7, 2012

No video today and I felt much freer! I think this project is best documented with still photos. I don't want 60 hours of video to wade through. Making time every day to knit is helping me realize how much time I actually have. It's expanding time instead of shrinking it. A man asked me what my knitting rate is. I told him I'm not keeping track.

Grace and Rachel came by. Grace says she plans to weed under the bench because the grass is soon going to touch my bum.

### Afternoon Knit.

My tall neighbor who looks like a former basketball champion pushed a noisy gas-powered beast across his lawn and mowed under my bench too. He introduced himself as Pete, gave me a high five and an "All right!" when I told him what I am doing. He invited me to just knock on the door whenever I get thirsty. I also talked to a woman in her 50s with kind, brown eyes. She asked the meaning behind my knitting. I told her about my longing for the ocean and that the project is called "For Longing."

I tied a stick to the end of the knit line so it wouldn't blow all over the place. Most cars are slowing down to go gently over the knitting; it feels like a metaphor for the vulnerability of putting my art out in the world. A UPS driver carefully drove on the wrong side of the street to avoid running over the knit line. I pray no one has an accident because of me! At the end of my sit, Pete who was talking on a cellphone on his front step, thanked me twice. I'm not sure why.

May 8, 2012

Today someone sat on the bench with me for the first time: Grace. She was dressed up, freshly showered, on her way to a Parent Teacher Association meeting. She watched the cars go by, noting that many cars are slowing down and trying to go around the knit line. I find it touching how much respect people have for handicraft. I'm thankful that the knit line is narrow, curling in on itself like a rope. I hope it's strong enough to

17

withstand the tires! I have decided to hide a camera in the bushes and try to capture some footage of the cars slowing down to go over the knit line. It's like a psychological speed bump. I love that in slowing myself down, I'm also inviting others to do the same.

So far, the friendliest people have been the stay-at-home moms, and the retired people with dogs. Grace talked about how few people stopped to chat with me as a reflection of how little time people have.

I said, "We need people like you to balance the rest of us nuts."

She said, "I love my stay-at-home mom life, and the fact that I have time for people and PTA meetings. We need each other."

## May 9, 2012

I hid a camera in my landlady's yard hoping to capture the cars slowing down to go around the line. Instead most cars zipped over it. Disappointing. Almost no one stopped to talk for the first hour. Even though the sun was shining, it was chilly and my hands are still numb now as I write. The man with the green and orange hat stopped again; this time he said hi, and introduced himself as Mike. Retired, plays guitar, and fixes up houses to resell as a hobby. Mike was on his way to the Firehouse Cafe to meet up with friends. He left and time stretched out again.

Grace and Rachel appeared and introduced a friend and her dachshund. Then an older guy wearing a submarine hat introduced himself as Donald. He entertained us with tales about his stint in the navy, sitting in a sonar tower, listening to the whales. His job was all listening, no seeing. And he only got to send one 15 word message a month to his wife. Talk about longing! We met Donald's dog too, Freddie. My neighbor Pete emerged from his house and gave me a fatherly pat on the back. Grace thanked him for cutting the grass under the bench so she didn't have to do it. I had five people hanging out with me at the bench and talking!

They said, "Look what you've done–you've created community, a happening!"

I said, "I don't take responsibility for it."

They said, "Then you're a catalyst for community."

I was very moved. The impromptu gathering was so unexpected and magical after the slow hour of knitting.

## May 10, 2012

I don't know how this experience could get any better! Today Grace brought me four skeins of Carron "ocean" blue yarn. She said they were a gift and that they were on sale when she went to pay for them. The checker refused her 40% off coupon because they rang up already discounted. As we visited, she began untwisting my knit line for me, and Rachel joined her like bridal attendants smoothing out my train. They added about three feet to the line so that it crossed the road.

Mike stopped by and said, "You're becoming part of my morning routine." He intentionally moved to 16th Street because the neighbors greeted each other, unlike other neighborhoods. "At around 13th Street, the neighborliness goes away when you get down to the condos and apartments where the more transient populations live," he said.

Mike said, "Your knitting to the sea is like a fairy tale."

I found out that he plays jazz guitar and invited him to come play his guitar at the bench sometime.

"That's funny, I was just thinking about doing that today!" he exclaimed.

So if the weather is good, I hope to enjoy live music tomorrow! I would really like to record it but I don't want to be invasive.

A mom and her son came up and the mom said, "I hope I'm not interrupting—What are you doing?" Then they came back later and the mom said her son had a question he was dying to ask me but he was too shy, "Do you knit all night?"

I got a good laugh out of that one. I love how this piece provokes a sense of wonderment and imagination. A lot of people start their question, "We were wondering…"

Today a lady actually parked her car, got out and came over to talk to me. Her name is Karen. She lives in the yellow house with the fragrant lavender in the front yard.

I also met Michelle, a woman with a soft voice. She said, "My kids recognized you as The Fates who also knit blue yarn from one of their sci-fi books."

I said, "This project connects to a lot of myths about yarn—the story of Penelope, for example, from *Ulysses*."

All this time, I was surrounded by amazing neighbors and I never knew it! What a revelation. I am now thinking of knitting the rope as a metaphor for community building. Up to this point, I've been guilty of being too busy and transient for community. I've always left the house in a rush, dashing to get groceries or catch the bus. It took me sitting still with this bizarre goal of knitting at a bench to open me up to the people around me.

## Afternoon Knit

I met Janelle with her flaming red hair from a bottle and her frowning daughter Camellia. Janelle has a baby on the way in one month and is very pregnant.

After she left, I sat thinking about this knitting project as an embodiment of constancy.

Then my friend Vanessa and her daughter came and we sat on the bench together and Vanessa somehow picked up the conversation where my mind had left off.

"My middle name was Constance before I changed it to Elwa—the name of a river. There's no constant except change, right?" Vanessa said.

I thought about God and was silent. Her daughter posed on the bench wearing heart-shaped pink sunglasses. Oh to see the world through the eyes of love, with the heart of a child! I feel my heart opening as a result of all the positive interactions with people at the bench.

## May 11, 2012

The only person who stopped to talk today was Mike. He brought his hiking guitar and played "Sunny Side of the Street," "Blue Skies," and several love songs while I tapped my foot to the music. Whether on purpose or by coincidence, most of the songs had "blue" in them. It made the knitting go so much faster. I had hoped he would sit but he stood on the corner like he was serenading me, which made me a bit self-conscious. He's been playing for years, and is excellent, but really shy when it comes to playing in public. My project inspired him to bust out his guitar; he was going to take it down to play at the Firehouse Café next.

## Evening Knit

This afternoon I was in a funk. Discontented and ill-at-ease for no good reason. In my "not enough" and "too much" state of mind. Not enough love–life is too lonely, long and hard. Not fast enough—I was even frustrated with my vegetable seeds for not growing more quickly. I had too many dishes stacked in the sink…and I lugged grocery bags and milk up the hill which was too steep. I bought new underwear and discovered they're too big like elephant undies. I finally decided to just knit. My funk lifted and my mind became clear and serene.

I chatted with Alice (Donald's wife) who was walking Freddie and a stray pug. Alice is a sparkly lady in her late 60's.

She said, gazing fondly down at the pug, "It's a dog inside that monstrous body and I love it anyway."

She said the pug went on a joy run—it still had its ragged leash on when it showed up in her yard. She's a dog magnet. Lost and stray dogs go to her yard and she returns them to their owners.

Some people came up as we were talking and said to me, "Who knows, you may change the world."

I said, "I doubt that, but I do know that I am being changed."

And Alice chimed in, "Yeah, look at all these neighbors

21

you're getting to know."

The sun started setting. I could smell the intoxicating wood-smoke from a fireplace, and a scent like crab apple blossoms or lilacs nearby. Seagulls shrilled, a train whistled, two teens drove by and slowed down to ask what I was making.

"Cool beans!" they said, and hopped out to take a picture of me with the sunset.

I'm trying to knit some extra sessions early on in this project. The weather is so favorable right now. It feels like what I'm supposed to do.

## May 12, 2012

A very uneventful sit (which, I imagine, will be the majority) so I had to endure my noisy brain. Today, it was abuzz with thoughts of gallery representation. I think I'm stuck on this topic because I recently spent time with an artist friend who has stacks of unsold art and it really depressed the hell out of me. Again, the question, What is my purpose, my vision? And how do I get there? Two young people asked how to walk to Amtrak but did not comment on the knit line stretching across the street.

## May 13, 2012

It's really warm, my hands are no longer going numb. Mike sat and chatted with me for about half an hour. His concert down at the Firehouse was such a great hit that he hopes to play every week now. He said I was the kick in the pants that he needed. One of his friends saw him "serenading" me and said maybe he'll bring his guitar down to the café too.

At the end of my sit, a woman came by. "It's so beautiful," she kept saying, fingering the yarn.

I told her my dream to knit down to the water and she loved the idea.

"I've watched it grow every day," she said.

I like that word *grow*—evoking generativity, time, change.

This project keeps growing in wonderful ways that I can't anticipate.

## May 14, 2012

Another sunny day. I'm still on skein number two! The line has passed the level sidewalk on the other side of the street and started going down the hill. Cars are slowing down and waiting for my permission again. It was pretty quiet though I had a couple of good conversations. I enjoyed talking to Art (who still has not introduced himself.) He teaches Qigong. He said he tries to avoid healing people except as a kick start because he wants them to heal themselves through a regular practice. It made me think about the importance of time as medicine, and the necessity of our full participation in our cure.

At the end of my sit, I received another gift. A pile of dirt fell off a truck right in the middle of Taylor Ave, at the steepest part below the stop sign. At first, I thought, how tacky. Then I saw it for what it was–rich, dark compost for my garden which has terribly depleted soil. So I scooped up four pots worth.

## Afternoon Knit

A man with a leaf blower apologized for kicking up dust. People in cars went by grinning from ear to ear, some slowed down to ask my permission to pass. A young mom pushed a wailing baby and two children in a stroller up the hill.

I met Pete's wife, Cynthia, and felt an instant connection to this tall, fine-boned woman with large hazel eyes and a brown pixie hairdo. Pete sat on the bench a minute or two. They've been on vacation in North Carolina.

As the minutes tick by on this project, I've been thinking about the difference between Christo's installations and mine. Christo claims his work is about joy, aesthetics and nothing else. My piece is fraught with symbolism and meaning and has a title that is poetic rather than descriptive. But I love and admire Christo so. Giving all for love.

23

## May 15, 2012

Sunny and clear. Today I found a gift of lamb's ear leaves on the bench. The project is beginning to feel endless. I'm worried people will just start to ignore me as the novelty fades, and I'll be so bored!

## May 16, 2012

Grace came and sat with me for a few minutes and I noted that Rachel hasn't been walking with Grace much lately.

Grace said, "Rachel is taking a class...Walking uphill alone is a lot harder."

I said, "Knitting alone is hard."

She said, "Everything is harder alone."

Mike said hi but he was too cold in his sleeveless shirt and carried on. He's writing music down at the café so his buddy can play with him.

Two large boats and a top-heavy tug boat floated in the bay below. I've just about finished my second skein of yarn. The project is losing its novelty for me. From here on out, it will probably be sheer plod! My mind wandered a lot, and I started writing an artist statement in my head. Then I debated whether to apply for a grant for this project. Christo would disapprove—he raises all his own money through the sale of his drawings.

## May 17, 2012

Started skein three today. I got goosebumps knitting in the cold wind, even though the sun was shining. Rachel told me about her daughter and friend who finger-knitted enough multicolored yarn to make a huge ball.

"They were doing it for World Peace. They didn't know how the world works, but they were very passionate about it," Rachel said.

I didn't tell her about my "Knitting Meditation for Peace in the Middle East," a 10 day "knit in" at a gallery where I knit a 40-foot long blood-red scarf. I was moved that her girls had had the same instinct as me to knit for peace.

Grace and Rachel are calling my project, "River to the Sea." They advised me to attach a little note to the end of the knit line so people would know not to pull on it or cut it! Grace asked me if I could knit faster if I used fewer stitches but the main thing that slows me down is reversing the needles at the end of each row—fewer stitches wouldn't solve that problem.

## Evening Knit

A lady told me that if I was waiting for the bus, I must have been waiting for a long time! I have decided to commit to doing three hours of knitting per day. [Note: this resolution lasted a day.] I feel the weather is holding steady for me and I need to do my part. The sky was dramatic tonight. Big piles of clouds that went from lilac to rose. Stunning but my camera couldn't capture it.

## May 18, 2012

The dark-eyed woman who wears dresses to work said, "So you're knitting to the bay?" She must be really busy because she rarely stops to chat.

Art did some calculations and said, "You'll be knitting for the next 200 days."

I said, "I've added some shifts."

"Maybe you should add graveyard shift," he said and I laughed.

## May 19, 2012

Gorgeous, quiet Saturday but for the murder of crows cawing nonstop in a tree nearby. In the absence of visitors, my mind was very busy today with money-making schemes and how to get into more art shows.

A group of young blond women drove by blasting loud music. They had crossed the road and were heading up the hill when I heard them scream, "Oh my gosh! It goes all the way across the road. That's crazy!"

People ask me every day, "How far does it go?"

I would like to say, "Come on people, that's the point. You're supposed to walk down and find out." But I say politely, "A little ways down the hill..."

## May 20, 2012

A bald man in a red truck stopped to tell me there had been three deer standing behind me.

I've been thinking about the blue rivulet flowing down to the ocean as a metaphor for the love within me merging with infinite Love beyond all knowing, both immanent and transcendent. Not empty me reaching, yearning for what I haven't got, but an overflowing of love towards Love. This gives meaning to the process and not just the destination.

## Evening Knit

Misty rain. The wet yarn stuck to my fingers so the going was slow. A woman rolled down her car window and said, "Magical realism?" I liked that.

A man and woman came by. The man sang his own mash up of *Hansel and Gretel* and *Amazing Grace* to me, "I once was lost, but now I have the blue rope..."

This project is funnier in the rain. I quite enjoyed myself.

## May 28, 2012

Grey and cold. The knit passed by quickly because my friend and journalist Cheryl arrived and with great energy and chutzpah, began interviewing passersby about my project. I wish we had gotten a picture of Cheryl typing on her Apple laptop while I knit beside her on the bench.

## May 29, 2012

The sky is bright despite the cloud covering. My busy, dark-eyed neighbor surprised me on her lunch break by coming and sitting on the bench with me. After weeks of minimal interaction, I felt victorious as if I'd tamed a wild animal.

She said, "This knitting is such a joyful way of connecting the community. My husband and I are wondering how much the total purchase of yarn will cost you?"

I said, "I don't know but if you want to save your JoAnn fabric coupons for me that would be a great help." She was excited to support the project.

People have started comparing the project to Christo which is appropriate because I probably owe him for my inspiration. [Christo is an artist who constructs sublime, large-scale installations like buildings wrapped in shiny fabric or temporary silky fences stretched across miles of ranch land.] Even though I wasn't thinking of his piece *Running Fence* when the idea to knit to the bay came to me, it was whispering in my subconscious.

## Afternoon Knit

Gorgeous and sunny now! I feel like I am living the dream. Heartbreakingly beautiful out with a little breeze. So glad I'm here to see it. You can never knit on the same bench twice.

## May 30, 2012

Cloudy day, strong chance of rain. I can feel the cars going over the line when it's at a certain tension, like it's an extension of me. I'm hoping to finish this knitting project before summer which means I only have three more weeks.

## Afternoon Knit

Scent of lilacs on the breeze. I am grateful the rain has held off. I met Steve the Gardener who does edging and yard work. He used to live on South Hill until he lost his job and got divorced and couldn't afford it anymore. He told me to beware of motorcycles with dragging kickstands. Two cute, confident grade school girls came and chatted for a while. They explained that the reason I don't see many girls go past the bench is that the girls use a different (secret) route. Three boys put up a poster about recycling as part of an inane school project.

A man told me from his car, "I saw you from a distance and I thought, she looks like she's knitting, but I didn't believe my imagination!"

I am starting to tell people it's a fairy tale and that seems to answer the "why" question very nicely.

## May 31, 2012

I knit in a soft rain today as water trickled down my ear and dew drops collected on my fingers. I asked a boy with an umbrella to videotape me knitting in the rain but he said he didn't have time even though he was early for school. I said good morning and tried to talk to two boys but they totally ignored me. I hate that! And I hate the dark tinted car windows that shun all exchange and the earbuds that block communication. But I enjoyed my knit. Accepting the warm, fresh rain made it just another experience to relish. Grace videotaped me knitting in the rain but it makes me seasick to watch because she taped it while hiking up over the hill.

## Afternoon Knit

When I returned for my late afternoon knit, the sky had brightened and the bench dried off. Jay birds scolded while a lawn mower droned on and on. The enthusiastic lady with the shade hat came by excited to see the progress.

A man said, "That's a long leash you have there."

I retorted, "It's NOT a leash!"

## June 1, 2012

Warm gusts of wind and I overheard a man telling a girl it was 69 degrees today. I finally learned the name of my dark-eyed neighbor—Carla—who reminds me of a former flower child with her long hair and flowing dresses. She wanted to know if I could use other colors of yarn since she has some extra skeins lying around but told her that I'm very particular about the color.

I'm still shocked by how anti-social the children are. Today I said "Morning!" to a boy about five years old and he looked right through me. It was a most disconcerting experience, as if I were a ghost.

The wind gifted me with beautiful mental snapshots like the pink rhododendron flower that landed upside down on the line, or the line running through a patch of fallen red leaves. I am like the weather today. Sad, tossed about by change. A friend of mine is moving far, far away.

## Afternoon Knit

The rain held off the entire two hours and a warm wind caressed me. I had a remarkable conversation with a small woman named Frances.

She said, "I've been defending you to my critical friends as we drive by the knitting bench together in the car. I feel a real attraction to the piece and want to know what is going on in your head. I know that's personal."

I listened as she told how she had lost her job, gotten divorced, and was now selling her home because she couldn't afford the mortgage anymore. But God had gotten her through it and always provides. She grew up Catholic and is of the Baha'i faith now.

## June 2, 2012

Today was rainy and overcast. I met a tall man with a white beard wearing a "Canadian Academy" hat, and holding the leash of his boxer, Indigo. I noticed his dog's leash was the same color as my line so I asked to videotape it, and just then three dogs converged on the street corner from multiple directions with their owners. Indigo tugged on his leash, gazing intently across the street at another (female) boxer and we all laughed.

## June 3, 2012

No knit today.

## June 4, 2012

Drizzly and cool out. Started my sixth skein of yarn. I am becoming a part of the landscape. Birdsong surrounds me. A hummingbird hovered briefly above my head. The joggers continue to ignore me but the school boys have started going down the sidewalk on my side of the hill with the blue line. A

Hispanic truck driver stopped to get directions back to the freeway. No Grace, Rachel or Mike sightings today. I miss them.

## Afternoon Knit

Frances brought two Baha'i prayer booklets. She said she couldn't stay long and asked if we could pray together. I said sure and she prayed from the booklet a beautiful prayer that ended with these lines:

> *O God! Thou art more friend to me than I am to myself.*
> *I dedicate myself to Thee, O Lord.*

## June 5, 2012

Light drizzle, cold.

## June 7, 2012

I'm soggy, still stubbornly knitting without a raincoat.

## June 8, 2012

I wound the knit line around a larger stick today to transport it. Rachel and Grace said that soon I would have a muscular young man (preferably oiled and shirtless) helping me move it like the Ark of the Covenant.

My favorite part of every knitting session is walking home. I see so much more clearly after an hour of knitting.

Stillness leads to vision.

## Evening Knit

Tonight I witnessed the clouds turning purple and candy-pink during the lovely sunset. Two older ladies asked what "possessed" me to do this project and I answered in a vague way. The line is getting very long and heavy now. I got rid of the stick that I had been wrapping the knit line around and wrapped it around my arm instead. A hose reel is so ugly. What else could I possibly use to carry my line?

## June 9, 2012

My mind wandered a lot today because of the cutting wind. I use thoughts as a buffer against unpleasant sensations! A helpful idea came to roll up the knit line in a ball. It looks massive next to the smaller balls of yarn like a cuckoo in a nest.

I met Michael, Michelle's husband and a kinetic sculptor, with his black Lab, Finn. It's wonderful to meet artists while I'm making art. I feel relaxed and self-assured unlike the nervous jitters I get in the gallery scene.

Frances stopped by on her bike and I was struck by the quality of her voice like a deep, slow-moving river. I asked if she's from the East Coast and she confirmed she's from Connecticut. Also, the petite woman with the Sheltie dogs came by. I need to get her name.

A rush of wings! A flock of black birds suddenly rose into the air, and landed in the Douglas fir. I felt awe. I felt God then.

## June 11, 2012

Big news—Cheryl's article on my knit finally got published in the *Herald*. A huge antidote to the doldrums I've been in! Cynthia stopped and chatted. She just retired from being a nurse. I find her face so beautiful like a queen with kind, deep eyes.

On warmer days like today, my muscles don't clench up and I actually enjoy the sit. Finished my sixth skein of yarn. Though I was tempted, I decided not to put out a piggy bank for donations towards yarn—it's too much like panhandling. Wrong connotation.

## June 12, 2012

Patience connects time to eternity. Not sure where I read that. Today an elderly lady parked and sat with me, Marilyn of Michigan, a knitter and a quilter. The first person who has sought me out after reading the news article. How does it feel to be a celebrity? Very normal. And humbling. I've got a long way to go!

## June 13, 2012

A Coast Guard cutter and a large ship were parked in the bay. I saw a lot of my regulars today. Our culture is short on two things: community and contemplation. And I get to have both.

Rachel and Grace visited for a long time. Grace had a headache and Rachel massaged Grace as we talked about breathing to get through pain. This led somehow to the topic of childbirth and African women giving birth alone in the bushes.

## June 14, 2012

My neighbor Roxie (the owner of the Shelties) came and tucked a windbreaker and a fleece over my cold legs as I knit. The wind had been nippy and I was wearing a skirt since it is laundry day so I was grateful. I said good morning to a scared hunched over woman and she said—almost inaudibly—good morning. It's a start.

## June 15, 2012

Gorgeous, warm morning. The little boys gave me a big WOW in passing. Cynthia said hi. I'm curious what she is doing every day as she comes and goes like clockwork but it seems to annoy her when I ask.

I had trouble focusing because my genitals were on fire, I'm not sure why. Birds sang like they'd lost their minds, while my mind wandered a lot. I'm knitting only one hour a day now because the rest of my day was feeling too short, bookended by two hours of knitting.

## June 16, 2012

Light rain. Carla came out in her slippers with a cup of coffee for me.

## June 17, 2012

A gift awaited me at the end of my knit rope when I went to collect it to roll back up the hill. Someone had tied a pink peony bud to the line like an offering, a valentine. No wonder a guy asked me if I was fishing!

## June 19, 2012

It's cold out today. My friend Ann who taught Psychology in Eastern Washington came by again (in shorts!) She's a strong, honest woman who loved the challenge of working with teens from low income, Native American backgrounds. It was a way for her to test whether her academic knowledge works, she told me.

My neighbor Mollie drove up and gave me $10 for yarn and invited me to the block party. Grace and Rachel's walking schedules are changing because this is their daughter's last week of school so I probably won't see them anymore.

I was surprised by a cop in a car, and nervously wondered if he would shut down my knitting across the road but instead he asked in a squeaky voice what I was doing with a curious and open expression on his face.

"Be careful or your line might get caught on a car," he said as he drove away.

I just laughed. It must be so hard to be an emergency responder, always hearing about what goes wrong.

## June 20, 2012

The mailman drove by and said, "You go, girl!" Started eighth skein of yarn.

## June 23, 2012

Knit in downpour this evening. My yarn basket is molding. Staying present is much harder for me right now. Lots of mental rabbit trails, and it's hard to return to the moment. But sitting here allows people to share with me and connect on a much deeper level than they would otherwise, and that makes it feel worthwhile regardless of my ability to stay concentrate.

## June 24, 2012

This hour felt very long. It turned out my alarm didn't go off so I knit an extra 48 minutes. Michael stopped and talked about interactive art with me.

I asked what he meant by *interactive*, and he said, "Art that allows the viewer to physically change the art within certain parameters."

Interactive artwork is the ultimate form of receptivity. This knitting project is my most interactive artwork yet—people talk to me, they touch the knit line, they touch me. We get rained on. Today I was winding up the ball and a rambunctious blond dog charged over and crashed into me, knocking the ball of knit line right out of my hands. It made me laugh.

The clouds have lifted since last night when I couldn't see the horizon. The ship down in the bay has shifted to the right, and the rhodo blossoms have turned brown and fallen. Daisies are out in abundance as are lilacs festooned with raindrop jewels—perfect spheres, convex mirrors. I wasn't really present last week. All these changes were happening in my environment but I didn't even see them. Sleepwalking through life.

## June 25, 2012

The islands looked very soft today like a delicate pastel drawing.

Roxie said, "You have almost knit one block. It's marvelous! Thank you Christen."

That warmed my heart. Roxie is the slight, grey-haired woman who jogs past regularly with the Shelties. She lost her husband a year ago and now leaves the blue lights in her tree shining all year round instead of taking them down after the holidays. Her friends tell her, "You're an artist, you can get away with it," Roxie carves rocks into animals by hand, then gives them away. She invited me to stop by.

## June 26, 2012

Chilly and cloudy today. The knit passed quickly.

"Bonjourno!" Carla called out as she pointed a banana as a gun at Cynthia and me.

"The perfect fruit," Cynthia smiled.

Carla crossed the street in her classy black-and-white dress to give me a coupon for yarn.

While Cynthia mowed the lawn with her noisy lawn mower, the mysterious man with the pack who walks by every day trudged silently past the bench.

## June 27, 2012

A boy, probably three years old with curly blond hair, came up to ask what I was doing. He and his mom wore matching striped shirts. The mom said they would carry on along 16th but the boy insisted that they follow my line. So they changed course and disappeared together over the hill. I was moved by the child's profound response to my work.

## June 28, 2012

During my ritual unwinding of the line down the hill, I've enjoyed glimpses of Karen's garden—it's a multi-layered, textured affair with lavender and heirloom roses that waft their fragrances onto the sidewalk. Karen has a bird in her yard that cries in a high wobbly voice like a hybrid of dove and turkey. I wonder what it is?

Someone asked me, "So do you have an end date?"

"It's not that sort of project," I told him. "It's about the moment with all its drudgery and bliss," I add. I can't believe how long it's taking me to get down to 15th! I thought I'd have reached it weeks ago.

## June 29, 2012

At the end of my evening knit, I solved the mystery of the funny bird in Karen's backyard. Cynthia and Pete came by on a walk just as I got up to wind the line in for the day so we walked down the hill together. To my surprise, I was as tall as Cynthia. From my low vantage point on the bench, she looked much taller. As we approached Karen's yard, I told Pete and Cynthia about the exotic bird sounds I had recently heard. Suddenly Karen appeared and invited us into her backyard with a pink dogwood in full bloom. The sound came from male quails. Karen gave us each three quail eggs covered in brown freckles and showed us her tiny quail egg cartons. I met Karen's husband Mel too with his mad scientist mop of white hair and we lingered together for about 25 minutes.

It was the perfect temperature, comfortable, not hot. Soft clouds dotted the sky while the sun made an appearance here and there. I speed knit today. I'm learning to push the yarn off the needle the way a cyclist effortlessly lets the pedal rise after a downward stroke. Effort—non-effort.

### June 30, 2012

A group of joggers walked by and I overheard, "Then he got his shorts in a knot. Just because I enjoy a good-looking male stripper doesn't mean I love my husband any less."

A train went by sounding extra mournful and a crow cawed in response. I could imagine it thinking, that must have been a very large bird to make such a racket. Rain, rain, rain. My pants got soaked through. Art and B.J. made an appearance but the emperor's lap dog decreed an early retirement due to inclement weather.

The mountains were shrouded in white clouds.

### July 1, 2012

Cloudy, but dry. My yarn is still wet and it grows heavier by the day. Quiet knit with only two comments from pedestrians: "Perseverance!" and "That's going to take forever!" However, my mind was not quiet. It was very, very busy.

Cynthia went to church and came back. (I had noticed a tiny golden cross around her slender neck.)

### July 2, 2012

I didn't heed my intuition to knit earlier, and got rained upon. Alice came by with her daughter and Freddie the dog. She raved about the fragrant white roses in bloom near Roxie's house. It feels ironic when people tell me I'm making a lot of progress. I still haven't even reached 15th yet. I did a lot of thinking today and didn't even try to stay present to my knitting. I am grieving an impending move away from Bellingham to enter a monastery.

**4**

# The Call

Ever since I lost my teaching job, I had been making a
concerted effort to listen to God. I felt so lost, only God could
help me find my way again. I had started meeting monthly with
a small, wiry Catholic woman who practiced yoga and belted out
Alleluia at every possible moment. "Look at these daffodils!"
she'd say in ecstasy, "Alleluia, hallelujah!" I told her about the
unfortunate chain of events leading to my unemployment, and
expressed my anger at a God who seemed to thwart me on every
side—employment, art career, relationships. I told her about the
series of abject relationships I had cobbled together, and how
each had been worse than the last. I had decided to go cold
turkey for a year and not date at all because I was attracted to
men for all the wrong reasons—I was magnetically drawn to men
with the most baggage, and the greatest likelihood of abandoning
me.

"Have you told God how you feel?" my spiritual director
asked as we lounged side by side gazing out her office window at
snowy Mount Baker. "Have you told God you're angry?" she
pressed.

"No way," I said. It sounded dangerous and off-limits like
saying "I hate you" to my dad and getting spanked for it.

"Then that's your homework," she told me. "Tell God exactly how you feel and then listen for God's reply."

Later, I doubtfully got down on my knees and feeling foolish and awkward like someone talking to myself, I tried to give God a piece of my mind. "God, I'm so mad at you for letting my heart get broken over and over again. I'm so mad and sad I almost hate you right now. Please speak to me," I added desperately. Then I cried a while.

But a feeling of spaciousness started coming over me and my heart no longer felt raw as it had moments before. Softer than a whisper, the words presented themselves: "You've tried all these other men, why don't you try Me?"

It left me speechless. Being a rather literal-minded person, I decided God wanted me to become a nun. I didn't know what else these words could mean. Ever since I fell headlong in love with God in my mid 20's, I had been haunted by a hunch that I might be called to the religious life, and had scrupulously avoided the question except for halfhearted visits to local convents that were—Oh sweet relief—a terrible fit for my personality. Now I felt as if God had said checkmate, and like Jonah swallowed by the whale, I could not run away anymore. The knitting—the very thing that was meant to tether me to this place—had made me realize my intense longing for union with God. It was bittersweet. So many puzzle pieces seemed to fall into place—my knitting meditation, my need for ritual, community, rhythm. So I threw myself into researching monastic communities and began planning visits.

July 3, 2012

Mists obscured the islands as I knit in the rain. A woodpecker gripped Carla's chimney. Art went by in his yellow smart car; Pete blew me a kiss. I miss Grace and Rachel's cheery voices on rainy days like this. The ball is getting too heavy for me, and I am not sure what to do now. Rain somehow got inside my sleeve and now my elbow is wet. I'm going to start wearing a raincoat.

40

## July 7, 2012

I wonder if the integrity of this project will be broken if I knit on the train with it when I go visit the monastery. I'm worried that I'm not going to finish the project otherwise.

## July 8, 2012

A couple of joggers said hi, and Art's family drove down the hill evacuating their home in time for the house cleaner to arrive. The daisies have faded and purple star flowers have taken their place. I am letting go of the need to complete the project or worry about the outcome. I am letting go of the need to understand (in other words, control) what is happening in my body. Today I felt a river flowing through my head and into my groin and a pulsing sensation that was pleasurable in an intense way. Even now as I write, I am interrupted by an intense feeling of penetration, and energy coursing through my legs and feet.

## July 9, 2012

I'm annoyed that people refer to the knit line as a "rope" but I don't correct them. The difference between the people who just "happen" upon the knitting and those who have previously read the article in the paper is enormous. The first group is baffled, awed or delighted. The second group are like smug insiders who think they know everything.

At the end of my knit, I was rolling up the ball of knit line when suddenly the wind shook the boughs of the Douglas fir tree making a susurring sound. A crow glided by. Wind chimes rang. The sacrament of the present moment. I had just witnessed perfection.

## July 10, 2012

A milestone! I reached 15th Street today. I almost couldn't see the end of the line, the sun was so bright. The mountains hid in a haze. I told Art I was learning a lot about patience (and my own impatience.)

He said, "Try relaxing when you feel impatient and see what happens. Patience is not the opposite of impatience, relaxation is."

Lynn came by wearing a NO COAL button and a group of us started talking about the coal trains that are threatening our region. This is how political action starts—people stopping to talk and share, and the bench created a space for the exchange to happen.

Ann said hi on her way to use the computers on campus, and left calling over her shoulder, "A little bit a day—if you don't do anything, nothing gets done, just like your knitting."

Carla gave me another coupon for yarn and said she wants to have me and my landlady over for dinner to get to know me better.

## July 11, 2012

I spent the whole hour untangling and winding the line into a ball. I didn't talk to anyone today except Cynthia who put an old armchair out for grabs. I'm feeling lonely, hungry for conversation. I thought someone had tied a dead crow to the end of the line but it was a black shadow cast by the street lamp. Funny how perception fails.

## July 12, 2012

Fog on the water today. I could only see the near edge of the shore. Lynn stopped by with her fluffy dog to ask me lots of questions about garbage pickup in Bellingham because she just moved here.

She said, "Well, I better let you get back to your peaceful meditation."

I said, "This is part of it."

Then Mollie came with a bouquet of fragrant purple butterfly flowers and soft rabbit ear leaves from her garden. She wanted to thank me for bringing the neighborhood together.

She said, "You're probably not aware how much of an impact you've made. Usually, I get almost no RSVP's to the neighborhood block party. This year, I've gotten a lot, many from people I don't even know."

Mollie used to be an installation artist but she hasn't made an installation in 10 years. She's too busy working, cleaning, living. But she does make jewelry art. She said she loves how installation art changes the way people relate to a space and even though it might not last long, it stays in the perception of the people who experienced it and that makes it totally worthwhile. There was an awkward silence when she had told me what a gift this project is and I realized how poorly I handle silence.

I said, "Thank you," and, "Cool, cool." I wonder what I'm afraid of? I think I'm afraid that the other person will be embarrassed and leave.

## July 13, 2012

This morning, about seven people passed rolling giant caterpillar tires up and down the hill, and one guy pushed a full wheelbarrow. They kept sweating up and down the hill for several hours in the blazing sun while their fitness coach cheered them on. Very surreal! In the Third World, a person would never believe that some Americans pay to do meaningless physical labor.

Tonight was one of the most dramatic sits so far. Big clouds, thunder like someone was rearranging the furniture upstairs, and sunshine. Forked lightning flickered in the corners of the sky. One lightning bolt touched Lummi Island. A lot of people walked or drove past. Pete sat on his front porch holding a pink umbrella and waiting to watch the weather "show" even though it wasn't raining yet. About 45 minutes into the sit, it started dumping rain and the thunder sounded like a bomb exploding. It's Friday the 13th, I thought, and tried not to worry about getting struck by lightning. In a few moments I was soaked through. Huge drops of coolness slipped down my chest making me flinch. It was exhilarating to sit and take it, like a particularly rocky meditation session. I thought, this wasn't the kind of shower I wanted, and the rain stopped abruptly. By then the line was drenched.

A blond couple drove by laughing in a red sports car and called out, "Have you caught anything? There's a fish on your line!" They laughed uproariously at themselves while the sun shone through a frame of black clouds.

## July 14, 2012

The islands are swathed in fog like a baby blanket. Very quiet knit in terms of social interaction. A stitch got added somewhere so I knit two together to drop my count back down to seven. The knit line reached the curb today and will soon start crossing another street soon. Mike drove by and made eye contact and smiled.

Carla came out her front door in black shorts, then went back inside again.

## July 15, 2012

Socked in with clouds, good weather for sweaters. I hope the rain clears up for our block party this evening! I had cramps today so the knit felt very long. I saw a couple with ridiculous mini Schnauzers like old men with moustaches. I notice I judge people by their dogs. They said that the rope was flexible and tenacious like me. When I returned to my knitting basket after bringing in the line, someone had left a donut hole in it for me.

## July 16, 2012

Yesterday evening I went to the block party which happened despite the cool, cloudy weather. I was afraid that as the local knitter, I'd be treated like a celebrity but I blended right in and enjoyed meeting new people. I am dismayed by the anonymity of car culture. I hadn't seen or talked to 2/3's of the guests and we live on the same neighborhood block. All the food was vegetarian except for my beef cacciatore (my pan was scraped clean by the end of the night.) For dessert we had strawberry ice cream with blueberry and raspberry toppings freshly picked from neighbor's gardens. Mollie and I hula hooped.

When I went inside Mollie's house to use the bathroom, I saw her installation made of long woven lines of movie film and cassette tape suspended from the ceiling. I was struck by her father's artwork on the wall with the text:

*Is anyone listening?  Or is everyone talking at the same time?*

## July 17, 2012

Grey, cloudy day. The scent of roses on the wind, drifting from Roxie's yard and the smell of freshly cut pine the window workers sawed up. A window installation truck pulled up in front of the bench. The truck made a great sculpture in itself—lined with windows and ladders and a hand-painted sign that said "Lyndale Glass."

The driver told me, "You know, it's rare that I see someone sitting on a bench, knitting a line across the road, and a blue line at that...Very rare."

One woman wanted to know if I was going to "make art" out of the line when I am done.

"This is the art," I said.

Ann stopped on her walk to campus and said, "You probably won't feel at home at the local Catholic church up the street from here for another 10 years—that's the downside of a close-knit community. Some of these people's grandparents built the church. I started attending it in 1977." She advised me to get involved and start serving as a way to connect.

## Afternoon Session

A woman in a sun visor and aviator glasses walked up to me and I judged her when she asked where the ocean was. She introduced herself as Keiki and sat down on the end of the bench (a rare occurrence) and asked me why I was doing this project. She got teary-eyed and said she loved it that I was doing this art as the result of a private conversation, a response to the little voice inside. She does coaching with people to help them tune in and follow that inner voice.

"That's what changes the world," she said. She saw the knit line as living and active. "It's a mind stream," she said.

I said shyly, "The knit line is like a spring of living water coming from within."

She invited me to come to her analytical meditation group.

"It's all about connecting one's self to the infinite and

learning to listen," she said and continued, "I am a baptized born-again Christian but I've been attacked for attending meditation groups outside the church. Once I asked a man with a 'Jesus Saves' sign to please explain what *Jesus saves* means to him and he couldn't."

She said, "Tragically, clichés and slogans often shut people down to God instead of opening them up."

It was a profound encounter—quite possibly the deepest conversation I'd had on the bench so far—and I thanked her.

## July 18, 2012

Cynthia and Pete appeared and Pete 'fessed up to being the donut hole fairy who had planted the donut hole in my basket a few days ago. The sun started setting over the bay, blinding me and turning the people out walking into black silhouettes.

## July 19, 2012

I am so glad I knit this evening instead of at 8 a.m. because I got to witness the sun setting tonight behind an infinite strata of pink clouds. Knitting across a street is easy, I've decided. It's the blocks in between that are so hard! I'm already halfway across 15th street. I bumped into my landlady in the garden. Our relationship has relaxed and deepened over the past couple of months and I think this knit has had a lot to do with it. Just seeing each other more has helped immensely!

## July 21, 2012

Partly cloudy today and quiet. Donald and Freddie came by. Freddie had discovered a pork chop in someone's yard and was proudly carrying it in his mouth. B.J. and Art went the other way to avoid a dog confrontation.

A man clutching a coffee cup said to me, "It's all about the journey, not the goal."

"It's all about the journey AND the goal." I said. "The project wouldn't make sense without the destination. I am focusing on the journey so I don't get discouraged."

Small increments—today, I knit one foot!

I have an idea for the culmination of the piece. I will knit and the neighbors will unwind the ball down to the water, passing the knit line like a bucket brigade. I will make the journey without moving an inch. Paradox.

Yesterday I had a wonderful visit with Mollie. She invited me to a flash mob art gallery where artists will line the trail and suddenly pull their art out to flash a passerby.

I said, "You're an artist of community, or as Joseph Beuys coined, a social sculptor. This is probably the most needed kind of art today."

She had let down her sandy brown hair and it swayed around her waist. I can see why her friends call her Rapunzel. It feels right that she's part of this project—I am letting down my hair too—so to speak—with my long knit line.

I am haunted by my awareness of our neighborhoods as a kind of wasteland. With the automation of everything from garage doors to sprinkler systems, there is almost no need to be outdoors where you could exchange a few words with your neighbors. We've created cocoons or bubbles for ourselves that are rarely disturbed. But a cocoon is made to be broken open.

## July 22, 2012

Suddenly as I knit, I realized I am a caterpillar spinning my cocoon and the bench is my tree branch, the site of my transformation. A line from *"The Four Quartets"* by T.S. Eliot popped into my mind: *In my end is my beginning.* Last night, I told my parents I am becoming a nun, and to my surprise, they gave me their blessing and told me I would probably suit it very well because I love both solitude and community. All the hurdles and obstacles are rapidly disappearing from my path. It's like the knitting—I just sit and all is accomplished.

Be Still and Know. I want to write this phrase on the bench, and paint the bench blue and gild the sides with gold. It will be my chrysalis. Thinking about this while knitting, I got choked up with emotion, my tears flowed freely and I sat and knit through it all. Becoming a butterfly is a lonely process!

Karen walked up to the bench with two visitors. I have stopped coveting her raspberries now that my landlady invited me to eat hers and Carla has given me a Tupperware full. Abundance.

A beautiful policewoman circled around the neighborhood several times in her patrol car, and finally asked what I'm doing in a tone that was friendly and curious.

## July 23, 2012

When I went to roll up the line, someone had carefully lifted the end off the road and doubled it back up the sidewalk. Michelle stopped to chat with her dog Finn. She knits English style, yarn wrapped around her left pointer finger. I had no idea that was even an option. I heard a woman tell her partner as they went down the hill, "Do you see that girl? I read a story about her in the paper." A cyclist carefully lifted her bike over the line. I was crabby tonight, waiting for a phone call that never came. I had to let go many, many times.

## July 24, 2012

Keiki walked by and said, "Hello dear one."

Pete blew a kiss out the car window.

In the silence that ensued, I sat pondering a phrase that came mysteriously into my mind: *Quiet the disturbance within.*

## July 25, 2012

Sunny and warm after yesterday's clouds. Carla's lawn is strewn in dandelions, their yellow heads bobbing merrily against the azure blue sea. I felt content and happy for a change, my mind buzzing from the lecture I gave this morning.

Roxie reported attending a quilting bee in someone's front yard with everyone helping to piece together the quilt. I think we're seeing a revival of people coming together to help each other. I hope so. The FedEx guy told me I wasn't making much progress which was a fun change from the flattery I've grown used to receiving! I broke my commitment not to answer my cell phone during my knitting today—I just couldn't ignore my friend's call.

## July 27, 2012

A blond lady drove up and said, "I know it's none of my business, but my curiosity has gotten the better of me. I've been watching you for months. What are you doing?"

It's amazing that after three months and counting, I'm still getting this kind of response.

Pink sunset while I knit tonight.

A kooky idea suddenly flashed upon me, Finals Week Fairy Godmother. I pictured myself on the university campus during finals week dressed up like a fairy godmother with a star wand, a cream puff wig, glitter makeup, gloves, and a basket full of chocolate. I saw myself plunked down in the middle of one of those huge anonymous lecture halls during a Scantron exam, or skipping across the square. I love the idea of putting together a team of fairy godmothers. It reminded me of the time when I spontaneously opened a pink umbrella in my high school math class and my math teacher was not amused.

## July 29, 2012

Sunny and warm. My mind is anxious and unsettled, flitting from worry to worry. I feel that I've hit a new wall of inattention. When I first sat on the bench in May, all the sounds and sensations were so novel to me, it was easy to stay present. Now they have become background noise to my busy mind and it is only with effort that I hear the crows or the train or even the sound of footfalls on the sidewalk. However, I am still enjoying the scent of the lilies as I wind and unwind the knit line up the hill.

## July 31, 2012

I did a lot of knitting and almost ran out of yarn. I was grateful for the sheer uneventfulness of the hour.

"So, you're knitting...how mundane," a man said and we

both laughed.

I paused by the lavender to listen to the resonant humming of the bees. The air seemed to be vibrating, there were so many.

## August 1, 2012

A neighbor James stopped by with his leg in a splint. His leg is slowly healing from a recent fracture. His dog Cody had wandered off so he had a walk without his dog. He seemed a bit naked without his dog.

## August 2, 2012

Today I knit under a cloudy sky. Tom and Carla's hose fell off and water gushed out of the spigot. I rang the doorbell twice and Tom finally appeared. I felt like a good neighbor.

I've started telling my regulars that I'm leaving town for three weeks to go to a conference and visit a monastery.

## August 3, 2012

Ann stopped and entertained me with her sharp recall of stories. She's going back to Colville in a few weeks so I won't see her again until Christmas. I broke my rule to stay on the bench the full hour and jumped up to hug her.

I said, "I feel apprehensive about an upcoming art residency in Cottonwood, Idaho because I know my work will change in ways I can't predict or control."

She said, "Those shifts are known as growth; think of yourself as blossoming like a lily."

"Saint Kateri was called The Lily of the Mohawks—Are you going to her canonization?" I said.

Ann said, "I can't because I'll be working at the school in Colville."

"But I thought you would go because she's our first Native American saint," I said.

"I'll be surrounded by Native Americans at the school," she said.

St. Kateri would approve of Ann's perspective, I thought. Ann introduced me to several others including a woman with a white Yorkshire terrier. They talked in hushed tones about the woman's son who had dropped out of school and is addicted to drugs.

Roxie and I chatted a while. She asked, "Are you taking the line with you?"

I said, "No."

"That's good—every artist needs a break when working on a major undertaking like this one. And you will come back more inspired. Who knows? It might be a mild winter and the neighbors will bundle you up and bring you hot cocoa. You're making a line down to the water, where we all come from! No one else can knit this line, it has your energy traveling through it. You've touched every inch of it, do you realize that?"

I said, "Yes, it's like my umbilical cord."

Her comments made me think of a creepy film called *The Red Violin*; the violin gets impregnated with the spirit of the woman whose blood was used to varnish the exterior. Do I believe that the knit line carries my energy, and if so what does that mean?

I think my growing edge is open-endedness. I had a dream recently where I was taking a Scantron test and I said to myself, there is more than one right answer. I had no anxiety, just a realization. The South African artist William Kentridge talks about the open-ended messiness of actual political reality and how he's trying to reflect that ambiguity in his work. By refusing to commit himself to just one medium, he stumbled upon his film techniques. The very broadness of his inquiry and the refusal to specialize and master a single medium led him to his breakthrough. But it's taken him years. Each of his 15-30 minute animations take him about six months to draw, working steadily. What impresses me is his daily commitment to practice, and the patience that reveals.

I am finally starting to knit past the chain link fence of Lowell School. Today was a perfect ending to the first segment

51

of the knitting journey. Now I take a break. To think that I believed I would get there before school got out. So glad I was naïve enough to think the project could be completed in a couple of months. Had I known the truth, I would never have undertaken it. Sometimes counting the costs of an endeavor before beginning something is not such a good idea.

## August 3-26, 2012

During the gap in my knitting, I took the Amtrak train to an art conference near Boston, then to Our Lady of the Redwoods Monastery in Northern California. I chose the six-day train trip across the country to allow me to slow down and experience the vastness of the land.

## August 26, 2012

Today my bones and muscles ache from the long train trip. But when I sat down to knit, I was full of excitement and my fingers danced. I thought about time, the mystery of it. Like my line, it doesn't flow steadily at the same rate. Time bunches up when lots of things happen, and then it meanders lazily. There are rapids, and there are slow-moving sections just like the Colorado River that I contemplated through my train window.

Art's wife surprised me by stopping her smart car and calling out to me, "You're back!"

"Only for one day," I said.

"You better do a lot of knitting today to catch up!" she replied.

A truck driver called out, "You've been gone a long time. We missed you," and gave me a thumb's-up.

Carla stopped and chatted before grabbing the Sunday paper and turning in. Pete and Cynthia pulled up in their car. Pete gave me a lei from his dad's luau at the retirement center. Outside of these encounters, it was quiet. My mind was busy and the hour dragged on. I am going to trust that I'll have enough money to pay my rent until I've completed this knit line. Whenever I finish, that's when I'm supposed to enter the monastery.

## September 3-24, 2012 No Knitting

### September 25, 2012

It's my first day back after a three week art residency and I enjoyed observing the changes. The school kids crossed the street in droves to walk down the hill with the line. Roxie has now hung prayer flags from her flagpole. Carla and Tom are having their house painted olive green. (Poor Tom, I have now called him Pete and Don. Some names just don't stick.)

"That's a long-ass rope," one of the painters said to the other about my knitting. The rope caused a minor traffic jam when a man slowed to ask me what I was doing. Pete blew me a kiss and came over to chat. It feels good to be back.

### September 26, 2012

"I'm jogging over it for good luck," a blond woman said as she ran over the blue line.

Rachel and Grace suddenly crested the hill. Grace said she was so happy to see the line. They had actually knocked on my landlady's door to ask about me in my absence. It was wonderful to see them again, back in their fall walking routine.

"It's quite a journey of faith you are on," Rachel told me.

I am really working on focusing on today, not the unknown future. The thought crossed my mind to put a box of my stuff out and a donation jar. I feel that I am supposed to complete this project but I don't know how I can afford to live here without a job.

### September 27, 2012

Roxie came and sat with me for the first time. She was so open today, I could see her eyes because she wasn't wearing shades. She'd suffered through a painful medical massage then taken herself to the pub for beer and a steak sandwich. She was craving meat, even though she's usually a vegetarian.

She said, "You look sad. Was your trip good?

"Incredible," I told her. She encouraged me to take time to process it.

"Are you back for a while?" she asked.

"Yes, I'm not sure how long."

"Flexibility," she said, "is the key to happiness. Life is all about adventure. We come home to recharge sometimes then embark on the next one." Roxie invited me to come over sometime and tell her all about my adventures.

The sun broke through the mist, creating a saffron path of fire over the water. I watched the sun set while I knit furiously. I am not sure I will finish this piece before I leave for the monastery, and I'm filled with longing.

### September 28, 2012

I saw Grace and a woman running with her iPod strapped to her arm like a blood pressure cuff. Grace estimates I will get 25% more length to the line once I untwist it. I keep feeling that I am closer than I think.

Grace and I watched as kids passed walking to school.

"They're out walking in droves because it's fall and not raining and the beginning of the school year," Grace said.

It gives me joy to overhear kids saying to each other, "Let's walk slowly so we can see how long the line has gotten."

### September 29, 2012

I knit this evening until it was dark, and the sunset stole the show with fiery pink clouds. As the train whistle blew, I caught sight of a huge full moon tangled in the branches of dark evergreen trees.

One man decided to measure how many feet my line extends. According to his calculations, I'm a quarter of the way to the bay in three months of knitting.

## September 30, 2012

Went on a day trip with a friend and forgot to knit!

## October 1, 2012

A cyclist exclaimed, "That will be one long sock!"

A woman with a dog said, "It's really interesting to experience the knit line as a pedestrian. Even my dog is aware of its presence and carefully avoids stepping on it."

A mom and small son came up the hill counting. They told me the knit line was 350 steps long. "Thanks for helping us get up the steepest hill," the mother told me.

## October 2, 2012

Today was bright and clear but nippy! My muscles tightened against the chilly wind. I tried knitting with gloves on but it was too clumsy. I knit three rows in the wrong stitch before I realized it. There have been more of what I would call low-income people here this fall—people with shaggy haircuts, cigarettes, slang. It's easy to distinguish them from the inhabitants of the hill.

## October 5, 2012

Wednesday I knit twice, consciously knitting looser as part of life purpose to let go and unwind myself. This is my pilgrimage. The mystery man with the cap and the backpack is back in the hood, sauntering along. I just learned that *saunter* comes from medieval knights who were *san terre*, without land, or wanderers. Grace is helping out with a walkathon fundraiser, a modern version of pilgrimage, purposeful wandering.

Mike invited me to a presidential debate pizza party at his house which he said would be easy to find because it's yellow. I was tickled pink. I finally found his yellow house after knocking on two wrong doors of yellow houses. He had a plain but comfortable house with a garden patch. I drank two glasses of wine and consumed lots of pizza while watching Obama and Romney duke it out on TV.

## October 6, 2012

Today Carla came out in a black dress and watered her plants. She'd like to have my landlady and me over for a meal before I leave. I told her I am going to an "intentional community." Is it wrong that I don't want everyone in the neighborhood to know I'm going to a cloister?

I talked to Karen about her beautiful garden and how it goes through cycles of beauty and ugliness, growth and decay just like our lives. She said I must feel good about my knitting progress but I don't. I'm worried about not finishing the project before I go to the monastery.

I'm grieving the thought of leaving this neighborhood. The words "gentle and careful" came to me as guides for my leave-taking. Tears came and went as I knit thinking about how the bench evokes both presence and absence. When I'm not there, perhaps the neighbors will long for me.

## October 7, 2012

I hitchhiked home from downtown Bellingham, and started knitting just as the sun went down behind the mountains. Patty, the woman with the disfigured face, came by to ask me if I wanted two tattered sets of Beatrix Potter books—hers and her mom's. I said yes. She doesn't have any family members to pass them on to and couldn't bear to throw them away.

I knit in silence contemplating the sunset awash with saffron, plum and salmon hues until a man introduced himself as Dave and sat down on the bench to show me his photos of the sunset. For the past eight years, he'd been living on a remote island named Guemes where he moved with his multi-millionaire girlfriend, giving up his dotcom job in Seattle to help her convert a deluxe horse stable into a green home with its own solar water supply. All those years he'd worked with his hands, helping his girlfriend and volunteering as an emergency medic for the island. Then she dumped him. He's 10 years from retirement, and has no job. My knitting timer went off and I ran out of yarn but I didn't want to abort this fascinating exchange so we talked on, lit only by the light of the street lamp. Dave was now preparing to go back to the city to live alone and work.

I told him my circus values theory, that there are two values systems in the world, and they are mirror opposites. If you are suited to one but live in the other system, you will be restless and unhappy. Security culture values safety, wealth, and stability. Circus culture (including artists, monastics and activists) is founded upon adventure, beauty, camaraderie, and simplicity. Dave said that his time on the island had given him a taste of circus values and he'd had enough. I said my time in academia had given me a taste of security culture and I was sick of it. I told him about my plan to go live in a remote monastery with 10 women, which will be like living on an island. We shook hands and traded lifestyles, then he left to carve out a new life for himself in Seattle.

When I went to roll my knit line back up, someone had tied a daisy to the end of the line. I took a picture of it before putting the line away for the night.

## October 8, 2012

Today I spent more than an hour untangling the yarn. I was actually grateful because it kept me from starting my next skein. The line has gotten so tightly coiled in on itself that it needs to be stretched out and unwound and Grace has offered to help me. We shall see how much length we gain by untwisting it!

I can't help but see my tightly-coiled line as a metaphor for the current state of my soul. I'm not comfortable with the unknown. I get myself tangled up inside trying to see from every angle, and end up knotted in fear and confusion.

## October 9, 2012

Yesterday, in lieu of my knit, Grace drove me to a tall lookout tower at the top of the arboretum and we dropped the ball of knit line over the balcony like Rapunzel letting down her hair. The blue line spun releasing hours of pent up energy and finally hung quiet and still. Today the line had leapt from the 9th sidewalk square to the 24th, thanks to the uncoiling of the knit line, but no one but me noticed how long it had grown. I took a photo of a dead sparrow lying beside the knit line. The intersection of the crack in the sidewalk and the knit line made a cross. The wordless suffering of Creation.

October 10-11, 2012 No Knit

October 13, 2012

I knit in a light rain that teemed with the scent of sweet, green things. I continue to marvel at the beauty of this journey, aware of the moments in time when the static in my brain lifts and I hear the whooshing of the wind in the trees, the staccato of a nail gun, the strange tongue of the squirrel perched on the telephone pole. New signs of autumn: pine cone kernels in the gutter, courtesy of Mr. Squirrel.

I still don't know if I'll ever complete this work of art. Must focus on the rightness of the work itself rather than the outcome as Thomas Merton said:

> *Do not depend on the hope of results. You may have to face the fact that your work will be apparently worthless and even achieve no result at all ... as you get used to this idea, you start more and more to concentrate not on the results, but on the value, the rightness, the truth of the work itself.*

October 14, 2012

Powerful gusts of wind sent leaves scuttling like crabs on their tippy toes and my hair blowing in every direction. The wind and the rain have released earth's pent up scents: pungent lavender fragrance especially strong near Karen's house. I enjoyed the sound of the wind in the Douglas firs most of all, their branches swaying like giant kelp. I sat with a phrase that came to me in my sleep: *To behold, but not possess.* I want to be like the trees that let go their leaves to the wind, witnesses to a force that's strong yet ungraspable. A handful of people passed by, but it was mostly just me and the wind and the trees.

October 15, 2012

I chatted with Art and commented that he doesn't walk B.J.

around here anymore, but Art told me he still does, it's just that B.J. chooses the route.

"Why not?" Art said and shrugged. B.J. also decides how long they walk. I thought how great—total surrender, total receptivity. Dog is God spelled backwards, after all. Art is definitely a Zen Master of sorts. That my two friends on this journey are named Art and Grace is not coincidental. Both have accompanied me in important ways in this art project but also in my spiritual life.

I am practicing beholding the beauty before me. There is a gulf between beholding and possessing and the difference is life and death. Today sunlight streamed through the chain link fence illuminating the yellow maple leaf.

## October 18, 2012

It was raining this evening and I almost cancelled my knit. I had forgotten how much fun it is to knit in the rain. When I first got to the bench, I was delighted by a gift of six pinecones someone had placed in a row where I usually sit. I felt peaceful the whole hour of knitting.

Mollie (the artist with Rapunzel hair) drove up and invited me to a haunted house art gallery and Halloween party.

At the end of my knit, Carla came out with her hood over her head to ask me what time I wanted to come for dinner on the 21st.

## October 21, 2012

Yesterday I knit and left the line on the road while I had a garage sale at the bench. A transgender woman named Michelle offered to help push my wheelbarrow of books for sale up the hill. She said she was a frail old lady of 65, but she was taller than my dad and pushed the wheelbarrow uphill with great vigor. The sun shone down on me through a little window in dark grey clouds. Roxie brought me tea twice, and bought my sewing basket. Around noon, a friend came and relieved me so I could take a needed bathroom break and get lunch. Then it started to rain! We covered the books but somehow the tarp flew off and my big art books got wet.  Then the rain stopped as abruptly as it had started.  A friend brought hot chocolate for all of us.  Temperatures dropped and my feet turned numb.  Not exactly the time of year for a garage sale, but I couldn't help it.

To my surprise, my treasures weren't worth much to other people.  I parted with my wacky East Indian tin frog playing a banjo, and my golden bird earrings from my Grandma that weren't gold after all, but brass.  The one exception was my silver ring shaped like a wing.  I showed it to an older man and asked him what he wanted to pay.  He offered me $20.  That felt like grace.  I parted with about a third of my possessions in preparation for my upcoming move to the monastery.  My friends carried boxes of my leftover things back to my home.  By then, I was physically and emotionally spent, so their kindness meant a lot.

I bathed and went to Carla and Tom's for a gourmet meal of Sicilian chicken and pasta, salad, homemade blueberry crisp and ice cream.  Carla pried the secret out of me about my call to become a nun.  I felt quaint and misfitty as the other guests plied me with questions.  But that's ok—perhaps it's my form of humility right now, this gift of my vulnerable heart.

Carla said, "Sometimes I wonder what would remain if I were to set aside the house and the titles, the job, etc.  Strip it all off.  Who would I be?  What would remain?  That's what you're doing, isn't it?"

Her perceptive use of the word 'strip' startled me because that word has been on my mind a lot lately.

## October 22, 2012

I knit but it was so cold I could barely form stitches.  In one hour, I knit what normally takes a half hour.  It was a shock to realize that earlier this summer I had almost convinced myself not to enter the monastery because I wanted to continue my daily knitting practice.  It's clear now I wouldn't have been able to knit through the winter anyway!

## October 24, 2012

Today I put the raincoat over my legs as a windbreaker, wore my hood and hat, and sat on a cushion. It sure made a difference! The hour flew by. Art and his wife drove by in the smart car. She never stops to chat, but she waves—I still don't even know her name. A man said goodbye to his son and stood, looking out over the horizon after his son disappeared down the hill to school. I wonder what was passing through his mind.

## October 25, 2012

The rain pelted down as I knit this morning. My fingers grew so cold and numb, I couldn't feel my keys in my pocket. I got drenched—no raincoat, no hat. Art and wife were horrified that I knit without a hat or rain gear. My favorite comment today, "Oh honey, I hope it doesn't shrink. I hope the bus comes soon!" Then her eyes widened as she realized how long the line was. James came by with his poodle, Cody. I think Cody liked the smell of my goat wool gloves.

## October 29, 2012

Three day gap in the knitting while I worked and went on a road trip with a friend to Mount Angel to check out a Benedictine monastery. I debated whether to knit today then was glad I did. The rain let up right before I got there and the soft mists over the hill felt like a silence. I keep feeling invited to let go of my noisy thoughts and just be.

Carla has graciously offered to host a show of my art in her home. I have to make fliers today!

## October 30, 2012

Grace and Rachel stopped by in the rain to say hi. A drain repair man sidled up in his truck and asked if there was anything he could do for us.

"As a matter of fact, there is," Rachel said.

"Wow, what an offer!" Grace chimed in. They looked like Tweedledum and Tweedledee in their complementary green and purple neon sports jackets. Afterwards I asked if they knew that guy since they had chatted a long time.

"Nope, Grace just has that effect on people," Rachel said.

Grace denied it saying, "The two of us could strike up a conversation with a telephone pole!"

October 31, 2012

The bottom half of me below my black coat got drenched.

A woman asked, "Have you reached the ocean?"

I said, "I haven't but today is my last day of the knitting season." My last day on the bench for a while, maybe forever. The ocean was hiding behind a veil of rain and fog expressing the grief inside me.

At the end of the knit, Grace came and gave me two warm hugs.

"Look how big the ball of knitting is!" she crowed.

I patted the ball and said, "Good ball."

Grace patted my head and said, "Good Christen," which moves me again as I write it.

After I cleaned out the rental and loaded my car with my storage boxes for my parents' basement, my landlady came home.

"My one regret is that I didn't make time to get to know you better," she said.

She surprised me by most of my damage deposit with a small deduction for the black stain that my dripping wet coat had made on her rug.

Then I went to Mollie's party. She was dressed in a floral Hawaiian gown with flowers wreathing her head. Her mom, dressed as a nun, was speechless when I told her I was soon entering a cloister. The table overflowed with food including a cat head sculpted out of salmon cream cheese which Mollie had labelled "Cat Brains" and a scrumptious lemon-lentil squash soup. The best part of all was Mollie's basement converted into a Tiki Bar complete with wicker chairs, coconut shell bikinis, a bar, and schmaltzy Hawaiian tunes spinning on a vintage record player.

# 5

# Our Lady of the Redwoods

Deciding to become a nun was the relatively easy part, choosing a community and discerning a 'match' was slightly overwhelming, given the thousands of religious communities worldwide. A kind Vocation Directress helped me over the phone to narrow down my search to the Benedictines. She told me that I shared their "charism" or spiritual strengths: a life of prayer, manual work, and hospitality to strangers. So I began to visit Benedictine monasteries in the Northwest. I didn't feel any chemistry, although I met many lovely sisters who were eager to support me in my discernment. One woman in particular gave me a book about the Trappists, and I was astonished to find out that they followed St. Benedict's Rule, and were in a sense, more Benedictine than the Benedictines, because they observed the Rule much more strictly. I suddenly remembered a monastery in northern California that a friend had told me about whose website I'd secretly visited for the last 10 years. I decided to take a detour to visit them on my epic train ride across the country in August 2012. When I arrived at Our Lady of the Redwoods Monastery, I had the sweet feeling of homecoming.

I loved the Asian simplicity of the monastery chapel—its cool, quiet interior that looked out on a massive redwood tree. I stood in awe before those trees, ancient, timeless, like the elders of the community whose lives bore witness to the wisdom of slowness and endurance. Two of the original Trappistine nuns from Europe remained from the original founding Mothers of the community, one in her 80s and the other in her 90s.

I was also attracted by the beauty of their communal prayer. They gathered to sing prayers to God in a call and response Gregorian chant—Several sisters had angelic voices. I felt as if my soul would burst its ribcage, like I was giving God my whole self with my breath poured out in song.

Too, I thought they were beekeepers, and I had a bee fetish at the time. I had just read *The Secret Life of Bees*, and my recent sculpture "Honey in the Heart" was fresh on my mind. I was disappointed to find that they didn't keep bees but rather bought the creamed honey that they sold. However, they stirred flavors into the honey—lemon, cinnamon, orange—and I could eat as much of it on buttered toast as I wanted. They were unbelievable cooks—the food was mostly organic, and though simple and primarily vegetarian, it was prepared with a lot of love. Not to mention, the European sisters had brought with them a taste for gouda cheese and artisan bread, strong coffee and dark chocolate.

There were three other artists in the community—an icon writer, a weaver, and a watercolorist. I hoped that I might find both the likeminded community and the practical support that I needed to thrive as an artist. I so longed to take root in this spiritual and spirited gathering of women.

In the end, I loved Our Lady of the Redwoods for many reasons, but I entered for only one reason. One afternoon, I was lying peacefully on my bed in my cinderblock guest cell at the monastery when I felt Love wash over me and that inner voice spoke unmistakably to me: Consent to be known. As usual, no explanation came attached to this lovely phrase—God is a Poet of few words—but it felt like an invitation to intimacy with this particular community, an intimacy that I both yearned for with all my being, and feared. I can already hear the laughter of a skeptical friend telling me that I made up this inner voice, that it's not God, but my imagination. All I can say is, I don't talk like that. For one things, brevity has never been my strong suit! And my way of expressing things to myself doesn't involve commands to myself or words like "consent." When God whispers to my heart, the words often sound quaint, albeit irresistibly charming and romantic. Always in a tone of voice that's so soft and gentle I could easily brush it aside, yet with a clarity and truth that demands my total surrender.

When I returned to Bellingham after my visit to Redwoods Monastery, I couldn't get it out of my imagination, my heart. Though I hadn't planned to move down there until I finished my knitting project, I felt such a deep longing to return that I wrote to them and begged to enter.

* * *

All told, I lasted six months at Our Lady of the Redwoods Monastery, including nine weeks of observation before entering formally as a postulant. But in those six months, I had consented to be known, and it changed me at the root of my being. In the end, it was Father Kevin, a visiting Jesuit priest, who helped me make the difficult decision to leave the monastery. We sat down together in the private parlor and I told him unquestioning obedience wasn't my strength, and I was butting heads on a weekly basis with my novice director. I don't remember everything I shared with Fr. Kevin because it was an emotional conversation for me and I gushed like a leaky fire hydrant. Perhaps I told him I was not suited to a lifestyle of silence and introspection. I came alive each week during the two "talking" meals on Sunday, then crawled back into my shell to survive the rest of the week in silence. Or that I was growing increasingly depressed and bored by the repetitive work and the subdued surroundings. I survived each day through sheer willpower and the belief that God had called me there. (I didn't tell him this part: I was also proud and stubborn. I thought I'd be the next St. Teresa of Avila. I had a host of spiritual sayings to buoy my flagging spirits: "Whom God calls, God also equips" and "God alone is enough.")

Father Kevin listened intently to me. He was a small man with blue eyes and greying brown hair, exuding kindness and humility. He begged me not to over-spiritualize it. He thought it was clear that my temperament was not suited to the monastery. God had given me my strong personality for a reason and wouldn't force me to become someone else.

That was news to me—I'd been seeing my personality as a mistake, like a wicked stepsister trying to stuff my oversized foot into Cinderella's glass slipper.

"What do you truly desire?" he asked me.

I said, "I want to follow Jesus."

Fr. Kevin said, "That's good—but a little vague. God wants you to thrive more than God needs your help. What are your dreams?"

"I want to be an artist," I blurted out.

"What do you need in order to be an artist?" he probed.

"I need a supportive community, a job with regular hours, and some structure," I said.

"Go and find those things," he said simply.

And with that, I was tearfully reborn into the world that I thought I had left for good.

How strange it was to sit in the passenger seat as the abbess drove me down the twisting, tree-tunneled drive away from Our Lady of the Redwoods Monastery. I felt like I was in a giant birth canal, being propelled back to Bellingham. It was wonderful to be back in the vibrant world outside. I didn't even mind the young people cussing each other out on the train station platform. An invisible shield of serenity and irrepressible glee surrounded me as if I'd brought the monastery with me. Too, I sensed the sisters' prayers; I often fingered the red string that one of the sisters had tied around my wrist and hers, both of us promising not to remove the string until it fell off like an umbilical cord of friendship.

Once back in Bellingham, I moved in with my parents

temporarily (whose undisguised delight at my return was touching) and started looking for a job. It was the end of May and I was eager to start knitting again, but I needed to find work and a place to live close to the knitting hill first. One day as I was aimlessly wandering the aisles of the local grocery store, I felt a tap on my shoulder. I turned around to see a tall woman with silver hair asking me, "Would you like a job?" She said we had been in a Centering Prayer group together over a year ago and she felt I would be someone with a gift for working with her adult daughter who needed full-time care. Completely caught off guard, I rallied enough to say yes and gave her my phone number.

The next weeks were a joyful blur as I got fast tracked into a full-time caregiver job with benefits—knocking out two overnight shifts in two days, leaving the rest of my week free to make art. It was my dream job—I had finally gotten my break after years of juggling part-time, temp jobs. As soon as I got the job, I made plans to move into a house close to the bench. I had just bought a car with the money that the monastery had graciously given me for my relocation expenses, and had little savings so I decided to sublet something cheap while I waited for a more permanent place that I could afford. I found a large room for $350 in a charming student rental nestled among trees and a white picket fence. I can endure anything in the short term, I told myself, and tried to sleep through the parties past 2 a.m., listening to my roommates having noisy sex in the bedrooms nearby. Quite a contrast to the cloister, I chuckled to myself. Finally, I felt settled and ready to return to my post on the bench.

# PART TWO

# RETURN

# 6

# Picking up Stitches

July 1, 2013

Hurrah to be knitting again! Today was my first day back knitting since last November. It was one of those rare, hot summer days in Bellingham. The water shimmered like wrinkled tinfoil in the heat, even though I arrived in the evening. As I unwound the line down the hill, the sound of neighbors chatting over dinner wafted out through screened windows. To my delight, two neighbors came out and gave me warm, sweaty hugs!

New things have popped up, such as a Little Free Library on 14th St—take a book and leave one for someone else. I see people I've never seen before. A bespectacled man walking his spotted dog. A young girl with satin black hair who wished me good luck.

I sat knitting and I dropped a stitch. As I fumbled to pick it back up, more neighbors appeared. The unspeakable joy of picking up where we left off. Offers of a future get-together, perhaps a meal, and peace be with you. Also, the use of a bathroom as needed—a logistical issue I had not taken into consideration until today. I'm now living in a sublet, a 20 minute walk from the base of the hill.

I learned that Art's name is actually Arnold. I had misheard it, and he never corrected me because it made no difference to him! How embarrassing.

## July 2, 2013

Recently, I asked a friend how to keep going despite all the challenges. She said to keep a Fat Head File where you put all the nice, complimentary things people say to you. On a down day, whip it out to encourage you. So today I started my Fat Head File. I put a drawing in it of the knitting and the bench given to me by a girl who used to pass me every morning with her mom on the way to school. I love her drawing because the knitting needles are green and living, with what look like coiled-up chromosomes inside. And the knitter is invisible, totally absorbed into the knitting, which is what happens when I'm in the zone.

## July 3, 2013

A man rode up the hill on his bicycle, his cowbell tinkling, (only in Bellingham!) Patty and a friend walked past the bench, canes in hand. She introduced her friend saying, "We've been friends for 54 years."

It appears my knitting has shrunk since last year. The knit line used to be at 14th but now it's about half a block higher up the hill, only reaching the school driveway. It's either shrunk, or wound tightly in on itself. It's discouraging to lose ground before I even begin! Some neighbors offered to pull on the line to stretch it out for me, but they didn't.

However, near the end of the knit, someone started tugging very hard on the line. I looked down over the hill and saw a bunch of highschoolers trailing away down the hill. They let go but left the line lying in a zigzag on the sidewalk. I liked it so much, I took a photo. If I could take a picture of my mind today, it would look like that zigzag.

People who write (paint) traditional Byzantine icons say that what happens in the process of writing an icon reflects what is happening in their life. The icon is a mirror of sorts. I think my line is telling me to relax, move outside myself and quiet my monkey mind. Or maybe it's encouraging me to see beauty even in this tangle!

## July 4, 2013

*Every day, we are offered chance after chance to practice staying in relationship ... more than mentally receiving each other, this involves daring to imagine each other freshly through the heart.* ~Mark Nepo

Lots of firsts for the knitting bench this week. I have arrived to find people sitting on the bench for the first time, enjoying the view. Sitting on the bench has made me hyper-aware of the people who pass by every day, the ones who choose to speak to me and those who don't.

After months of walking past the bench without saying a word, The Silent Man stopped.

"You haven't been knitting for a while have you?" he said.

"No, I've been in California," I said.

He said, "I used to live in California...I was part of a hippie camp...I was there for two winters." He spoke haltingly like someone who was shy, who didn't talk much. We exchanged names. His name is Jerome. Then he went on his way. Forget Independence Day, I thought, this is Interdependence Day, a powerful moment when a familiar stranger became my new friend. A movement from isolation to connection.

## July 5, 2013

Huge white ship in the bay today, close to shore. I knit from 8 – 9 a.m., and the morning light cast wonderful shadows. I couldn't stop taking photos. Delighted to see Arnold and Jane and their dog B.J. this morning. After much contemplation, Arnold decided to put my drawing of a girl knitting in his meditation shed. I am honored.

A very sweaty jogger came up and talked to me. She said twice, "It's an act of devotion."

The line got tangled, and a young mom with her son and daughter were excited to help untangle it. They are a military family, going to Korea soon. I really hit it off with the little girl who had straight brown hair and a Hello Kitty shirt and ruffled skirt.

## July 7, 2013

Knit in the evening today to avoid the hot sun on my fair skin. I felt refreshed as soon as I encountered my neighbor Alice and her silky dog Freddie. She said that Taylor Ave (where I knit) is a legendary sledding hill. It's extremely steep and scary in a car but exhilarating on a sled or toboggan. One day, she was out walking in the snow, and suddenly three men zoomed down on a sled. They stopped sheepishly at 15th St and said they were out looking for their kids. Yeah, right.

We talked about the difficulty of becoming conscious, the realization that everything you do and think has an impact, positive or negative on others. And true honesty, how rare that is! Not saying what you are thinking can be an act of dishonesty and cowardice too. And we discussed how mindfulness and integrity could express itself in a small act like cooking a meal or sewing a quilt. Anything done with loving attention has the power to heal.

Soon others joined us at the bench. The evening passed quickly, and I hadn't taken any photographs because I didn't want to detract from the wonderful conversation. Close to 9 o'clock my neighbors left. Jerome, the silent man who I'd met on July 4th, walked by without saying hello. I said, "Hi Jerome," because he had stopped to adjust his sock just past the bench. He said "hi" without looking up and continued on his way. (I wonder if we'll ever talk again?)

As I wound the line back up the hill, my eye was caught by the sunset reflected in the back of a car, an unplanned movie screen.

## July 8, 2013

Jerome did a downward dog stretch off the back of the bench

before I arrived at 6:30 a.m. today. The sky blurred into water with a wooly fog that obliterated the horizon line. I had a meditative knit, saying hi to only a few passersby. I enjoyed the sound of the chickadees. How can these two blocks of city sidewalk continue to reveal fresh delights? The linear shadows cast by the horsetails were especially gorgeous in the morning light. The quality of attention that I bring to this hour of knitting is something I hope to sustain throughout the rest of my days. Every moment would then feel like the miracle that it is.

### July 9, 2013

Sometimes this project feels like something straight out of Dr. Seuss. In fact, at times I feel downright silly! But as George Bernanos wrote, the ridiculous is always so near to the sublime.

# 7

# Uninvited Collaborations

July 10, 2013

*The soul, reaching, throwing out for love, as the spider, from
some little promontory throwing filament after filament, tirelessly
out of itself, that one at least may catch and form a link, a bridge,
a connection.* ~Walt Whitman

Today a tiny spider landed on my arm as I was knitting.
Then before I could grab my camera, a puff of wind blew it
away. Throughout this knitting project, I have enjoyed
imagining that I'm a little spider throwing out my line. One of
my favorite works of art is the Uninvited Collaborations series by
artist Nina Katchadourian. She used tiny red stitches to mend a
spider's web, and tried to help its marketing by stitching "Web
Repair: Low, low rates" into its web. Her attempts were rejected
by the spider, who tossed the bits of string on the ground.

Josh came by the bench and lingered for a visit before
heading to the art department to teach. "In the end," he said,
"teaching is about being a servant." He wears himself out taking

college kids on field trips to Seattle and Vancouver but finds it fulfilling at the same time. He asked, "Where did your red cowboy hat go?"

"My mom's dog ate it," I said.

"That would make a good country western song," he said and continued on his walk.

I ran into Mollie as I wound the line back up the hill. She described an installation for me where she tacked a black plastic line down to the ground, tracing her journey all over campus and into her classroom. People followed the line trying to figure out where it went. I love this idea of drawing the invisible paths that we make.

Today I noticed that my neighbor Carla had changed the poem in the poetry altar located in her backyard to "Digging" by Donald Hall. It is a lush gardening poem about death and resurrection.

## July 11, 2013

dumb line, blunt line, line that remains stubbornly line, line as tension, line as pilgrimage

## July 12, 2013

Today I had a wonderful conversation with a woman who teaches learning strategies. She told me about time management, and how it can be distilled down to one word: purpose. It's like being a farmer–if you keep your eyes focused on the end of the row, you will make a straight line with your tractor, she said. (She grew up in the Midwest.) She said that's what I am doing with my knitting, the ocean as my vision. She's a person of faith, and believes we're each given a unique purpose like a coal burning inside us. One daily action aligned with that purpose, even if it's just 10 minutes, will tend the fire and make it grow. That reminded me of my favorite quote by St. Catherine of Siena: *Be who God meant you to be and you will set the world on fire.*

At the end of this project, I'm going to have a huge ball of knitting, and that won't be the art. The art is the daily practice, and all the experiences, thoughts, and people that come my way. The challenge is how to document that. I find that people clam up the moment I break out my camera. So I think that writing is my best bet for capturing the experiences that make up the artwork itself.

## July 13, 2013

Quiet Saturday morning interrupted briefly by shrieking seagulls tailgating a bald eagle. I thought about rejection, and my experience of being a misfit American kid who grew up in Thailand. My childhood has given me an intense longing for connection, a desire to welcome people who are different. My wound is my greatest strength.

## July 14, 2013

Top 10 Ways to Meet Your Neighbors

1. Get a dog and walk it every day. Dog owners talk to each other. (Or you could walk your pet tortoise on a leash like the poet Baudelaire did...it helped him slow down and savor the sensations of modern life.)

2. Work in your garden and say hi to passersby.

3. Go to the same coffee shop at the same time every week and get to know the regulars.

4. Push a baby, dog, or other being in a stroller. (My grandpa swears he saw artist Emily Carr pushing her pet monkey in a perambulator in Victoria, B.C.)

5. If owning a dog is not an option, ask dog owners questions about their dogs.

6. Do something creative in public.

7. Walk instead of driving. Keep your gaze lifted, earphones off, and your arms hanging at your side. Make eye contact and smile at oncoming walkers.

8. Say, "I don't think we've met. My name is
_____."

9. Wear a benign but provocative shirt.  For example, a shirt with the words "Free Hugs" on it.

10. Throw a regular garage sale.

## July 15, 2013

I had just finished unwinding the line down the hill and was coming back up to begin my hour of knitting, when I saw a woman already sitting in "my" spot knitting on the blue line!  It was almost an out-of-body experience for me…as if someone had picked up a paintbrush and started painting on my canvas, or raided my closet and dressed in my favorite clothes.  Thankfully, she knew how to knit and purl, and completed several beautiful rows before handing the needles to me.  Another chance for me to relinquish control.

# 8

# Present Tense

*Patient Trust*

*We are quite naturally impatient in everything*
*to reach the end without delay.*
*We should like to skip the intermediate stages.*
*We are impatient of being on the way to something*
*unknown, something new.*
*And yet it is the law of all progress*
*that it is made by passing through*
*some stages of instability—*
*and that it may take a very long time.*
*And so I think it is with you;*
*your ideas mature gradually—let them grow,*
*let them shape themselves, without undue haste.*
*Don't try to force them on,*
*as though you could be today what time*
*(that is to say, grace and circumstances*
*acting on your own good will)*
*will make of you tomorrow.*

*Only God could say what this new spirit*
*gradually forming within you will be...*
*Accept the anxiety of feeling yourself*
*in suspense and incomplete.*

~Teilhard de Chardin, geologist and priest, excerpt

## July 16, 2013

A woman stopped and told me, "I used to walk past you many times without ever stopping to talk. Then one day you were gone, and I started missing you."

## July 17, 2013

*Nature does not hurry, yet everything is accomplished.* ~Lao Tzu

The man with the cowbell on the back of his seat puffed up the hill, much to my amusement. Today I have been as impatient as a wound-up tin bear beating its tin drum. I usually feel the most impatient when I am actually exercising a lot of patience, the way my stomach muscles ache after I've done a bunch of sit ups.

## July 21, 2013

*To live in the past and future is easy. To live in the present is like threading a needle.* ~Walker Percy

I went to the block party this evening. Each neighbor chose a word out of the Hawaiian dictionary to write on their name tag. Inspired by the Dada art movement, I decided to flip open the dictionary and use whatever word my pen tip happened upon. To my amazement, I landed on the word "koi au" which means "flowing current" or "eloquence."

A neighbor brought his guitar and used a broken beer bottle as a slide, spiriting us away with soulful tunes. We lingered well into the evening, gorging ourselves on ice cream topped with fresh berries as the kids hula hooped and threw bean bags to topple tin can towers. I wish we did this more than once a year!

## July 22, 2013

Today as I was knitting, I thought about repetition and the many artists who have returned to the same subject or action over and over. An example is Uta Barth's breathtaking series of portraits entitled "You Are the Weather" where she photographed the same adolescent girl 100 times between 1994 and 1996. Rather than inducing boredom, these portraits awaken a sense of mystery. I am reminded of the wonder of each morning's tide yielding a seemingly inexhaustible offering of new shells, crab carapaces, and sand dollars. Similarly, knitting at the bench every day has shown me that each day is singular and unique. Familiarity breeds awe. Today, for example, two people that I have never seen before talked to me at the bench. One was a painter out photographing the beautiful landscape to use as references for paintings. She left calling back over her shoulder that she had to chase the light.

## July 23, 2013

When I arrived to knit late this morning, the ocean was completely obscured by mists. The ocean still exists down there, I reminded myself, despite being invisible today. So much of my life feels like a journey into mystery, putting one step in front of the other, hoping that I'm pointed in the right direction. I wait for a flash of illumination to break upon me, but it only comes after long intervals of groping my way forward like a nearsighted mole. "I see feelingly," the blind Gloucester says in Shakespeare's play *King Lear*. It's an apt metaphor for the creative process, and life.

## July 24, 2013

Every day, as I unwind the line, I enjoy the explosion of yellow vetch and dandelions growing beside the fence at Lowell Elementary School. What if Community is a weed? What if it's a virus or a rash that won't stop spreading? What if it sprang up suddenly, and people left their cars and locked homes to stand together on the grass laughing and sharing stories, singing, dancing and making music? What if children jumped rope on the sidewalk, climbed trees and rode their bikes to their friends' house? What if the beauty of what I experienced at the block party were an everyday reality?  Why not?

July 25, 2013
"What are you making?"
"I'm making a line to the ocean."
"What are you going to do with it?"
"That's what I'm doing with it."
"Oh, to find your way?"
"Yeah."

A few days ago:
"So you're making one?"
"Yes, I'm making One."

Another woman asked me today, "Why are you doing this?"
"I'm knitting a line to the ocean."
She said, "I know, but why?"
"To connect myself to the Infinite.  It's about communion."  It
was so hard for me to open myself up to a stranger who I doubted
would understand.
She said, "Well, I better get back to work."

   Cynthia came and sat on the bench with me.  I feel like I'm
going to melt whenever she looks at me, her eyes are so kind.
She's also got a naughty sense of humor.  She pointed out how
funny our neighbor looked from this angle—as if standing and
peeing—but he was just blocking the garden hose from our view
with his body.

July 26, 2013
   Almost every day I am asked how many feet I knit in an
hour.  We Americans adore efficiency and progress!  Today, Pete
asked me how much it cost per inch!  I still don't know how
many feet I knit per hour, and to be honest, I don't care.

July 27, 2013
   Knit tonight, still trying to avoid the blazing sun.  I spent the
first half hour untwisting the line—It's gotten wound up again
like a twisted telephone cord.

Jerome talked to me again! (The third time in four months!) He told me that he's taken part in various protests, once wearing a cardboard box "television" on his head. Another time, he held a sign that said "Eat Microwave Pancakes." He walks 10 miles every day, staving off depression after having a stroke.

Sound of Carla and her guests laughing on the back deck wafted to me as I watched the florescent pink sunset.

## July 28, 2013

I love the surprised looks and smiles that I get every day from people who see me knitting a line that flows over the road and down the sidewalk. I hope it brings a sense of expansiveness and possibility to each person's day. I think of my musician friend who infiltrated a grocery store with his band members and played jazz instruments spontaneously at a preset time in various parts of the store until they were escorted out. Another time, they played slide whistles in the changing rooms at the mall.

On a more serious note, Cynthia came out and shared a precious card she received from a Trappist monk after her dad died. He sent her a few thoughtful words that still make her tear up with their generosity. It really doesn't take much to make a difference in the world.

## July 29, 2013

Today I got engrossed in painting watercolors and setting up my new online shop. Suddenly it was almost 7:30 p.m. and I hadn't completed my daily knit. I was almost at the bench when I heard my neighbor Sandy calling my name and hurrying up the sidewalk toward me. She asked me if I would cat-sit for her and Marvin this weekend. I said yes, and she invited me into their home for a glass of wine and chocolate. I couldn't resist, so I didn't start knitting until 8:30 that night.

Fortunately, my neighbor Ann appeared walking down from the university where she checks her email. She offered to unwind the huge ball of knitting down the hill for me. I have never let anyone do this for me before (not that anyone has ever offered). It felt luxurious not to have to unwind the ball–which feels like 40 pounds–and then walk back up the steep hill again. I was in a rare, generous mood towards myself–the wine and chocolate and kind neighbors helped. Normally, I would have berated myself for procrastinating, but this time I just embraced the opportunity and had a blast taking night photos during the knit and on my walk home. Photos of daisies lit by moonlight, lace curtains across a bright bedroom window, the school building eerie and dark.

# 9

# The Daily Practice

July 30, 2013

My knitting project is teaching me the power of maintaining a daily practice, no matter what. Over time, I've realized that a practice is more important than the successes and failures along the way, in fact the practice creates the way. I'm thinking of artist Richard Long who "draws" a line by walking a path across the same terrain over and over. A single day's work might not matter, but the accumulation of days of patient work makes a significant impact. I think about my habits, the actions that keep me pointed towards True North, the ocean, what truly matters. When I get up in the morning, I write three pages of uninterrupted, unedited, often terrible writing. It clears my head for the day, and helps me to feel connected to myself and God. (This practice came from *The Artist's Way*, a book that has given me many breakthroughs, both personal and artistic.) If I don't have any appointments, I knit in the morning for one hour, then write about the knitting. *Write every day, without hope and without despair*, the author Isak Dinesen counseled. I hope to take that to heart.

## July 31, 2013

How do I write about an hour when nothing happened? I'm learning to savor the sensations of urban life. From 2:10 – 3:10, I listened to the sound of the leaf-blower, waved okay's to drivers to roll over the line, felt the sun burn through the clouds and warm my shoulders. The sweet nothings that comprise most of my life are easily overlooked, yet they are often times when I feel most peaceful and alive.

## August 2, 2013

Rain! I wasn't fully awake when I stumbled out the door this morning wearing yoga pants, a couple T-shirts and a light blazer. I had to steel myself to sit down on the rain-drenched bench. I could feel the two wet bands of the bench imprinting themselves across my pant seat. A cute chimney repairman in a red truck told me, "I like the way you aren't wearing a rain hat, soaking the rain in like a plant."

Honestly, I don't enjoy knitting in the rain very much. Mostly because I don't have proper raingear, and the knit line gets heavy and dirty, absorbing all the water and debris on the sidewalk. I did have fun photographing a brown slug slithering along the wet sidewalk. As I was putting the knit ball away in the basement, my neighbor Arnold invited me to help him out with a mysterious project. He had two clamps, and a golfing umbrella.

"It's better than getting rain on your head," he said, as he clamped the umbrella to the bench. He asked me to sit down again, and test it out. Hurrah! I felt like a queen.

## August 3, 2013

A young handsome doctor sat down and talked with me for a while. He told about growing up with a developmentally-delayed brother, the joys and challenges. (I've just started my caregiving job so could relate.) I rolled up the line which was still damp from yesterday's rain just as it started to get dark.

August 4, 2013

Today I noticed a second Little Free Library has cropped up in the neighborhood! The accidental pairing of two books "Really Bad Girls of the Bible" and "So Brave, Young and Handsome" made me happy. How's that for a codependent relationship? I knit from 6:30 to 8 p.m. today after feeding and poop-scooping Sandy and Marvin's cats.

I stayed at the bench extra long because Alice came and sat with me. She said I might consider starting to love and care for my body, not just my mind and spirit, which is just what I needed to hear. And that prayer is not limited to talking. Prayer is a posture of listening and receptivity to God—which could surely encompass many different things including my knitting practice.

I also met another woman as I wound the yarn ball up the hill. Wiry and tan, with lots of silver jewelry. She was at a party recently, and her friends all wanted to know why I was knitting a line to the ocean, so she had followed the line down to talk to me. This time, I didn't evade the question. (I have been catty lately–making tautological statements like I'm knitting a line to the ocean to knit a line to the ocean. I know, really annoying.) I told her how hard it is for me as an artist to explain my work but that I had made a decision to be open about it as of yesterday. Feeling vulnerable, I told her the piece was called "For Longing" and it's about my yearning for God. She didn't bat an eye, and expressed gratitude that she had come to talk to me on a day when I was willing to share. She said she was a Buddhist, and was trying to practice every day, all the time. I had been so afraid of offending people, or worse yet, being labeled a religious wacko. I'm realizing I don't have to manage people's opinions about me, I just have to be myself. It feels pretty damn awesome.

August 5, 2013

Beautiful, quiet morning knit. The hour passed very slowly. I enjoy the way the line changes shape depending on the speed and direction of the cars that cross it. A woman interrupted her phone conversation to give me a hug. I hadn't seen her since last June. Keiki. The first person to cry in response to this art work.

## August 6, 2013

Foggy and cold.  I enjoyed taking a picture of the city water meter truck with the slogan "Make Every Drop Count" in large blue letters on its side.  I thought about making every stitch count in this half-mile knit "stream" to the bay.  Karen says her husband is concocting a method for me to transport the ball of knit line up and down the hill when it gets too heavy to carry.  Karen and Mel are the people with the quail in their gorgeous backyard.  They told me they grew raspberries by the sidewalk for folks to munch on as they walk by.  Their generosity moves me.

Keiki gave me another hug today.  She was talking on her headset again.  I don't know how people can be so talkative at 8 in the morning.

## August 7, 2013

I climbed the 80-foot observation tower in the arboretum again yesterday to drop the knit line over the edge of the railing.  When I knit, I turn my needles at the end of each row and this in turn winds up the line, filling it with tension.

A shirtless jogger named Craig told me that rock climbers have the same problem with their lines getting twisted.  He asked about my project, and said sagely in response, "Small drops of water can fill a very large vessel."

A dad came up with his two kids, herding them carefully to the opposite side of the tower to avoid the crazy lady with the rope spilling all over the floor like blue spaghetti.  The kids were fascinated with my project—while Dad carefully pointed out the wonders of the Cascade Mountain range, the kids stole glances at the yarn spinning like a top down near the pavement below.

As I waited for the line to unwind, I happened to glance down at the rail to read some faded graffiti that said, *I can't justify buying more yarn.* I almost got goosebumps! It's this kind of recurring serendipity that makes me sure I'm on the right track.

## August 8, 2013

Since untwisting the line, it has stretched across the 14th St intersection, and is rapidly heading toward 13th. The ocean looks closer now, like a blue planet looming. I can't get enough BLUE in my eye sockets. As I wound the line back up the hill, some women came up and asked me, "Now, is it a sweater or a scarf?"

I was so taken aback, all I could say was, "Really?!" Then I realized they were laughing, so I joined in. I was grateful for a quiet knit today, a buffer for a busy day ahead of me. (I'm duck-sitting tonight. A new line to add to my resume.)

## August 9, 2013

For every driver that barreled through the intersection of 16th and Taylor, there was a driver who slowed down and made contact. A mother and daughter drove past smiling and waving. A man in a truck honked and nodded.

I felt buoyant today. It had something to do with wearing yellow, I think. I feel so cheerful in yellow, like a human daffodil. I bought my ruffled yellow shirt immediately upon arriving back in Bellingham to celebrate my return to the noisy world so full of color.

Jerome stopped to chat. I no longer think of him as the Quiet Man because he has become quite talkative. He walks 10 miles every day in all weather conditions. He said the forecast is sunshine for the next four days. If you live anywhere in the Pacific Northwest, you know that golden days like these are a rare gift.

## August 10, 2013

I only knit 35 minutes today because I ran out of yarn. That was fine with me because I needed to put my friend's ducks back in their hutch before the "witching" hour when the owls start craving *foie gras*.

As I wound the line back up the hill, I saw Harry, an oil painter who lives all alone in a huge house enclosed by tall cedar trees. The yard is full of mythological statues created by his father. (I know because I peeked.) Harry and I have a history. We made each other's acquaintance briefly one day about a year and a half ago, and he gave me his artist card. Months went by, and we never talked. One dull winter's day, I was on a treasure hunt, searching for beautiful things to inspire me. Suddenly, my eye was caught by a small red tree with no leaves by the sidewalk. I had just picked a scarlet twig off the tree, when suddenly Harry burst out of the brush, and thundered, "Leave that tree alone!"

Harry is tall, barrel-chested, with a bushy beard and a fat dreadlock on either side of his face. Suffice it to say, I quit the scene as quickly as possible. Later, I emailed him an apology and a link to my website. The next time I saw Harry, he came towards me open armed and gave me a bear hug! He said how much he had enjoyed my artwork, and that he liked 75% of it, which is more than he could say about his own work. Today Harry and I talked about the knitting. I told him it has taken me five months (not counting winter and spring) to get down to 14th.

"To make this *stripe*?" he exclaimed. (No one has ever called the line a stripe before...a rope, a string, a ribbon, yes, but not a stripe.)

Unfazed, I said, "Yeah."

He said, "That was an odd idea...but then who am *I* to say that?"

## August 11, 2013

The magic never struck for me today, but if I keep knitting, it's bound to come back. That's what a practice is for. A practice is something I define as an activity that I do regularly whether or not I feel like it. I've knit every day at 16th and Taylor for 41 days in a row now and I don't want to break the continuity. But today I did not feel like knitting at all. The sweet aroma of bread from my bread machine filled my bedroom and there was a chill in the wind outside. I finally got myself out the door and up the hill by 8:00 p.m.

As I arrived at the bench, Jerome walked slowly up. I said hi, and continued on my way to fetch the ball of line out of

Arnold's basement. When I returned, Jerome was still at the bench, doing stretches off the back. Partly because I was in a hurry to unroll the line, and partly because I'm worried that he thinks I'm romantically inclined, I just said a quick goodnight, and headed down the hill.

## August 12, 2013

I let the ball of line roll down the hill as it pleased and it swaggered delightfully. I wonder what to do when the ball of knit line gets too heavy for me to carry in the near future? I have a wheelbarrow but winding a ball and pushing a wheelbarrow uphill at the same time sounds awkward. Maybe I need one of those giant wooden spools that fishermen use to wind up their nets.

The challenge of knitting in the early evening is the glare of the sun off the water. My red hat pulled down over my eyes helps, but it also shuts people out.

## August 13, 2013

When I went down to roll up the line, I almost got goosebumps at the sight of Taylor Dock below me. The destination is looming! I brought a paper bag to stuff full of all the wormy, bruised apples that rot on the neighbors' lawns. With some judicious cutting, a drop of lemon juice, a few minutes of cooking, and a drizzle of honey, they will make the most delicious applesauce.

On my walk home, I heard the quacking of ducks. Looking up over the embankment, I saw them in a kid's plastic wading pool, preening themselves.

## August 14, 2013

Another quiet morning, cloudy and warm. A woman drove by in her car, then came back to chat. She told me about a yarnbombing project in Sunnyland neighborhood, a tree cozy with a heart on it.

"You never see the knitter, but she keeps adding to the cozy, a little at a time," she told me.

I like to think that what I'm doing is not yarn bombing but rather a daily ritual, presence performed. But who knows?

A hybrid approached then slowed to a purr as the driver drove mindfully over the line. My friends jokingly tell me that the knit line is a psychological speed bump.

All over the neighborhood, I've spotted "Marshall's Lost" cat posters. I liked this one especially because of the description, "fat, friendly male," like a dating profile. A little boy about three feet tall was out by himself riding a red bicycle. I have never seen an unattended child here before. He told me my ball of knitting was really BIG. I asked him if he wanted to try holding it, and warned him that it was heavy. He took the knit ball in his arms and said, "Easy-peasy!"

### August 16, 2013

The magic has returned big time. Giant clouds piled up over the ocean, and the sun burst through in a dramatic light show as I knit this evening. The smell of wood campfires. Lots of people out walking. A family on bicycles passed sounding their bells. Noisy crows, train whistles, a child hammering on a toy piano, a car blasting reggae. A woman with bouncy hair jumped out of her car and started snapping photos of me with her iPhone.

Suddenly, I heard a man's voice saying, "I'm going to talk to this knitter—I'll catch up to you in a bit."

Then I was face-to-face with Dave who I hadn't seen or talked to since last year when we met at the bench. At that time, we were both facing massive upheavals, and choosing new paths—he recovering from a breakup and moving back to the city after years on an island, and me entering Our Lady of the Redwoods Monastery. We were both sitting on the edge of the cliff of our lives before taking the next plunge. Now the river of time and grace had worked its wonders, moved us further downstream, and gently set us down. He looked happy and relaxed as he shared about his new job and digs in Seattle. He was visiting family in Bellingham, and just happened to be out on a stroll when he chanced upon me. Wonderful to come full circle.

## August 18, 2013

When I came up the hill from unwinding the ball of line, a lady was sitting on the bench knitting while her husband looked on. The same guerrilla knitter that appeared on July 15th. I wonder if this will be a monthly occurrence?! She made a knot in the yarn–the first knot in the project, and I accepted it. She was very apologetic for the mess she had made of my knitting. While we chatted, a man in a truck drove up to the line, then in a rage, put his truck in reverse and drove the other way. This is the first time I've seen the knitting cause road rage.

A girl about nine years old strode down the hill. Suddenly she stopped and stared at me for a long time. Her blonde hair flashing, she ran up the hill past me. Then she came back down. She had a silver camera hidden under her arm, and she took pictures of me knitting for about half an hour, on the sly, as if I wouldn't notice! She paid me the biggest compliment by spending so much time with the art. I got shivers down my legs imagining this could be the moment when she vows to be an artist.

The sun broke through dark clouds in four different spots, beaming shafts of light down on the ocean like four UFO's preparing to land. My neighbors pulled up in Carla's jeep and tumbled out. They had just watched *The Butler*, a film about a man who was the butler during four presidencies in the White House. I feel a bit like a butler here on the hill. I'm part of the landscape, the background of people's lives.

On my way to roll up the line for the evening, I heard the twitter of birds in the privacy hedge to my left, where a flock of tiny chirping songbirds had settled in for the night. I took some photos which disturbed them and they flew away.

## August 19, 2013

Very quiet knit this morning, and shorter than usual. I listened to the planes taking off from Bellingham Airport, and felt the misty rain on my arm. At the end of the knit, I locked eyes with a young buck, his velvet antlers just starting to show.

## August 20, 2013

Cloudy skies overhead. I could barely hear my neighbors' greetings over the roar of the cement truck down the street. The smell of diesel on an empty stomach made me queasy. However, I was fascinated by the long arm of the truck, like a giant spider leg.

A woman drove up in a yellow VW Bug and asked what I was doing. Then she drove around the block and came back. She was early for work so she decided to park her car and follow the knit line down the hill. She loves Fairhaven neighborhood because people care about connecting with each other. "Is that part of your motivation for your knitting practice?" she asked.

Josh came by on his morning walk, and we visited for a while. I told him I have only one Facebook friend (having deleted my account in a desire for monastic simplicity the year before), and he said he would like to be my second friend. I have returned to Facebook, with much feet dragging, to set up an artist profile.

## August 21, 2013

I didn't make it to the knitting bench until 8:03 p.m. The sunset was seamlessly executed—all the colors blurring into one another like a giant melting sundae. It's one part magical, one part lonely, and one part creepy to knit at night. I did come face-to-face with a deer who submitted to having his photo taken twice. People asked me "why?" a lot tonight, and I am back to giving poetic and cryptic explanations. One girl walked by wearing a tangerine sundress with a cloth sunflower tucked behind her ear—the perfect outfit for a summer evening stroll. The smiling bicyclist with the cowbell pedaled up the hill. Two doors down, a child who landed wrong in a somersault finally stopped crying and fell asleep. The lady who always wears black shades and a huge white hat came by. It was getting dark, but she was still wearing the shades. She said she bets I have some interesting conversations. I hope she will eventually open up more, but we're making progress as evidenced by this tiny exchange.

Marvin and Sandy strolled by with their dog. Marvin always has a fat, stinky cigar in hand. I love their relationship–both of them are nerds (historian and librarian) and whenever I overhear them, they are having the most wonderful conversations peppered with lots of laughter. Sandy offered me her granny shopping cart should the knit ball ever become too heavy to carry up and down the hill. We talked about how big I think the ball will get. I have no idea–maybe three feet in diameter?

## August 23, 2013

Cloudy and windy today on the knitting bench. Cynthia came by teasing me that if the bench becomes a dating hot spot, the neighborhood will be in trouble!

I said, "I have to work on my sex appeal."

She said she's seen guys stop to chat with me, and the next thing, they are sitting on the bench talking the whole hour while I knit. Parenthesis–this has only happened once or twice this summer.

I asked, "What kind of nursing did you practice before retiring last year?"

"Obstetrics—I got paid to witness miracles every day," she said smiling.

I would have guessed hospice care. She has the perfect bedside manner, so warm and gentle. She crossed the street saying that she was going to check email at the neighbors' house since her internet was down.

I said, "That's what friends are for."

"Especially if they don't know it," she called back over her shoulder.

This hour's knitting zipped by because in addition to Cynthia, I had another guest, Karen, who followed the knit line up the hill to visit me. We happened to be wearing the same black shoes with round, silver buckles. It was the first time Karen had ever sat on this bench, even though she's lived in this neighborhood for years. Cynthia came back and chatted with us near the end of the knit. I left Karen and her visiting while I hiked down hill to roll up my ball of line. Heading home, I saw a pink Victorian house with matching hollyhocks that almost exploded my cuteness barometer.

## August 25, 2013

I almost cancelled my knit because I felt ill from eating some questionable leftover lentil spaghetti. A cup of ginger tea, a hard-boiled egg and three pieces of white toast later, I was raring to go again. As I knit, a neighbor walked by and told me to look behind me at the rainbow! I had been knitting under a rainbow and didn't even realize it. Two college women happened to walk by just then carrying a printer box; I asked one of them to take a picture for me. Patty came by. Her face scared me the first time I saw her. She was drooling, and didn't have a chin. I learned that she battled cancer 42 years ago and the doctor had removed her infected jaw. She courageously continues to go about in public, and has helped raise awareness about "Let's Face It," a support group for people living with disfigurement from cancer.

## August 26, 2013

I spent the hour wondering if it would rain, feeling like a giant yellow sculpture in my full-length raincoat. Cynthia said the weather was moody and couldn't make up its mind. The guerrilla knitter greeted me and speed-walked by. When I crested the hill after rolling up the knit line for the night, someone had carried my knitting needles and line across the street, presumably so they could drive past without running over it. So I have a new theory for why some drivers look grouchy going by–maybe they feel bad about driving over my knitting.

## August 28, 2013

Roxie, the dog trainer, walked up and we chatted briefly. I asked how the preparations for her art fundraiser for the homeless were going.

"I've been trying to design a brochure, but I get so frustrated with my computer that I go on walks to clear my head. Hence, I have been going on lots of walks lately," she said wryly.

At the end of my knitting session, a blonde woman flagger drove up in a construction truck, and put out a "Road Work Ahead" sign. Soon I could hear the grinding of a mixer up the hill from me. I have a fondness for construction signs because they are so bright and garish. Where else does one see neon orange in this land of respectable greens, browns and blues?

## August 29, 2013

I was in a foul mood tonight because I'd just ruined a painting of a wiener dog and the last thing I wanted to do was go out and knit in what looked like a hurricane. But I pushed myself out the door, whining to my roommates all the while. Coming down the hill, unwinding my knitting, I happened upon two guys with joyful faces, chatting and lounging on the grass by the school in anticipation of their AA meeting. One guy, Ken, asked if he could take a photo of me for his girlfriend who has just started knitting. He had Jackson Pollock pants, splattered with dry wall plaster, so I asked to take a photo of him too. The other guy told me that he knits, and pulled out a partially-knit, checkered headband from his knapsack. They asked me where I knit, and I told them about the abandoned bus stop, and how I fell in love with the old bench and wanted to give it a new purpose in life. "It wasn't ready to retire," Ken said. I loved his spectacles, round like the wheels of his bicycle. We said goodbye, and I finished unwinding the line and sat down to knit on the bench.

I had a long chat with Jerome today. He once earned a living filleting salmon in Alaska, spending the winters near Guadalajara, Mexico. His dream was always to open a café in Mexico that served breakfast and lunch, so that he could spend the evening on the beach. But he never did it.

The bicyclist with the cowbell pedaled up the hill smiling as usual but not saying a word. When I went to store the ball of knitting in Arnold's basement, I found that he had set out his rainboots for me. So thoughtful.

It was a blustery but warm evening. I felt like shouting, the wind teemed with life. It reminded me of one of my favorite childhood stories, *Mr. Widdle and the Sea Breeze* about a grumpy, old man whose life is turned upside down by a girl and her pet seagull. When the Sea Breeze comes, Mr. Widdle is pulled out of his rut, into the big, wide world. That's what this daily knit is doing for me too.

### August 30, 2013

It's open house at the school today. Kids flocked past dressed in new school clothes, bright and clean, filling the air with excited chatter about meeting their new teachers.

# 10

# I Am An Artist

September 1, 2013

A boy came by, talking on his walkie talkie to his parent. He was half black, half white, and his shirt said, "I'm different. Yeah! I'm different." He asked me some questions about the knitting project and was really into it. I asked to take his picture, and he stood very straight and proud. I loved him. A leader in the making.

I met Alan, an older guy with a small backpack. He walked by a couple of times, and finally sat down to chat. I asked him what he does, and he said, I'm a Walker. He said that when he was young, he asked himself, what am I good at? He concluded that he was very good at walking, so he's taken up walking in a serious way. He's walked from Canada to Mexico, and also done the Appalachian Trail. While we were chatting, Jerome walked by. What timing! After Jerome, Alan is the second urban hiker I've met. He walks from Bellingham Technical College to Fairhaven, about 10 miles a day. He's training for his next major hike. I didn't get a chance to ask him where the hike will be. How refreshing that Alan did not give a standard reply, "I retired from _____."

Just this week, I've made a decision to tell people I'm an artist when they ask me what I do. It's a scary step for me because I feel committed like I have to take my dream (myself?) seriously. Too, it can be humbling to face the raised eyebrows. I might as well tell people that I make balloon dogs, or sell popcorn. I don't like the question that inevitably follows, So do you support yourself as an artist full-time? I feel like I'm not legitimate until I can answer yes. Anyway, none of this really matters, and it's good for me to eat humble pie, I suppose. It's just so unfair. A lawyer, for example, doesn't have to say, My passion is law, but waitressing pays the bills. However, I think when people ask me what I do, they want a window into who I am. Telling them I'm an artist gets to the heart of me, really quickly. I suppose that's another reason I don't like it. I'm shy and self-protective. Hah, but I'm saying it anyway, so there!

## September 2, 2013

This afternoon, I knit less than usual because my neighbor Carla invited me for a Sicilian pork roast dinner, and I didn't want to arrive late. The highlight of the knit was my splendid neighbor, Camellia, who informed me about teeter totters, washing your hands, and how her silly baby brother rubbed black beans in his hair. I could have listened to her all evening. She has always held back, and barely even said hi up to this point. Suddenly, she has blossomed, just in time for preschool this fall. Also, two women jogged up over the hill and nearly split themselves laughing when they saw me knitting. I told them they'd worked so hard, jogging up the steep hill, they deserved a break. They'd been discussing the blue knit line, trying to figure out what it was. Their theory was that it was going to guide someone to a message, such as a marriage proposal.

## Evening Knit

I knit in the evening again after the party.

A lady came up over the hill and said, "Do I dare ask what

you're doing? Did you come straight out of a fairy tale where a wicked gnome cast a spell on you?" Later she came back and asked if she could take a photo for her blog about Bellingham's musical scene.

A man and a little girl came huffing and puffing up the hill on their bicycle built for two...They also stopped and asked if they could take a photo of me! (Two in one day, not bad.)

The man said, "This is my out-of-breath-daughter Sophia, and I am her out-of-breath-father, Alex." They had just moved to the neighborhood from Klamath Falls.

A couple drove up in their car, and the woman called out, "You're a yarn sculptor."

It was not a question, but a statement of fact. I didn't say anything, but sort of bowed in acquiescence while wondering how one sculpts yarn.

## September 3, 2013

The quiet knitting ended abruptly when the knit line began to pull me down the hill. I was being dragged along by a force stronger than myself, like I was on jet skis. Finally I dropped the knitting needles, and headed down hill to see what was causing this bizarre tugging. Worst case scenarios flashed through my mind—what if the line had gotten snagged on a truck? But then I saw three young males doubled over, running away. I was irritated, to put it mildly. But also curious to see what they had done. I ran back uphill to get my camera so I could photograph the detour that the line took today: the boys had draped the knit line through the trees, over the crosswalk sign, and across the street at a diagonal angle. I hope they don't do this again because it could be a tripping hazard, and I don't want anything to stop me from knitting to the ocean.

## September 4, 2013

I had so much free time before work today, I decided to knit all morning just under two hours. The cool, overcast weather was perfect for knitting; I enjoyed the drops of mist on my face. No more sunburns. In other good news, the guys who wrenched on the line yesterday did me an unexpected favor because the line extended several feet longer today. Deacon Larry and Christina from Sacred Heart Church were out on a walk together. Deacon Larry said that when I finish knitting to the ocean, God will show me what to do next. And Christine chimed in, "Or maybe you'll see a mermaid!"

I met a woman named Renee who is a textile and fashion design artist. Her stitched business card says "Social Fabric." I loved the play on words.

Grace and Rachel stopped to chat. I hadn't seen them this year—probably because of summer vacation. They're the soccer moms who walk together every day for two hours, after dropping their kids off at school. The first brave souls to talk to me at the bench last May.

## September 5, 2013

Today I heard thunder rolling as I sat down on my crunchy yellow raincoat to knit. A very quiet knitting session ensued, punctuated by cars full of passengers whose smiles lit up their dark interiors. How beautiful when nothing happens. Three crows perched on the electrical wire, one flew away reminding me of these lines from "Thirteen Ways of Looking at a Blackbird":

> I do not know which to prefer,
> The beauty of inflections
> Or the beauty of innuendoes,
> The blackbird whistling
> Or just after.

I heard the screeching of the train's brakes on the rails below. Sea gulls. A beautiful blond woman pulled up in her white bug and told me that my project was cute. She then parked in the young doctor's driveway.

I took a photo of the knit line's sinuous curves and captioned it, *Speak to me in cursive, darling.*

## September 6, 2013

Chuck, the mailman, was on vacation, and a young guy with a nice beard subbed for him. He said that the postal workers have been discussing my knitting project, and offered me the choice of either his cheese stick or a ziplock bag of graham crackers. I was touched, remembering the book, *The Gift: Creativity and the Modern Artist*, by Lewis Hyde, who writes that artistic inspiration is a gift that the artist receives, gives in the making of it, and which is received as gift by the audience who then give back. Those graham crackers were gift to me, nourishment and encouragement to knit on.

A blonde woman drove up in a red truck. She said that a lot of people in her group knit, even the men. I asked her about the gathering and she said it was a 12 Step Group.

She said, "We knit and we kneel." Then she said, "Serenity Now!" gave me a thumbs up and drove away.

Several people asked me if I was knitting for peace. More and more people want to know if I'm knitting for a cause. You aren't allowed to do something for the beauty of it; you have to have an explanation for everything. (That's one reason being an artist is so challenging.) I love the idea of "holding space," a ministry of presence. But how do you tell that to someone impatient for a practical explanation?

## September 7, 2013

Today's knit was uneventful, even dull. The sun came out against all odds, hot and bright. I have been thinking about the decisions we make in life—marriage, childbirth, career, or in my case, this half-mile knitting project. If anyone had told us what we were getting ourselves into, we would not have started. Thank God for naïveté. It makes us do brave and bold things, that would make our knees knock had we known better. When I started this project, I anticipated a charming summer project. Six months of knitting and counting, I am still glad to have said a wholehearted yes.

## September 8, 2013

The lawn across from my bench has exploded in fluffy dandelion heads. Spiders have suddenly appeared, spinning webs across garden pathways and gates. I thought I felt a sneaky one crawling on my arm, but it was just one of my hairs stuck to the side of my shirt. The whirr of birds, flying together like planes in perfect formation. I knit as the birds chirped and squeaked themselves to sleep in the bushes and trees around me.

Lately, I'm thinking about changes with the transition from summer to fall in full tilt. Sometimes I crave permanence and security, and my life gets miserable like an airtight container that doesn't let any sunlight or oxygen in. Embracing life as an adventure rather than a script has been so liberating. As the voice told me in the dream last year, Behold, don't possess.

More changes: Cynthia and Pete are leaving for Italy tomorrow for a month. I used their bathroom at the start of the knit today and told Pete as he fried breaded chicken breasts that I don't know what I'll do without their bathroom for a whole month.

Cynthia told me she and Pete had spent some time at church yesterday praying for Syria. I so hope her prayers, and all our yearnings for peace, are answered.

I spotted Karen harvesting tomatoes and chard; she invited me to check out the cabin in their backyard. She and her husband are willing to rent it to me. It has no running water, but a cozy wood stove, two wooden deck chairs, and a loft for a bedroom. Extremely rustic with handwoven floor rugs that Karen makes for a living. (But no toilet. This is fast becoming an obsession for me). I told her I liked roughing it. For now, I'm moving in with my brother and sister-in-law since my sublet has ended, but it's nice to have a backup plan.

## September 9, 2013

A woman stopped to ask, "What will you do with the half-mile knit ball of line once the project is done?"

I said, "I will probably transform it into a new artwork."

She said, "With all the time and energy you have put into it, it has value in and of itself, and should be preserved in a museum."

"To most people it would probably just look like a ball of rope, unless they knew the inside story," I said unconvinced.

She said, "If you left the knitting needles attached it would raise questions in people's mind as to why anyone would knit a line that long..." She paused and said, "My kids think you're crazy. They think I'm crazy too, but they still love me."

"How old are they?" I asked.

"12 and 16," she replied.

I said, "Ah yes, I was cynical in my teens. I had very little sense of humor back then. I too thought my parents were crazy when I was a teen–and I still find them eccentric."

She said, "It's a good thing, because they have given the world an eccentric daughter."

Mollie's parents Wendell and Emily and their friends stopped by on a walk. Emily asked me what would happen when the knit line gets to the ocean. I told her I want to have a bucket brigade of friends and neighbors pass the ball of knitting down the hill all the way from the bench to the ocean. The closing act will bring everyone together in an extravagant outpouring of love and community. At least, that's how I'm picturing it, and things rarely turn out the way I envision. She said that when the line touches the ocean, it will draw the water uphill due to capillary action.

By the end of my two-hour knit, I could see the tops of the San Juan islands like blue ribbons suspended over the fog.

## September 10, 2013

Knitting in the morning is so magical. I adore the swooping shadows, the dew on the tips of grapevines, the shiny newness of everything. A man said the knit line helped him find his way. He had followed the knit line down the street, and then drove off to check out some houses. He got lost, but when he saw the knit line, he knew where he was again. This pleased me, like a scene from a fairy tale.

Arnold told me I should get a golf cart to drive up and down the hill now that it's taking so long to unwind the line.

I hemmed and hawed about how it would not fit in with my ritual, but he said, "It would be a new ritual, an electric one. Isn't your goal to electrify people? Well, golf carts are electric, you know."

A young guy drove up the hill on a blue motorcycle. He turned off his engine and said, "I saw your line running along all the sidewalks. It's beautiful."

Finally! Someone besides me thinks it's beautiful, I thought.

I asked the window delivery man if I could photograph the makeshift canopy on the truck. He said the guys at the shop affectionately refer to it as the Frankentruck. A middle school boy wearing bright blue sneakers said hi with an open smile. I let him hold the ball of knit line with one hand, and he said, "Holy crap!" when he felt how heavy it was. That sent me down a mental rabbit-hole about Jung and Freud and one of my favorite words, *scatalogical*. (Where else do *scat* and *logic* meet in the same breath!) The sacred and profane collide or embrace all the time, depending on your point of view.

## September 11, 2013

A doozy of a day! I was in a foul mood that hadn't let up when I crawled onto the bench to begin knitting at 5:35 p.m. for the next two hours. I said, Ha ha, I'm not afraid of you, and got in touch with the calm, brave warrior inside. But the sun beat down, and I felt as calm and brave as wilted lettuce. I knit on. First surprise: the young doctor cycled up to me on his road bike in a skin-tight red racer outfit, a crop of sandy chest hair peeking out the open neck of his spandex shirt. I told him I've been lamenting the absence of my bicycle all summer (it's stuck at the monastery), and he said I could choose from the two additional bikes he owns. The trouble is, they are all one speed bikes—slight problem considering this is Bellingham's best sledding hill.

Mollie pulled up in her truck and yelled stories to me through her lowered window like she always does, her truck on the wrong side of the road. This scenario usually ends when another driver gets road rage. Today, she gave in and parked across from me in an illegal parking spot next to the fire hydrant and sat down on the bench to visit for over an hour.

She said, "Artistic ideas are in the air–they don't belong to us, they come and go. All we can do is make ourselves receptive."

The sun finally dipped down behind the giant Douglas fir and we sat in the blessed shade. And Mollie had the good heart to go home and bring back four beverages for me to choose from–concentrated cold coffee, green juice, coconut milk or water. I mixed the coconut milk and green goo together (per her recommendation) and it slipped down my parched throat. It looked like swamp water mixed with Elmer's glue, but I was past caring.

She was having a rough day too—a difficult anniversary of sorts. In addition, her furnace had broken down: "I told the repair guy on the phone to send someone with a sense of humor. "Why?" they asked me. "Because I have a Tiki bar in my basement."

After she left, I watched the glaring sun dip below the powder-blue mountains. The dreadlocked artist and his lady friend were out on their porch watching the sunset as I collected the knit line for the day. They waved and I waved back. I saw testosterone-pumped guys with huge trucks, smoking and hanging out in the church parking lot, their animated voices enlivening the air. Not your typical church crowd, I thought to myself, probably 12 Steppers, but when I asked a guy he gave me a vague answer. Maybe he was just practicing anonymity like the three inch wolf spider that just crawled out from under my bed where I'm typing. This day's not over yet.

## September 12, 2013

I was grateful to knit in the cool morning air as I watched dads walking their kids to school. I said good morning to a little blond boy on his way to school and he looked right through me. I said it louder, and he ignored me again. That's taking never talk to strangers a little too far, I think. Josh and Thomas came by; Thomas asked me to sub for him at the Art Department for a day. He encouraged me to bring the knit ball to show the students. Hurrah! Josh said he had inherited a giant ball of string compiled from vintage parcel wrappings from his mother. Mom used to exhibit the ball of string on a Victorian pedestal in her home. Now they have it in their living room, their cat's favorite place to nap.

As they turned to go, a woman walked up to the bench. She introduced herself, and said she and a group of meditators were following my blog! I was delighted and surprised. Her friend, the host of the group, owns a portrait I painted in 2000 of myself in a red jacket with buttons. And this friend has been quietly reading and sharing my blog. I was delighted to know a thread of connection still exists, since I thought we had lost all contact. (We had been coworkers at the Frye Art Museum Cafe in Seattle over a decade ago. I have lovely memories of this strong, clear-eyed woman.) A feeling of gratitude washed over me at realizing how this knitting project has brought me back into relationship with others. A web of relationships, virtual and face-to-face, that nourishes and inspires me daily.

Transcendence of self begins with community. The whole is so much greater than the sum of its parts. The ocean has come to symbolize for me not just the Infinite, but this sea of humanity. I am enlarged by each person that comes my way; my narrow preoccupation with my own pride and fear gives way ever so slightly before this great tide of life coming and going.

September 13, 2013

Overcast and cool today, the ocean hidden by white. I picked up a beefy apple from a neighbor's lawn, and pondered food throughout the hour of knitting. Artist and art offered as bread to nourish the community. A transubstantiation of sorts. Human beings do not just crave food or sleep, we hunger for beauty, meaning, and wonderment. I'm still reading *The Gift* which describes the momentum that is generated when we give without expecting anything in return.

I like it (in theory). But it's a very challenging practice to embrace long-term. In my experience, everything I need is provided (with some bonuses thrown in), but it doesn't come from the direction I'm expecting nor in my time frame. How to live this radical trust, this self-abandonment in every moment? Maybe I'm too smart for my own good. The deer, on the other hand, don't worry about the grocery bill or the rent. I snapped a picture of the leggy molting deer today on its way to the neighbors' apple tree bonanza.

Jerome came by and chatted with me. I was happy when he stopped to talk to Roxie too. He's slowly finding people to trust. Walking all day without talking to anyone would get very lonely. I met Arnold's gardener—German accent and blond ponytail—who tends the front yard. Arnold is concerned that I find a large colander to hold the wet knit ball when it starts raining. He wants to make sure the ball will drain properly while it sits in his basement. And the rains are coming any day now!

September 15, 2013

Last night I intended not to knit today because my family was leaving for Portland at 7 a.m. for a ceremony for my brother. But my sister suggested I knit *before* 7 a.m. I decided I would, provided that I woke up by 5:30. I didn't set my alarm, but my heart must have wanted to knit, because I woke up on time. My sublet has drawn to a close, so I am now living with my parents on the other side of town. It's terrible for the environment, but I hopped in my car anyway and drove down empty streets. The red streetlights turned green for me as I approached, the way fear dissolves when we move forward, regardless.

When I got to the bench, it was still dark although the street light provided enough light to knit by. I could feel droplets of mist on my skin. The thought occurred to me that if I entered my neighbors' basement in the dark to fetch the ball of knitting, they might think I was a thief. Or B.J. might start barking and wake them up. I had just had an experience yesterday where I showed up at someone's house to drop something off without giving advance notice–and they were not happy. So I decided to sit, rather than knit, out of respect for my neighbor Arnold. At least, I could hold space for one hour.

I enjoyed taking pictures in the dark, and watching the sky lighten without ever seeing the sun through all the fog. The fog horn tooted, two trains whistled by, a blue jay screeched, a dog barked and fell silent. A man pulled up in his car and asked me, "Are you doing your knit in the dark?" He sounded impressed. He was heading out early on his way to Steven's Pass to rock-climb. I took a photo of the telephone pole with a Douglas fir in the background, shrouded in fog. I imagined that the street pole was dreaming of its past life as a Douglas fir, the ghost of its former self standing behind it. I saw my neighbor Arnold at the end of the hour, and told him I had just sat.

He said, "That's a good thing to do." He is a meditator, a lover of silence. He said he wakes up earlier than I'll ever come, and that B.J. doesn't usually bark. I said I didn't want him and his wife to mistake me for a thief breaking into their basement and he said, "Bah!"

So now I know that I can knit in the dark whenever I like.

## Evening Knit

As it turned out, I made it back in time to knit again that evening. Thank God, Tom and Carla were home with company for dinner. When the knit line suddenly began moving, pulling me downhill, I started yelling. Tom and two male guests came running outside. I told them a "hooligan" was yanking on the line.

Tom shook his head in disbelief, "A hooligan? A juvenile delinquent maybe, but a *hooligan*?"

I was not feeling eloquent at that moment. We could see a guy down below circling the intersection on a bicycle; Tom thought he discerned the knit line tied to the back. One of the dinner guests jumped into his car in sock feet and drove down the hill to try to stop him.

Tom said, "We have to tell them to stop. This is history in

114

the making!"

By the time Tom's friend reached 14th Street, the kid had pedaled away. I sat down to knit again, watching the line for every twitch, feeling paranoid. But there were no more disturbances.

Alice stopped by for a visit, and her grandmotherly presence comforted me. I was glad to have a distraction to keep me from stewing. When I went to roll up the line, it was a giant tangle, but came loose easily. Tom advised me to keep my knitting to school hours as much as possible. Point taken.

## September 16, 2013

I'm enjoying the signs of autumn. The sweet smell of rotting leaves recalls rose petals and apple cider. The ornamental cherry tree is oozing sap. I was sorely tempted to touch it, but I've learned my lesson that it's impossible to wash off tree sap. Harry's little maple is blushing yellow and orange and neon green. How is it possible to love this place so intensely? And how can I see something new on the same street every day in such a little space of time? I think it has to do with a relaxed and open frame of mind. I wish I could say that I'm always this present to the wonder around me, but I'm not. This hour of knitting meditation does something to quiet my inner noise for a few moments of pure awe.

I took a picture of a brick driveway, split down the middle like a pair of red pants.

Tom teased me as I marched down the hill to unwind the line, "Watch out for those hooligans down there." He asked if I expected to complete the project by the holidays.

I said, "Probably not."

He said, "Well, at least it gives you something to do. Keeps you off the street—er, I mean on the street, and out of trouble."

## September 17, 2013

"Is there a coffee hidden in that ball of yarn?" Josh kidded me. It was a good day for coffee, overcast and cool. Josh and

Thomas were out this morning on their work out walk up the hill, wearing matching black nerd glasses and shirts.

Josh told me about an art installation "Slumber" by Janine Antoni, where she wove the REM pattern that her brain made each night into a huge blanket that is now over 200 feet long.

Josh and Thomas made a laundry list of everything that could possibly go wrong with my knit installation. "What if it caught on the motor of a boat, and you were dragged down the hill into the ocean? To be prepared, you might as well start wearing a dinghy and water skis now," Josh said.

They continued on their way up the hill, having given my brain a wonderful buzz. I love the way their minds work.

A man drove up in his car, parked across from me, and walked into Tom and Carla's house. Soon, I could hear majestic piano music emanating. Tom is a musician, and he gives the keys to his house to friends so they can play his piano when he's not there. The concert only lasted a few minutes, and then the guy came out again.

"Did you get your fix?" I asked him.

"Yes," he said, "I only had two or three minutes today. Are you getting your knitting fix?"

"Yes, two whole hours of it today," I told him.

"We're all behind you," he said.

September 18, 2013

*The pale yellow flowers of the dogwood outside this window are saints ... The lakes hidden among the hills are saints ... but what about you? What about me? For me to be a saint means to be myself.* ~Thomas Merton

After taking a photo of the rambling rose, I sat down to a delicious knit on the bench today. Sunshine for the first half, a light breeze and cool shade for the second. Michael came by with his huge black dog, fresh from a week of making a sculpture in another state. A graceful kinetic sculpture like a giant

116

pinwheel, but much more elegant. He said he had forgotten how fun it is to make art.

"I felt alive again, you know?" he said.

"I *know*," I replied. Today was one of those rare times that I felt alive, felt I was doing what I was created to do. Every cell in my body singing.

I have been savoring the film I watched last night, *Like Water for Chocolate*. Several people have asked me if the film inspired my knitting project so I had to see it. I will never forget the image of Tita unfurling her knit blanket which trails behind her carriage for miles as she is carried away from home. According to the therapist in the movie, each of us contains a matchbook, and every time we connect with our passion, we set one match on fire. The trick is to light one match at a time, rather than the whole pack all at once.

## September 19, 2013

Today I got an email from Harvey, a man who stopped to talk to me yesterday at the bench. He could have wandered off a ranch with his wild hair and wonderful drawl. He wrote:

*Well, it certainly made my day – meeting you today. I have to laugh when I think of the image of you sitting there knitting into infinity. It was like I crossed over to Wonderland.*

## September 20, 2013

People often come up and ask, Are you trying to set a world record or something? So I decided to look up some knitting records in the Guinness Book of World Records just for fun. My favorite is "Most People Knitting Simultaneously." 1805 people gathered on December 3, 2011, in Kaohsiung, Taiwan to knit scarves for elderly and low-income people. I just love their matching, psychedelic outfits! For a long time, I've wanted to stage a "knit in" like this in D.C. to protest war in a feminist, nonviolent, and fresh way.

## September 21, 2013

"I'm miling you," the lady said through her car window

while two collies barked from the back seat. She drove the length of the knit line up the hill to get the reading of .2 miles long. Then she put her hands together, bowed, thanked me and drove away. (I found that simple gesture profoundly moving.)

This means I'm almost halfway to my destination. The total distance down to the ocean is .4 miles and 400 feet according to Google Maps. A bit depressing, because I thought I was halfway there a month ago when I reached 14th Street. An artist should never attempt math. However, support for this project is growing, and my web of relationships continues to expand in wonderful ways. If the project takes another summer, that might not be such a bad thing.

A skinny hour of knitting yesterday; I only put in 40 minutes.

## September 22, 2013

The spicy smell of a log fire in Karen and Mel's woodstove announced the arrival of autumn, as did the slugs scrawling gooey paths across the wet sidewalk. Knitting in the rain has its challenges. The yarn sticks to your fingers, and slips off the needles without warning. I dropped two stitches today, but picked them back up. As I sat, the folds of my raincoat at my waist directed a stream of water down through the front opening, drenching my thighs. Time to get rain pants. I can't believe that last year I knit without any rain gear.

The major challenge today was winding the line back uphill. The rain-soaked line felt at least twice its normal weight! I took the wheelbarrow down with me to carry the extra weight. Winding up the line took three times longer than usual, around 35 minutes. I may have to compromise my aesthetics and get one of those ugly garden hose reels.

Stopped and chatted with Michael for a few minutes. He's sort of a mad scientist—art for art's sake, all the way. He turned his property on Lummi Island into a sculpture park full of kinetic sculptures, some of which are sonic.

## September 23, 2013

At the end of my knit in the rain, a woman approached wearing a striped hat that matched her poodle's sweater. She asked to take a photo of her dog by the knit ball. This kind of absurd cuteness makes my world go round–and it made the ordeal of knitting in the rain with a cold and sprained neck worthwhile! Yep, I pulled a muscle in my neck yesterday while lifting the waterlogged ball of line, the kind of neck sprain that makes you turn your whole body to check your blind spots while driving. In short, I'm a bit of a wreck. So, I decided to be gentle with myself and only unwind the line across one street instead of down three blocks. You'd think it was Mount Everest. I told my mentor about my tight neck muscles and all-over-aching and she asked me to consider getting a half-hour massage.

I said, "That's all I can think about too, but I feel so guilty about it."

She said, "You're NOT eating a whole cake, or stealing government documents. You're just getting a $35 massage."

This put it in a new light. It may become a monthly tradition.

## September 24, 2013

After my knit, I scooted downhill to Chrysalis Inn, and booked a 30-minute chair massage to heal my sore neck. The cashier handed me a key with the word "Ritual" on it. The quote on the back hit the bull's eye of my heart: *You get peace of mind not by thinking about it or imagining but by quieting and relaxing the restless mind.*

Later the cashier woman came and asked if I'd be okay with a table massage for the same price?

"Are you kidding?! I'd love it!" was my incredulous reply. I found myself in a waiting room with a waterfall, wearing a fluffy robe, sipping Creme de Earl Grey tea, munching almonds and apricots and basking in the warmth of the toasty fireplace. This is Bellingham's best kept secret, I thought to myself. Can a massage be a spiritual experience?

At the end of my massage, I set my feet back on the ground, and I was a new human. My ears rang, and my balance was off, like I'd just emerged from an hour of deep meditation. I showered and shaved with the complimentary razor and shampoo, then slathered my body with white tea and ginger lotion. Delightful!

## September 25, 2013

Last night, I dreamt a friend was shooting a movie of my huge ball of knit line when suddenly it started tumbling down a cliff, bouncing off crags until it splashed into the ocean. I watched helplessly as the ball of knitting bobbed up and down in the waves, drifting farther and farther away.

I wonder what it means. Loss of control? Fear? Freedom and exhilaration? Is the project gathering momentum, taking on a life of its own? I hope so. I love the fact that the knit ball seemed animated, taking off on an adventure without me.

My eye was caught recently by a needlepoint with these words stitched across it: *There are two lasting gifts we can give our children. One is roots–the other is wings.* And this sums up the great paradox of my existence—I need both commitment and freedom. Looking at the knit ball plopped on the other side of the road, I've been wondering, is it a ball-and-chain, or an anchor? Last night, I told a friend that knitting every day has comforted and sustained me through the unexpected ordeal of moving four times this summer.

My wise friend replied, "It's an anchor."

And so it is. As much as I'm a commitment-phobe, I realize now how much stability a commitment provides whether it's a regular job, a marriage, or simply the daily practice of knitting.

## September 26, 2013

I hope to get a spool and crank for the knit line soon. I miss the process of unwinding the knit line downhill. Each block offers the possibility of multiple encounters, human or otherwise. And it is so delicious to document these experiences with my camera.

Roxie came by the knitting bench with three Sheltie dogs. She introduced me to her newest trainee, Sophie, a puppy who is replacing the one she just sold. I asked Roxie how much the people paid her.

"Just enough to cover the costs," she said.

"Oh Roxie!" was all I could say.

"They needed the dog, because their last one just passed away."

Roxie has a tough exterior, and a heart like melted butter. She used to invite homeless people to stay with her, but her neighbors felt threatened. She realized loving your neighbor is more complicated than you'd think, and decided not to invite the homeless over out of respect for the people who lived next door. Now she's throwing the art show at St. James Church, and donating half of the proceeds to the homeless. Some people never give up.

### September 27, 2013

Roxie came by the knitting bench today with her pack of dogs. When I caught sight of three neon leashes hanging from Roxie's neck, I laughed.

She said, "An irritated man once asked me 'Don't you know about the off-leash law?' to which I replied, 'The off-leash law is for dogs, not puppies. I'm the only dog. They're all puppies.' The man cracked up and didn't bother me anymore."

Roxie's dogs would not hold still for my photo of them except the new trainee, Sophie, who is trying very hard to obey.

I knit in the rain today. Today an older stocky man told me, "Knitting in the rain, now that's dedication."

Later, Jerome came by and asked me how I was doing.

"I'm dry!" I crowed with delight, and showed off my new rain pants. I congratulated Jerome for walking despite the rain, and told him he was dedicated.

He smiled brightly and said, "Thank you!"

I don't remember ever seeing him smile before. I thought about the ripple effect. What if Jerome told someone else that she was dedicated, and the compliment passed along several more exchanges, brightening each person's day along its circuitous path?

## September 28, 2013

My bags lie packed on my parents' basement floor to load into the car. My brother and sister in law have invited me to live with them temporarily until I can find an affordable apartment so I'm moving again after I knit at the bench. Before the computer gets packed, I've typed this entry.

If the whole cosmos is in a state of flux, why do I long for permanence? The shifting of the earth's tectonic plates under our feet, the movements of clouds, fall colors spreading like a rash over the leaves. Can I begin to see this movement as a sign of life, a creative act more spectacular than any dance, symphony, or film? Yes, I can—some of the time—but for right now, I'm ready for gradual changes, barely perceptible ones, like the quivering of an eye beneath closed eyelid, or a slow motion kiss.

# 11

# Knot

September 29, 2013

I am having serious writer's block tonight. I take people's words so damn seriously–and today at the end of my knit, Arnold told me that I watch too much TV (I don't own one) and that I'm filling the air with meaningless chitchat. It makes me want to crawl into a tight space, hold my breath and not make a peep for a long time. So I am writing this just to fight that demon of fear and creative paralysis. (This is the hazard of making art in public. Hopefully my skin gets thicker.)

The hour of outdoor knitting at the bench was wild—strong winds blew my hair in every direction. I finally tied a scarf over my head to keep the hair out of my face. It was cold, and I had a full, quivering bladder the whole hour. Also, in my recent move, I've misplaced all my socks. Mind over matter.

Two guys strode up, pants dirtied from pouring concrete for a neighbor's balcony. The older guy invaded my bubble– touching my scarf, standing too close, chewing his tobacco, while the younger guy stood across the street staring at the turbulent, grey sea. The older guy kept flirting with me—his ex's name was Kristin too. He restores Barracuda cars for fun. Blah, blah, blah. I was not interested in him—to put it politely— but I was glad for any distraction from the chilly wind. Then they walked down the road to ask the neighbors for their King apples, and I heaved a sigh of relief.

Mollie drove up in a red truck and introduced me to her brother who said he was "Fish Boy," aka Randy, an artist who makes fun folk paintings. I used to visit his gallery years ago. He's still painting, and is planning an art show with one of my favorite local artists, Thomas, whose imaginative paintings transport me to a land where bears, humans, and birds ride rowboats together, and mermaids swim in the sky.

## September 30, 2013

Lots of rain fell on me during my knit today! Chuck, the mailman, came by and we enjoyed a three-minute sun break. Several women jogged past in soggy T-shirt and slacks—impressive dedication. The yarn got tangled around the knit line, and I thought about how resentment can so easily tangle me up, or as the *Big Book* of Alcoholics Anonymous puts it, "block the sunlight of the Spirit." Here we go loop de loo! The only kind of knots I'm interested in are knit ones. I wasted so many years in resentment, I just can't afford to luxuriate in its sticky grip. I knocked on Arnold's door and rang the doorbell to talk to him about his upsetting comment yesterday but he didn't answer. I will keep trying.

Last night I dreamt the phrase, "bodies of light." And I believe that's my calling—to be utterly transformed into Light. Resentment, when given too much energy, act like a shutter that blocks the Light. Thank you, knitting meditation, for giving my mind an hour to untangle yesterday's knots.

## October 1, 2013

Today's knit was calm and soothing. I enjoyed the sunshine, although I still needed my fingerless gloves.

## October 2, 2013

In just two weeks, I have gone from thinking that a hose reel was a lively Scottish-Highland dance performed in tights, to a knowledgeable consumer of garden hose reels. Who knew that a whole world awaited me in Hose Reel Land? On my internet search, I came upon sleek, mechanical hose reels that Marcel Duchamp would have loved, and frilly, overwrought Victorian ones that made me gag. My favorite for design and portability is a green contraption with bouncy tires for $179. Who spends that kind of money on a hose reel? I found a used $15 hose reel online. I am not thrilled with the aesthetics of this hose reel. It's made of thick grey plastic like what's used for cheap playground equipment. I just couldn't bring myself to spend $150 – $300 for a garden hose reel.

I marvel at the unexpected twists and turns in the process of making this work of art. The initial naïve and blurry vision I had has crystallized into something unimaginably richer and weirder than I ever imagined.

I drove to the knitting bench after picking up the used hose reel on the other side of town, but didn't bother to hook up the hose reel because I only had 40 minutes to knit before it got dark.

## October 3, 2013

The hose reel looks less ugly today. But it's clear I will soon need a bigger one! I bumped the noisy cart down the hill, almost to 12th St, much to Marvin's amusement, who was outside building a fence and trellis. Moms were arriving to pick up their kids from school as I wound the line back onto the hose reel and up the hill, feeling ridiculous! Yes, but my imagination leaped from one spinning wheel to the next—a Sufi's enraptured whirl for the Beloved, the fiery, angelic wheels in Ezekiel, or a Tibetan prayer wheel casting the longings of a devotee to the four winds. As a human being, I need tangible, physical acts to carry the spiritual, rituals to connect me to the invisible. And so, I offer up these 15 minutes cranking the handle of my hose reel as an act of devotion.

Arnold drove by in his yellow electric car and gave me a long thumbs up for the hose reel parked by the bench. Later, he came up with B.J. on the leash to chat. I asked him about his comment earlier this week, that I must watch too much television. He said his rant was not directed at me at all, it just hit me the wrong way. I had been taking a photo of the wind blowing through his maple tree, and he took it as an opportunity to decry the "hot air" broadcast all day on TV. He was very apologetic, and grateful that I brought it up for clarification. This is how misunderstandings start, or in this case, end.

# 12

# Reel Change

October 4, 2013

I enjoyed the new dance I'm learning of keeping one hand on the hose reel handle, while using the other to unspool yards of knit line off the drum. Beautiful fall day, the bittersweet smell of cut grass filling the air. I met Gale, the male gardener, mowing the grass on the church lawn. At the corner of 14th, a young dad was out walking, coffee mug in hand, with his toddler whose round blue eyes drilled into my skull as only a child that age can do. He was still staring at me and the blue knit line when I turned to go back up the hill.

Back at the bench, I chatted with Chuck the mailman. He loves his route, a combination of houses and college apartments, walking and driving. He's been doing it for over 20 years. He told me his greatest fear is that with the budget cuts, the government will install metal mail lockers, one to each block, and he won't get to wander the neighborhood on foot any more. I hope this doesn't happen–we need as many face-to-face interactions as possible here.

My soul feels several sizes too big for my body right now, a kind of psychic growing pain, telling me there is important inner work that I need to do. What that is, I'm not sure yet. I'm being emptied out which I hope is 'clearing me out for some new delight' as Rumi, the Sufi poet, put it.

## October 5, 2013

*Sometimes our light goes out but is blown into flame by another human being. Each of us owes deepest thanks to those who have rekindled this light.* ~Albert Schweitzer

I showed up for my knit, not knowing what to expect except that Harvey had emailed to say that he was planning to shoot some video footage. Thankfully, he was running late, and I got a few minutes to breathe and center myself having just gotten off an overnight caregiving shift. The day was cool and overcast but not raining. I've been knitting daily since July 1st this year, and I'm tired.

So, I felt encouraged when Harvey arrived, eager to carry the hose reel down the hill and unwind the line. His excitement about the project rekindled my flagging spirits, while his questions revealed a depth of perception.

For example, he asked, "What is the relationship between art and spirituality?" Later he said, "It's as if you're making a sidewalk rosary."

As if on cue, the neighborhood came alive today. Suddenly my bench was surrounded by a flash mob of women joggers, posing, smiling and making quips like "she's a knitting fool!" Then Mollie pulled up in her truck and handed me a one-pound donation of yarn and talked to Harvey's camera about my project. As we wound the line up the hill, a man called out, "It looks like time to call Homeland Security!" I swear, I did not bribe these people but the timing was perfect for the video.

## October 6, 2013

An older couple drove up and asked if it was okay to drive over the line, and I said yes.

The man said, "My wife knits and she would kill me if I drove over her knitting!" They drove away beaming.

Sandy bicycled up the hill and sat with me on the bench, telling me all about the Artist Studio Tour; she had visited 10 studios with her friends today and bubbled over with inspiration from the artists she'd encountered. She said, "I'll miss you when you're done with the knitting project, you'll have to come up with a new project to do at the bench." I was touched.

As I wound the line back up the hill—a 25 minute ordeal now—a man came up with two dogs. He asked if I was trying to measure something, but I told him I was knitting a line to the sea. He told me how many fathoms long the line was. According to him, fishermen measure with fathoms as they reel in their nets–when your arms are outstretched like wings, that's about one fathom.

# 13

# Resilience

October 7, 2013

"Will I be interrupting you too much if I ask what you are doing?" A slight brunette drew near to the bench, cradling her dog in one arm, a yellow bag of dog doo in the other.

I said, "Not at all. I'm knitting a line to connect myself to the ocean, a metaphor for the Infinite. Do you live in the neighborhood? What are you out doing on this cold day?"

"I'm nursing a recent concussion. I have a 'bucket list.' My son doesn't like the name, so I call it my 'Adventure List.' One of the things on my list was to go ice skating. I had just started classes at Western Washington University, and the next day, I went ice skating, fell and got a concussion! It can only go up from here. This experience has really deepened my trust. I was giving lip service to what you call the Infinite, and this concussion has changed all of that..." she said.

"Blessed are the resilient, for they will never be broken that's also what this project is about. The knit line is resilient, cars drive over it all the time," I said.

"I keep tearing up," she said. "This is such a moving experience for me. I know I'm in the right place because I keep meeting people—like you. When you do something for the joy of it, there's real power. This is the first time that I've done something for the joy of it. I mean, taking education classes just because I want to. Do you mind if I tell you a story?"

"No, please do!" I said.

"I was newly married with a child and a baby when suddenly my husband died. I didn't have a car–my baby rode between the handlebars, and my child rode her bike with training wheels to preschool. I was in college, but I decided that my kids should be my first priority, so I quit classes, and started working. I worked 17 years in Licensing, doing service for the government. I just quit that job, not unhappily, and moved here to study education. I want to teach literacy to preschoolers." She teared up more. "When my son recently graduated, he turned to me and said, 'Mom, now it's your turn.'"

Her words resonated with me. I had just finished speaking with my mentor about my fear of failing to become a full-time artist, and she said that no matter how many times you fall down, you have to get back up again. Successful people have had failure upon failure, but what distinguishes them is that they get back up and try again. Failure is part of the reality of the universe. It doesn't mean that my life will always be this hard. If I fail, I'll just get up again, and maybe I can tweak my approach and learn from it. In my neighbor's case, she is giving up ice skating and taking up the hammered dulcimer instead.

# 14

# Awakening Beauty

October 9, 2013

On my way downhill to unwind the line, I snapped a photo of moss growing out of the grommet of a manhole cover like hair sprouting from a belly button. I enjoyed chatting with the two guys who came around to inspect the sewer. I asked the younger guy with earrings what he does for fun. He said that he makes mountain bike trails. "Kind of like what you're doing," he said.

"Yes," I said, "blazing a trail."

I've got my mojo back again. The knitting needles knit by themselves today. It took me half as long to unwind the line. All this because I got clear about my direction. For the last two days, I've had an internal war raging over whether to expand my art tutor hours in addition to caregiving and making art, or whether to focus on making art, and just keep caregiving to pay the bills. Today, I quieted myself, closed my eyes, and asked the question three times, and listened. Each time, I heard, Focus on your art. And the second time I asked, I had a vision of myself using a sword to slash thick vines that kept trying to entangle me like the prince in Sleeping Beauty. And how appropriate that image is. Art unrealized is a kind of sleeping beauty.

Each time I clear a space in my schedule to make art, it gets filled up again with something else, like morning glory vines on testosterone. Or rather, I fill it up again with something, anything at all, except making and promoting my art! I'm starting to realize that the good is often the enemy of the best. These distractions are often good things in themselves, and they are even more seductive if they're paid.

The only person to blame is myself. Why do I give away my studio time, and why don't I value my artistic gifts? I say I believe that my art is my gift to the world, my way of giving service, but I don't really live like I believe it. I need to take Frederick Buechner's words to heart: "Vocation is the place where our deep gladness meets the world's deep need."

So why does making art as my primary vocation feel so self-indulgent? Why do I feel guilty as if I'm dragging my finger through chocolate espresso frosting and licking it? When I'm radically honest with myself, I realize it's not guilt, but fear that has kept me stuck. Up to this point, I've preferred the comfortable clutter and distractions, the frustration, and envy, to the unfamiliar path through the dark woods that leads to a career as an artist.

## October 10, 2013

I told a class of 5th graders who were out on a service trip that I am an artist and the rope is a drawing, a decoration for the sidewalk. "It's really beautiful," an Asian American girl said.

## October 12, 2013

I went to Roxie's *Alice in Wonderland* themed art show at St. James Presbyterian church before sitting down at the knitting bench. I adored the grinning band of seniors plucking ukuleles and belting out oldies in sync like "She's ALL RIGHT!" I bought three of Roxie's psychedelic pink Sheltie dog cards.

Later I sat down to knit, and Roxie strode uphill, saying she had sold out of cards and was going home to replenish her stock. She introduced me to a man, telling him that I was another crazy artist. I asked the man if he did anything crazy in his spare time. In this case, it was the wrong question to ask because the man was a conspiracy theorist who thought that Rockefeller had suppressed the truth about health and hygiene so that hospitals could make money. He told me he has written two unpublished books about how to heal yourself, including a chapter about the healing properties of seminal fluid. Another chapter describes the time he broke his arm and a doctor put it in a cast. He feared his arm was getting gangrene so he cut it out of the cast prematurely. Shortly afterwards, he went on a walk, fell, and with a click, knocked his arm bone back into alignment and was healed. By then, it was time for me to wind the line back up the hill, so I shook hands with him and said a relieved goodbye.

## October 13, 2013

A cold knit today. At the end, Pete brought me a steaming cup of Earl Grey tea and plunked it down on the bench. He and Cynthia have just returned from Italy. I sat and gratefully sipped my mug of tea, looking out at the infinite fog below.

I will be taking a break from knitting to visit my 90-year-old grandpa. It's been four months since I saw him last, and he won't live forever. Some things are more important than art.

## October 14, 15, 16 No Knit

## October 17, 2013

I'm back to knitting, after three days in Canada. I was ready to stop knitting for the year, but the weather is balmy out–60 degrees today, and "not being in the mood" feels like the wrong reason to stop. As two East Indian women told me while driving by, "Weather good, you knit. Weather not good, you don't knit."

A brown van crested the hill, and the driver jumped out, leaving the van precariously perched at the stop sign and strode over to talk to me. I wanted to tell him to park his van and not block the intersection, but held my tongue.

"Bellingham's response to Christo! This made my day!" the man exclaimed.

## October 18, 2013

The world expands and contracts with my heart. Today the world feels infinitely beautiful after I let go of a fear about an unexpected bill, and opened up to the generosity of the Universe. I was treated to a concert of birds, hiding in the branches of the Douglas fir and singing their hearts out. When I was in college, I chanced upon an oil painting of a tree with a window cut into the foliage revealing luminous singing birds. In that moment, I decided to learn how to paint.

Roxie came by, looking exhausted but triumphant, and said she made over $1800 in her art sale, and has already donated half to the soup kitchen, and $100 to a cooperative art gallery. Now her church has decided to make the art sale an annual tradition, and has expanded it to include several other artists.

## October 19, 2013

Arnold was also out walking B.J., the Emperor's lap dog, as he fondly refers to him. He said, "Do you have plans to stop knitting soon?"

"Yes," I said, "when my fingers start freezing. There's not much I can do about that problem."

"We could look into getting an infrared heater for you," he mused.

"Please don't! I'm ready for a break!" I exclaimed and we both laughed. I urged him to restrict his research to hose carts since my overflowing hose reel is in need of an upgrade.

I also saw Jerome wearing his signature neon orange hat and jacket. He told me he had fasted for a day recently. I asked him why, because I'm nosy.

He said, "Ideally you fast to get closer to God. But you can also lose some weight in the process." We chuckled together. It was awkwardly awesome to see him again, after several weeks without our daily chat.

## October 20, 2013

A woman said, "It's funny to see you here knitting; this is

only the second time that I've seen you. After the first time, I told all my friends about it, but when I didn't see you again, I thought maybe I'd had a hallucination!"

Wendell pulled up in a truck and handed me another skein of ocean yarn for my project, courtesy of his daughter Mollie. The gift of yarn is such a blessing! It feels like a message that says, Don't worry, I've got you covered.

Wendell has eyes that dance like a moving stream, or liquid gold. I told Wendell how lucky he is to have Mollie for a daughter.

He said, "Yes, I'm so grateful. Not only does my family get along, we actually like each other."

They must really like each other, I thought, because they all live on the same block in adjoining houses.

## October 21, 2013

Dense fog filled the streets on South Hill today, muffling everything. I enjoyed watching people emerge like ghosts from the air as they walked towards me on the bench, then vanish away.

A woman and her dog stopped for a brief chat after work. She mused, "I love the fog. It reminds me of times long ago, steam punk, London." She paused and added softly, "I just noticed how loudly I'm talking." In fact, the fog did make us want to speak in hushed tones today.

At the end of the knit, I desperately needed to use the bathroom. I didn't want to bother Pete and Cynthia, but I gave in after holding it for the whole hour.

"Our *baño* is your *baño*," Cynthia called after me as I walked out their door. How free they are with their possessions, and their affection.

## October 22, 2013

Mostly quiet knit today in dense fog except for the drone of leaf blowers in the distance. Chuck the mailman came by, and said, "I almost don't want to say this out loud, but when was the last time it rained?" We are so spoiled this year. I'm grateful for non-soggy knitting sessions. It might have been otherwise.

## October 23, 2013

After about a week of fog, the sun finally broke through. I interacted with a record number of people today. A man drove up in a station wagon with his blind mother. As I talked about the project, I got the impulse to put the knit line in his mother's hands for her to touch. Her face lit up.

A lively group of kids came out on an autumn walk, paper leaves pinned to their shirts as name tags. They stopped and asked what I was doing.

One of the teachers asked the kids, "What's the longest you've worked on something?"

A boy raised his hand and said, "One hour!"

A spunky woman introduced me to her husband and two American friends visiting from Italy. Spunky had binoculars around her neck. She's a birder, and has recently spotted the rare and stunning cedar waxwing, much to her amazement. Since then, she always wears binoculars, just in case another stunner comes along. Cynthia, who was still working in the front yard, joined us to exchange stories and we spilled off the sidewalk and onto the street, as if the bench had become the neighborhood's front porch.

## October 24, 2013

The fog rolled in again today. I had a lovely visit with Aria and her older sister Luna, wearing matching pink backpacks and knit hats. Luna told me knitting a line to the ocean was a very silly thing to do. She is reading chapter books in school, and has the world all figured out! They both sat on the bench and told me they are planning to dress up as fairies this Halloween.

## October 26, 2013

Most human passersby didn't engage with me today—a quiet Saturday morning walk or jog to clear the mind for the weekend ahead, no doubt. However, a short-legged black collie named Skip decided to sit on my feet beside the blue line, and wouldn't move until his owners pushed on his rump! (I felt like St. Francis.) Roxie came by with her herd of Shelties, and the smallest puppy took a playful dive at the knit line, and briefly lifted it up in the air with her snout.

I keep taking pictures of the knitting and posting them on my blog like a doting parent of a plain child, who can't help showing off my pictures. I love how the line falls in new rhythmic patterns each day, unorchestrated and unplanned, like the lines left on the seashore by a wave.

# 15

# Generosity

October 27, 2013

"That's a funny looking backpack," Roxie teased me, as I walked with the hose reel slung across my back down three blocks to retrieve the knit line.

Karen was throwing a work party to tidy up her yard. Work Party–an oxymoron that reveals the truth that when friends work together, they party together. As Karen pruned back the grape vine, she exposed a branch of a raspberry bush that was covered in ripe raspberries.

"There's your lunch," she exclaimed.

I don't know if anyone will believe me, but I ate fresh raspberries today. The grape vine must have provided shelter to the raspberries from the harsh wind and rain.

In the past two weeks, I've been learning a difficult and liberating truth–life is not about fairness, it's about generosity. Somehow, I got it into my head that if I did X, I would get the result I wanted and deserved.

In the process, I've become a score keeper, and pretty controlling too. I called you, you didn't call me back, *et cetera, et cetera*. But life is a brutal teacher. Lately, I've become aware of many unfair situations, both in my life and the lives of those around me:

- compassionate roommates left paying massive utility bills for their alcoholic roommate who gets evicted.

- youthful, smart and loving grandmother gets stomach cancer and lands in hospice care.

- man tries to save drowning pregnant wife, and ends up drowning while she and her little one survive.

These fearsome events pierce me to the bone. And I could go on and on. The point is I don't want to. I have found that protesting unfairness gets me nowhere. I end up bitter, despondent and out of touch with the deepest level of reality. What I am slowly, painfully learning is that though Life sends these terrible curve balls, it also sends me blessings and lucky breaks that I don't deserve. Raspberries on October 27th? The friend that says breakfast is on me. The colleague a few years back who forgave me after I spread a malicious rumor about him that I later realized wasn't true. I don't deserve to wake up every day to creative work that I love. I don't deserve good health, decent looks, a loving family.

I would like to get my hands on the Cosmic Calculator someday, and see the ratio of painful to wonderful things. But, until then, I'm a happier, more generous person if I don't keep score, but rather do my best to tip other people's scales in a positive direction. As I'm realizing, this is not only the path of deep suffering and overwhelming joy, but also the key to a crazy adventure! And here's the biggest secret of all—each time I show generosity (and I struggle often to overcome the scared, stingy part of myself), I'm receiving more back. It's uncanny.

October 28, 2013

The weather has suddenly become wintry–despite brilliant sunshine, the nippy wind spells the approaching end of the knitting season. As soon as I learn a lesson, the opposite one appears. This time it's about saying no, simply and powerfully. A killer for me, as difficult as saying yes to

142

generosity. Jerome offered me a book today about his Seventh Day Adventist beliefs, and I took it, even though I might have said, 'No thank you, I have found my spiritual home.' My acceptance of his book may stem from my ironic enjoyment of all things strange. I still need to say no to the uncomfortable attentions of another man I'm not interested in. Partly, I distrust my read of the situation and I'm chicken, and if I'm really honest with myself—I've been starved my whole life for male attention.

I did say no to Cynthia who offered me a good book to read. It was probably the sweetest offering of the day, but I turned it down because I have a pile of four books that I glance at guiltily from time to time. I've already renewed one of them three times.

Do other people struggle this much to say no, I wonder? I feel like I have to be on guard all the time, otherwise someone will slip something by me that I don't really want? The stinky hand lotion full of chemicals, the ugly sweater, the party invitation that coincides with studio time. I'm reminded of my eighth birthday party when a boy who had a crush on me gave me used batteries and a stained handkerchief...This set the tone for my subsequent dating life.

I know it sounds terribly ungrateful, but sometimes I reach my saturation point with saying yes. I grant it, usually yes is the best stance to the world, and we often say no from a place of fear and selfishness. But oh, what a wonderful sanity no also brings, especially as the holidays approach. Time to reconnect with that inner two year old.

October 29, 2013

*The Holy Spirit is our harpist and all strings which are touched in Love must sound.* ~Mechthild of Magdeburg

A woman drove up, got out of her car and introduced herself. She said that the knitting project was lovely and poetic, and that she had read about it in the paper last year. I asked her if she was a poet, and she said no, she played the harp.

"Your knit line is just a long harp string to me," she said.

Aria and Luna walked by on the other side of the street with

143

their mom.  The mom explained that Aria was not allowed to visit the bench today because she had bit someone.  Big sister Luna chimed in, "And she broke my backpack!"  Meanwhile, Aria yelled and protested her way up the hill.

## October 30, 2013

Cold, overcast day at the knitting bench.  A mom passed pushing her sleeping baby in the stroller.  I listened to the clicking of my knitting needles, the crows, and the purr of passing cars.

Cynthia came by and gave me a small bag of candy corn.  I love how it looks, but hate the waxy, sweet taste.  Clearly I haven't learned my lesson yet about saying no, because I wavered a few seconds, and then accepted it.  But maybe the psychedelic orange and yellow will inspire a painting.

## October 31, 2013

I was daydreaming about Christian Zen when I suddenly slipped on some dog poo on the sidewalk.  It seemed appropriate because there is nothing like nearly falling on one's bum to bring one back to the present moment.

After I made it safely back up the hill and sat down to knit, a woman settled down on the bench next to me and started talking to me.

"I took my first dark walk yesterday.  I'm not going to stop walking just because it's getting dark sooner now.  In the dark what I pay attention to are the fragrances–of apples and wood smoke wafting on the night air," she said.  Then she headed home to prepare a Halloween dinner including orange bell peppers carved to look like jack-o-lanterns.

Halloween has always been one of my favorite holidays because it's everyone's chance to be an artist, to transform reality using their imagination.  And it's a sign of hope that, vulnerable as we are, we can still make fun of fear.

## November 1, 2013

A little Robin Hood left his quiver on the bench last night

while trick-or-treating. As I unwound the line, I also found some unopened Mini Mars Bars. This job has benefits.

## November 2, 2013

A wild, stormy day with sideways rain, but I was determined to do my hour-long knit. Also, I had a booth at a craft show today, but Cynthia volunteered to watch my booth so that I could run back to the bench to knit. I donned my yellow raincoat and cap, rolled the line out, and sat down. Looking crazed, I'm sure, I staggered to the bench as the powerful wind blew my hair all over the place. I sat down to knit hardly believing how cold and red my fingers already were. A truck driver gave me a thumbs up through bleary windows as he drove by. Moments later, the realization hit me–this is my last knit of the year. I couldn't bear to sit on the bench for the whole hour. In fact, I lasted all of 10 minutes on the bench. I went back to Cynthia who had sold a record 10 cards in 20 minutes. She'd entertained shoppers with tales of my knit to the sea, and handed out postcards.

As she exchanged goodbyes, she said, "I'll keep an eye out for you on the bench next year and your return will signify the coming of spring."

"I'm happy to be your groundhog," I said. I will miss her so.

# PART THREE

# FINDING HOME

# 16

# Holden Village

Harvey turned his video of me knitting into a short film called *Bellingham Subdued Quirk,* and, on a whim, submitted it to the Holden Village Snowdance Film Festival which was appropriately themed *Finding Home.* He scheduled his Mexico vacation during the festival, not dreaming that his first movie would get accepted and include free room and board for him and one guest. Out of the blue, he phoned and asked me to go in his stead and I said yes, not knowing what I was getting myself into, yet thrilled at the opportunity.

After a long ride in a shuttle, I arrived in Eastern Washington where a friend drove me to the ferry service that ran a few times a week across Lake Chelan. I went from the verdant Pacific Northwest into a wintry world bleached of all color, like slipping sideways into an Ansel Adams photograph. The pregnant white sky looked ready to dump snow at any minute. Our tiny ferry, laden with groceries, ski equipment, luggage, and Holden guests, lurched slowly out of the dock and over the deep lake carved out long ago by glaciers. I felt like an explorer and a time traveler, half expecting to glimpse wooly mammoths clinging to the sides of the snowy mountains. I kept my cellphone off since it had lost reception long ago, and instead took snapshots with my camera, marveling at the surreal, marshmallow landscape that engulfed me. We arrived at a dock and formed a human chain to transport the luggage from the boat up to the waiting Bluebird school buses. Then the switchbacks began and we careened back and forth, winding around the avalanche-prone cliffs until we finally pulled into Holden Village, a cluster of log cabins and buildings peeking out of the snow. A troupe of villagers greeted us with warm shouts and applause, even rolling a 70s red carpet out on the snow for me. I felt like a celebrity, as one of the only film people to have braved the trip. Harvey had picked the perfect audience for his film, I thought smiling to myself later on, as I counted the women knitting in the cafeteria and the movie theater. As a community, they celebrate the quirky, handmade and whimsical—and hilarity is even a core value on their mission statement.

We broke the record for snowfall that week, surpassing the 200-inch mark, and many times I wondered anxiously if I would be able to leave, or if I was snowed in for good. We faced potential problems I had never anticipated, like getting buried by a "roofalanche" of snow tumbling off the chalet roofs, and power outages due to the snowpack that often jammed the hydroelectric dam upstream. We carried on in prototypical Holden fashion with a T-shirt tie-dying party in the snow, and a 24-hour filmmaking competition and gala. Finally, the roads were deemed safe enough for us to ride the buses back to the ferry landing. Once we made it to Chelan, I rode back to Seattle with a family I had met at Holden. Most of the "drive" was spent sitting on the freeway for five hours. I'm not sure if the snow plows couldn't keep up or if there was an accident. I tried to entertain the squirmy kids in the back seat while we thanked God that we were in the warm car and not out in the darkness and snow that covered everything beyond our foggy windows. We ate snacks, told stories and took turns peeing as discretely as possible on the snowy bank of the freeway.

Coming back to Bellingham, Holden Village felt like a strange dream. I had met so many kind and generous people, and had gotten the red carpet treatment. Yet I hadn't really known anyone, and no one had known me. I had felt like a plant without roots. It's lonely to be a celebrity, I realized. I felt the old ache of loneliness and longing for a companion to share my adventures. I'd dodged my loneliness successfully since my last break up; now it hit me with a vengeance.

Immediately upon my return to Bellingham, I got news that my name had miraculously risen to the top of the wait list for a subsidized apartment in downtown Bellingham. Sweet relief. My days of drifting from college sublet to housesitting gig to family guest room had finally come to an end. I walked into the sunny, loft-style apartment with sturdy wooden beams and high ceilings and knew I was home.

# 17

# Knitting Again

May 1, 2014

My first day back knitting. One of the neighbors told me, "Summer is complete now that you are here." I enjoyed the hour so much. Parents and kids walked by me *en route* to school, snapping photos on their phones. My heart jumped into my throat briefly when the knit line got tangled up in a lawn edger. I thought for sure it would cut it in two, but the line survived. Lina, the lovely young woman who drives the white bug, stopped and chatted for a long time. I always thought she was a nurse, but she's a massage therapist, my age. A kindred spirit, I think. I saw some of my regulars including Roxie with her herd of miniature collies. She has two new puppy recruits in training, bringing the number of her dogs to five!

May 2, 2014

*The Bellingham Herald* sent Andy, a photographer, to shoot pictures of my knit. I'm not sure what he'll do with 500 pictures of me knitting, but that's his problem. He usually takes pictures of sports events, so this was quite a different assignment for him. He stood on the end of the bench with his giant camera, like a stork with a very long beak, waiting for the fishies to emerge. Of course, this scared almost everyone away!

May 3, 2014

A realtor and her daughter pulled up and talked. The woman was on the way to an open house, pleased that my line would guide people up the hill. Her daughter's smile was bigger than her face as they drove away, and I thought about how that was payment enough for me, my joy barometer surging.

A small inchworm suddenly appeared on my pants, looping its way towards the knit line. This is the second time I've been visited by an inchworm, and it reminds me to focus less on my goals, and more on action in the present.

And yet, I'm feeling impatient with almost every aspect of my life at the moment. Sometimes it is painful to have big dreams. I feel like a caterpillar crawling around, my butterfly wings waiting, tucked inside me.

I saw Tom in his front yard pulling dandelions. His wife recently found out she has cancer, their dreams shattered and forming themselves into a strange new shape. How peaceful they are in spite of it. Almost as if the awareness of mortality has made them more aware of what deeply matters, of this short, sweet gift called life. Carla has posted a poem called "The Seven of Pentacles" by Marge Piercy in her poetry altar off the back alley. It's another garden poem about living with intention and love, and reaping a bounteous harvest.

May 4, 2014

I only rolled the line across one street. It was raining and I felt justified in taking it easy since it was Sunday, after all. I met another artist. She liked "mindless knitting" like mine, the kind that doesn't require crazy amounts of concentration. I like the sound of a mindlessness practice. There is freedom in not concentrating too hard, letting my attention rest on whatever arises.

May 6, 2014

"I'm getting younger all the time," a man with a white beard sang out as he walked down the hill to pick up Aria and Luna, his granddaughters.

"You are," Steve the landscaper agreed, looking up from his work. "My mother is 93, walks 10 blocks every day and goes to jazzercise class twice a week. And she's dating an 83-year-old guy, ten years younger than herself! I tell her, 'Mom, stop robbing the cradle!'"

Lina and her boyfriend Tim drove by wearing 50s style sunglasses. Tim has started honking a handheld horn at me out his truck window, like the monster on *Sesame Street*.

A skinny man strolled up to the bench with a girl and said, "My daughter has some questions she wants to ask you."

His second grade daughter proceeded to fire off a volley of questions that would put most journalists to shame. "Do you knit at night?" "How long have you been knitting?" "Do you leave the knitting out after you're done?" "What made you think of doing this?" She started walking away, then came running back and said, "These are for you!" and handed me a tiny posy of purple flowers that she had gathered from weeds.

The cheery grandfather puffed back up the hill with his granddaughters, Ari and Luna. He urged me to put up posters announcing the grand finale when the knit line reaches Bellingham Bay. I was touched that he wanted to come—I don't remember speaking with him before.

Grandpa announced, "Luna is going to be a world-renowned scientist when she grows up."

"No, I'm not. I'm going to be an artist, a singer, or an author," Luna retorted.

"Well, you can be more than one thing. I'm sure the knitter does more than just knit," Grandpa said.

I'm sure he was trying to convince her to pursue a practical vocation, like my mom, who suggested careers for me as a dental assistant and occupational therapist, not that I listened. I flashed back to kindergarten when I dictated to the teaching assistant: 'I want to be an Artist...(pause)...a Swimmer, a Singer, and take care of orphans.' All very lucrative careers, I might add.

My attention returned to Luna who told me she is trying to

155

grow out her bangs. She is the author of a book called "Geometry, Geometry Everywhere" and wangdoodles are her current fascination. Luna had on a purple outfit with day-glo socks and Mary Janes. Her younger sister, Ari, wore a panda face appliqued on her pink jersey and stockings with a run in one leg. She is sulking because their grandpa always leaves the car at home, forcing them to walk up the hill.

Grandpa dictated to Luna to say, "It was nice to watch you knit."

"It was nice to learn about wangdoodles from you," I replied.

## May 7, 2014

"Enjoy the concrete music," Arnold said wryly as he walked by with B.J.. Jackhammers pounded in the background for most of the knit. As he moved on over the hill, I called after him to fess up to the puddle in his basement made by storing the soggy knit line after the recent downpour. He said he would show me an alternative storage spot when he returned.

Jerome stopped on his trek across town and pulled a Ziplock bag full of tiny slivers of notebook paper out of his pack. He handed me a slip of paper with www.isheavenforreal.com written on it in wobbly blue handwriting. He said he'd like me to visit the website. I was touched by his effort—handwriting on and cutting out all those slips of paper. I don't mind people trying to convert me. In fact, I find it refreshing. I wish it happened more often because it means that someone thinks he has something meaningful to share with me. I told him I already believe in heaven, but he is determined to make me a Seventh Day Adventist. He said he's a loner most of the time and enjoys the human contact at church. He used to attend a Lutheran church with a bunch of old White people; the Seventh Day Adventist Church is a vibrant mix of Blacks, Hispanics, and Caucasians, young and old.

## May 13, 2014

The line got tangled up today as I unwound it down the hill.

Operator error. Close to 12th Street, I saw an older gentleman power-hosing the cracks in the sidewalk. I asked him over the engine's din if he had a problem with me running my rope over his wet sidewalk. He said he did have a problem, because he planned to power hose for quite a while longer. He asked me what I was doing but he couldn't make out my reply over the roar of the engine. So I left the rope in a coiled up pile on the edge of the sidewalk.

Yesterday, the rope ended before the alley. Today it stretched past the alley, much farther than I could have knit in one day. It's mind-boggling, like my experience of Time as something that contracts and stretches like a bungee.

Cynthia stopped by and asked, "Are you doing okay?"

I debated which strand of tangled thoughts and feelings to share, then said optimistically, "My head is in a bit of a fog, but it's steadily clearing."

She jumped in her car to give a free haircut to a retired priest debilitated by a stroke.

A carpet cleaner drove by and asked, "Are you using the cars that drive over the knitting to add a bit of character to the rope?"

I chuckled.

Arnold guided B.J. down the hill with me to check on my progress, a departure from Arnold's "Dog is my Pilot" policy where B.J. picks the route and Arnold obediently follows. We crisscrossed each other often since B.J. couldn't make up his mind which side of the path smelled better.

Arnold asked, "Do you think the neighbor who offered to build me a new hose reel is the sort of guy who completes projects? The spirit is willing, but the flesh is weak, you know. Sometimes it's best to say 'thank you very much for your offer, but I've got a schedule to keep.'"

My schedule is currently dictated by the certainty that this hose reel is falling apart. The plastic handle lurches to one side, and comes undone regularly. In addition to a new hose reel, my shopping list includes a wide-brimmed hat because my skin is starting to sag in the sun.

## May 14, 2014

Dana and her husband Jim stopped by the bench at dusk, a brightly lit barge anchored in the bay below us. I hadn't seen them in ages. We all had on loose-fitting clothing after a sweltering day. Dana said that I should check out her daughter's blog about her epic bicycle ride from Alaska to Argentina. "A slow and patient journey like yours," she added.

A stranger approached to ask why I was knitting at night when I normally knit during the day. It's funny to realize that all my actions are being monitored, even by those who feign disinterest.

## May 15, 2014

Sailboat races down below on the bay and happy laughter from the balcony of the house where I used to live. I knit from 7 to 8 p.m. to avoid the blazing heat. I'm procrastinating on buying a better shade hat and hose reel. I tried to unwind the line down the sidewalk but it got so tangled that I gave up and just knit instead. My brother and his wife and son came to visit me at the bench; they tried to fix the hose reel but the handle broke. I felt embarrassed at my sorry state.

## May 16, 2014

Arnold and B.J. drove up in the electric car to give me some tips on my future hose cart purchase.

"Make sure the reel is pointed the right direction so that it unwinds down the hill, and that the handle is at the right angle," he said. Arnold's German, and has a mind for mechanical details.

I wish he'd make me a hose cart. I'm like a princess fainting in a tower, awaiting rescue. I don't know why I'm so resistant to taking the next step of buying a hose cart. It's almost amusing how lazy I am—how many days can I knit my one-hour minimum without unwinding the line? And cheap—I have the money to buy a hose cart but don't want to. However, this project is about serving the community, albeit in a quirky way. It's not about me—my money, my time, my energy. So, I hope to forge through this resistance soon, and take the next step of obedience to this calling.

Mike stopped and visited with me most of the hour. He has started playing jazz guitar with friends in local pubs. I'm proud that his musical debut was at the bench back in May 2012. After playing a few rounds of *Bright Side of the Street*, and *Blue Skies* beside the bench, he had gotten up the nerve to head down to the Firehouse Café and play for his friends there. And the rest is history.

## May 17, 2014

Honestly and nonjudgmentally facing my resistance helped me get unstuck enough to order a hose reel for $74.95 on eBay, a sweet deal. It's a dramatic improvement over the plastic variety—kelly green, plenty of storage and cushy wheels that will bounce right over the cracks in the sidewalk. At least, those are my high hopes. Arnold stopped to say he has located the perfect hose reel at Joe's Garden.

Too late! However, I am curious and will check it out.

Today several people came up to ask me why the line was not unrolled down the sidewalk. I can't get away with anything. I told them that it is a terrible mess, and has outgrown the plastic hose reel.

## May 18, 2014

I finally got my dream—an entire hour of quiet knitting on a Sunday afternoon. I wanted to gush thanks to my former landlady for using her quiet push mower instead of a noisy gas one. Clippety-clippety-clip. On a whim, I crossed the street to visit, happy to see her again.

Later, she sheepishly sat down on the bench. She had locked herself out. What could have been a disaster turned into a party as we headed up to Pete and Cynthia's to visit on their front steps while the dinner Pete had cooked got cold. My landlady's housemate Ben showed up with the key, and all was magical for 10 minutes of excited chatter as we caught up on neighborhood news. Call me crazy if you like, but I really feel that the knit line had brought us together yet again.

May 19, 2014

"Silly goose," Cynthia called out to me as I knit by the light of the street lamp. It was 10 p.m. I had 30 more minutes left. She came and sat by me, cradling a paper coffee cup between her hands. We talked about novels we had read and loved, most recently, *Broken for You*, a book that made me weep with the perfectly imperfect people that inhabited it.

"I'm sorry for making your dinner grow cold last night; you are the living definition of a good neighbor," I told her.

"Not at all; it was a moveable feast," she said.

I finished knitting, picked up my camera, and played one of my favorite night-time games. I take a photo of a light source while waving my camera hand wildly. The resulting picture made of painterly light lines are unpredictable and oh so free.

May 20, 2014

A woman asked if she could have my contact info because she was planning to move here from Tucson, Arizona. "I'm an artist too," she said.

I asked, "What kind of art do you do?"

She said, "Many years ago I made life-sized, electronic kinetic figures that filled a whole room. When I start making art again, it will be very small."

I asked her why, and she said, "Life is short..."

Puzzled by her answer, I didn't press her to elaborate. She looked like she had at least 30 more years of creative output left. After she drove away, I pondered the patient artists that I so admire. Jay DeFeo, who worked on her painting *The Rose* for eight years. Layered with nearly 2000 pounds of oil paint and mica, a moving company removed the bay window of her San

160

Francisco flat to get it out, lowering the painting by forklift down two stories onto a flatbed truck. James Turrell, who started carving skylights into the sides of Roden crater in 1974 so that people can contemplate the spectacular night sky. The project has cost millions of dollars and continues to this day. I thought of Antoni Gaudi, the architect charged with building Sagrada Familia Church in Barcelona, who began work on the church in 1883 and continued laboring on it until his untimely collision with a tram in 1926. As I write, the construction at Sagrada Familia continues. Most of the pillars, stained glass and sculptures are abstractions of natural forms. The building gives one the feeling of standing inside an enchanted garden.

And finally, I thought of Dominique Mazeaud's artwork, *The Great Cleansing of the Rio Grande* in which she ritually removed trash from the Rio Grande River over a seven-year period.

Life is short, but art is long. It doesn't spoil like food, and when it's good, it has the power to nourish and inspire generations of people. For me, it's men and women like these that deserve the title Artist.

Cynthia came out and sat on the bench with me for "moral support" and filed her finger nails.

May 21, 22 – no knitting. On retreat in B.C.

May 23, 2014

Rain. Picked up an earthworm that wriggled in my hand, covering it with sticky goo. I dropped it three times in the process of trying to photograph it. I long to be as transparent as an earthworm.

The woman who wears sunglasses every day whether it's sunny or rainy has recently walked by a lot with her black dog. She rarely says anything, although today she commented that I must be keeping the line rolled up because of the rain. I didn't bother to explain the fact that my line is tangled, and I'm between hose reels.

## May 24, 2014

Today I knit a therapeutic hour of 50 minutes. Just because I didn't get my act together to knit a whole hour, I don't have to cancel my knit for the day. As G.K. Chesterton said, "If it's worth doing something, it's worth doing it poorly."

Later that afternoon, my dad surprised me by suggesting we assemble the new hose reel that was still in its box, filling the back seat of my car. It stunk of spray-paint, so my mom banished us from the living room to the carport. After an easy assembly, I loaded it back into my car to take to the bench tomorrow.

## Sunday, May 25, 2014

Drizzling rain. Recently, the bicyclist with the cowbell spoke to me for the first time in three years and said "Happy Summer!"

## May 26, 2014

"What the heck are you doing?!" Cynthia called out.

"I'm knitting," I said. I had come woefully unprepared, having left my Frogg Togg rain gear at home. About halfway into the session, dark clouds gathered and started dumping rain. I kept praying *Thy will be done* as I watched my blue jeans turn from pale to dark blue, and the front of me grew wetter by the moment. Rain splattered my cheeks like tears. The garage door rumbled open, and Cynthia called me over, pulling Pete's coat off a hook for me and fetching a plastic bag for my purse.

"Are you going out?" I asked as I started back to the bench.

"No, I'm saving a knitter," she said, her eyes brimming kindness.

I am protected, I thought as I sat back down on the bench wearing Pete's warm oversized coat. A comforting thought. Immediately, the rain slowed to a drip as if I had gotten the point. In a few seconds, the dripping stopped, and the sun came out. The sky turned blue and boasted fluffy clouds. How strange this feeling of protection feels to me now as an adult. Growing up, I felt vulnerable so I constructed a fearless, independent mask to protect myself, and tasked myself with shielding my baby brother whose sensitivity made him a target. Sweeping him up in my arms, I'd carry him into my bedroom and sit him beside me on the bed, propped on cushions. Picking up my knitting or crocheting, I would work next to him, talking softly to soothe him as he looked up at me with starry blue eyes. The peaceful rhythm of the handiwork would soon have us taking deep breaths into our bellies.

After my knit today, I stopped by Ben's house to deliver a message. Then I asked if I could use the bathroom. He invited me to stay for tea. I wavered for a moment, knowing that this was the tipping point between business and friendship. I found myself saying yes, and sitting down at the table in his rental home that was mine a few years ago. He went back into the storage room to look for a new tea cup that had never been used. He showed me the cup telling me that the value increased in proportion to its thinness. A virgin cup, I thought to myself. It was shaped like half an egg, white with pink lotus buds painted on the side,  Holding my porcelain cup up to the window, I could see the sun shining through it like a tooth.

We caught up on a year's worth of adventures, tipping back cupfuls of Phoenix oolong tea that smelled of roses and incense. He said that he wanted to live his whole life as a poem. I had the awareness that I could easily fall for a man like this, but I hadn't yet and maybe I never would. The last time I fell for a Buddhist poet I got my heart so broken I wanted to die, but ended up becoming a Catholic instead. I am a smart woman when it comes to everything except money and men, so my motto is proceed with caution, if at all.

May 27, 2014

First sighting in a month of Sandy and Marvin (cigar in hand) out on an evening stroll sans Topaz, their old dog. I suspect Topaz died which is why I don't see them on their daily walk anymore.

"Where have you been for the last few months?" they asked.

"I was waiting for the weather to warm up," I replied.

"So you're a fair-weather artist?" Marvin said and they both laughed.

I also had my first visit of the season with Alice and Freddie, the Arabic dog with long wispy ears who drifts alongside Alice.

I asked, "Why haven't I seen you all month?"

"I've been going over every day to listen to a man who is under tremendous strain, taking care of his dying wife. He loves his wife, and can't imagine living without her, yet he wants her to die because her health has been failing for so long. I listen to him non-judgmentally," she said.

"I have often wondered, who will care for the caregivers?" I said. Caregiving is a difficult job, taking a psychic toll.

"Spending time with the dying has taken away my fear of death," Alice continued. "We're just spiritual beings having a physical experience."

"That smacks of Gnosticism," I challenged her. "How can you play a piano without fingers? I can't imagine Christen Mattix without a voice and a body."

"Well, maybe I was being too pat," Alice admitted. But we both wondered aloud why a corpse is just a shell, as if the lights had gone out. In the meantime, Freddie socialized with a greyhound passing by with a young couple. I told Alice to say hi to her husband Donald and she headed home.

May 28, 2014

Jerome and I admired the sunset together. I hesitated to break the news that his link www.isheavenforreal.com had not worked. especially since he'd handwritten the link on all those slips of paper. Unfazed, he said he actually had never looked up the link since he didn't have a computer. But now I feel bad, because I tried the link again tonight, and it works after all.

May 29, 2014

Tom emerged from the house to drive to work. "How are you?" he asked me.

"Tired and crabby," I said.

Tom smiled and said, "Me too. We have a lot in common...You just cheered me up. Thanks."

I'm not a fair weather artist anymore, no siree, I thought to myself as I knit in my winter coat. I watched a crow land on the fire hydrant and fly away. Red and blue recycle bins were stacked haphazardly on the grass. Passenger planes rose rumbling into the clouds above Bellingham Bay. The leaf blowers droned. Two young male joggers came up the hill, their neon shoelaces flashing. "That wasn't as hard as I expected," one said to the other.

Pete and Cynthia drove back from their stationary bicycle class at the Y. I once asked her why she doesn't bike. She said she is too afraid of having an accident. I'm sure she's not the only one. Pedaling my bike home, I remembered the principle of *alternatio,* articulated by Bernard of Clairvaux, a medieval monk. Just as the earth alternates between night and day, summer and winter, so too our psyches need periods of struggle as well as joy.

It's supposed to be this hard.
It's supposed to be this hard.
It's supposed to be this hard.

And when I get to the top of this hill called Life, I hope I will say, "That wasn't as hard as I expected."

May 30, 2014

Arnold approached with Roxie and her Shelty who had recently given birth to six puppies.

"They're not sleeping in my bed...yet," Roxie said.

"*Yet*—I appreciate the precision of speech," Arnold said.

A blonde Lab named Noodle trotted up with her owner to the bench where we were all congregated.

"She's a happy dog!" Roxie said.

Noodle just stood smiling on her tippy toes, perky and quiet.

Roxie pointed to the spot where Noodle's tail hit her leash at the end of each wag—there she had carved a notch nearly halfway through the leash with all her wagging.

I hope to wag myself right off my leash some day soon.

A guy strode down the hill, green smoothie in hand, and plunked himself down on the bench next to me. He's a new arrival, most recently from Hawaii. Before that—California, and New York City. He has a rich, gravelly East Coast accent.

I asked what he put in his smoothie and his incantation went like this, "Apples...Blueberries...Raspberries...Blue Green Algae...Protein Powder...Celery...Carrots...Wheatgrass."

My head spun by the end of it.

I got up to leave at the end of my knit, and he said, "I think I'll just sit here a while."

He looked so peaceful and content, pressing little buttons on his smartphone. The view of the bay beyond, absolutely stunning.

# 18

# Scent of New Hose Reel

May 31, 2014

I've been waiting to transfer the knit line to my new hose reel because Arnold said the reel needed time to cure. Judging by the smell, the factory workers in China sealed it up in a bag right after they spray-painted it. Today, the paint odor had almost disappeared. Arnold volunteered to help transfer the knit line from the old hose reel to the new one, so we met up at 2 p.m. on his lawn. Arnold kept telling me, "Relax!" I didn't feel nervous; perhaps my hovering put him on edge. The line on the old hose reel was severely tangled so we decided to gently unscrew both sides of the hose reel to take the knitting off. That junky plastic hose reel was much sturdier than I'd imagined—impossible to take apart because the side pieces were caulked to the reel. In the end, Arnold smashed the thing into four pieces with a wooden sledgehammer, like an Old Testament priest quartering a sacrificial bull. Not pretty, but necessary.

Even though I felt sorry for the waste, it made sense on a poetic level. I thought of the violence done to a cocoon when a butterfly bursts forth. Or a snakeskin cast off like a torn nylon by the snake that emerges, shiny and new. As a plant must split its husk to send forth a new shoot, there is a violence that is built into the heart of all becoming.

The line had outgrown the cheap old hose reel, just as I am in the process of outgrowing my old self. This week, I have felt stretched, as if someone is pulling my arms and legs in opposite directions. I'm expanding—which is great—but it's painful. If you listened quietly, you might hear my psyche emitting a high pitched "eeeeeeeeek!" I am that person who used to sit around envying other artists who were "making it" while I didn't lift a finger to apply for shows or grants. I drank a lot of tea, complained and stayed holed up in my apartment. This past week, by contrast, a curator in New York City asked me to knit a 15 foot line for an art show called *Hope*. Mind you, it is only a one-day show at a conference, but still, it's New York. So I knit 15 Feet of Longing in three days, powered by prayer, Earl Grey tea and a Neil Young CD, feeling stressed and crazy, my arm muscles aching.

I am so uncomfortable with change, especially the positive unscripted changes that are coming my way. The familiar is comfortable, even if it's shabby and worn out. I now know why I ran away from my dream of being a full-time artist all these years. Taking my dream seriously has required a letting go of my old, familiar self that was imprisoning me. I struggle on a daily basis to let go of clutter, fear, and procrastination and replace it with organization, gratitude, and self-discipline. But what an upgrade, I think, as I gaze down at my shiny new hose reel with its quiet springy tires, strong handle, and spacious drum.

Still, the old self was the container that carried me to this point. So I reverently gather up the four sections of my old hose reel and load them into the car to take home with me.

June 1, 2014

I told Arnold, "Your help with the hose reel yesterday was sure appreciated."

"You're welcome. It looked like more than a one person job," he replied.

Cynthia asked Roxie to see the new Sheltie puppies but she told her to wait a couple days.

"Way to go," Cynthia called out to the jogger as he went by, but he ignored her. "He's in the zone," she said.

Sunglasses glanced down at the hose reel. "Is that your new contraption?" she asked.

Even though I felt spent from this week's exertions, I enjoyed unwinding the line down the hill for the first time in nearly a month. The trek downhill took my mind off its preoccupations. I found myself faced with an entirely different set of questions. Have you noticed Karen's raspberry vines swollen with fruit? Have you gazed at the white irises rising like prismatic towers? Have you felt the refreshing breeze gentling your neck? Have you sensed the kindness radiating from the people that talked to you today?

For a moment, I had a wishful thought that perhaps the line had grown much longer, maybe even down to the bay! However, at its full extension, it just barely reaches 12th and Taylor.

## June 2, 2014

"I guess we have front row seats since we live on 16th St," Karl, the father of Camellia and Emmett said, surprising me by stopping on his walk home from the office. "Even though some of us neighbors don't visit with you on a regular basis, we are still enjoying watching it unfold. About a week ago, it was pouring rain, and my family was sitting around in our pajamas when we saw you outside knitting on the bench. My two kids pressed their faces against the window to watch you knit. You knit in just about every kind of weather. It will be sad when the project ends. But I bet you have mixed feelings about it. How long did you expect knitting to the bay to take you?"

I said, "A month...a summer max."

"The artwork is having a bigger impact on an abstract level because it's taken you three years," he said. "Some of the people who didn't give it a second thought in the first year, are now paying attention."

I agreed. "It's gathering momentum."

Suddenly his little girl Camellia came running towards him in her floppy purple hat with open arms yelling "Daddy" for a big end-of-the-day hug. His wife walked up too, barefoot and smiling in a long, slouchy dress, her faux red hair sparkling in the hot sun. They are a sweet family. I love hearing the children at play in the front yard.

Pete came and visited with me on the bench; Cynthia had gone to accompany Carla to the doctor's. I gave Pete my navigator sunglasses to shield his blue eyes from the glare off the bay and he looked so goofy.

Pete and Cynthia are leaving on a retreat. I'm going to miss them so.

## June 3, 2014

Arnold and his long-haired German assistant Leif stood on the roof vacuuming moss out of the gutters.

A flock of Canadian geese suddenly rushed over my head, honking, in perfect V-formation. By the time I had grabbed my camera, they were almost out of sight headed north up 16th Street. Reality is so hard to capture, either moving too fast or too slow for human perception.

I talked to Jerome for a long time.

"It's easy to be happy on a day like this," Jerome said. He was in a good mood, enjoying the warm weather.

"Roxie's dog gave birth to six puppies," I told him.

"Roxie and I aren't talking anymore since I showed her my letter to the city council requesting strict dog leash enforcement."

"But Roxie's dogs are so sweet and small," I protested.

He explained, "I've never had a problem with her dogs, but I don't like the precedent she's setting. As someone who walks from one end of town to the other, it only takes one unleashed, mean dog in 100 to create trouble."

I was sorry that they'd broken off their friendship—she was one of the only people that made a point of talking to Jerome. Relationships are fragile.

# 19

# Street Sweeper

June 5, 2014

Today my skirt got stuck in my bicycle wheel twice on the way over—a harbinger of things to come, though I didn't know it as I sat down at the bench feeling pleased with myself for arriving early enough to unroll the line down to 12th St.

Mike stopped to chat, guitar strapped on his back, when suddenly the knit line began to pull away from me. I jumped off the bench, running to keep up, needles in hand, attached to my knit rope like an umbilical cord. My hat fell off, but I kept tearing downhill. When I arrived panting at the school, I glimpsed a street sweeper lumbering away, my blue line caught in its rotating bristles. Tell me what to do, I prayed frantically, but couldn't think of anything but to catch up with the sweeper whose engine was so loud I could never have shouted above the din. Unable to keep up, I let go of the needles, and kept running. Finally, the sweeper released the rope. My worse fear had come true—the line had split in half, the ends horribly frayed. This is the world we live in, I tried to comfort myself. A world held together with glue, patch jobs, and mending. I wouldn't want it any other way, would I?

Mike sped downhill after me, angry at the driver but I assured him that the driver was completely oblivious to what had just happened. Mike helped wind up the ball of yarn and left to play guitar at the café. I retrieved the hose reel and started rolling the line up from the bottom of the hill. The gardener in front of the church offered his sympathy, said how worried he'd been to see the street sweeper. When I climbed back to 15th St, I saw Roxie carefully untangling the line. I don't know how she appeared exactly when I needed her. She also had my purse which a concerned passerby had given her.

"Putting together puzzles and untangling knots are my *forte*," she crowed. She thinks I'll be able to weave the two ends together so that the tear is not even noticeable.

I felt so supported throughout the ordeal.

Shit happens. But, as my spiritual director pointed out, shit is used in compost, generating a heat that's transformative. I've been in the compost a lot lately, experiencing both great growth and resistance. Recently, I'd felt loads of resistance to unrolling the line down the hill, but had chalked it up to my own laziness. It's not that simple, I realized after talking with my spiritual director.

She said, "Resistance is always a threshold, calling one to pause and ask some questions. Is this a threshold I need to cross over now? Or is it not to be crossed yet? Or must I never cross it? The goal in all of this is to move towards your true self. Resistance is like a knot, and when faced with a knot, the worst thing is to keep pulling on it, using brute force. Relax, don't tense. Let the "shoulds" lie. Then try different things, ask new questions, the way one gently tugs at a string to see what it's connected to and where it goes."

In this situation, the resistance was clearly warning me to stop unrolling my knitting downhill each day. As of today, I choose to lay the line across just one street where I can keep a watchful eye on it.

June 6, 2014

Clouds like white sand dunes in a bright, blue sky. Ari and Luna trudged up the hill with their mom, promptly plunking themselves and their pink gear on the bench. Ari showed me the disguise she had made out of a piece of grey paper that looked

172

like a mad scientist's mortarboard on her head. She also wanted to show me her "glove." Pulling a crumpled piece of Kleenex out of her pocket, she carefully worked her fingers into it— transforming the Kleenex into a fingerless glove with scotch-taped holes for each finger. Then she pulled it off and stored it in her backpack again for safekeeping.

Luna is sticking to her goal of becoming an artist even though she's not getting any external encouragement.

I told Ari I remembered the name of her book, "Geometry Everywhere."

She said, "No, it's "Geometry, Geometry Everywhere." She is smart, and very outspoken.

Her mom said, "She's been having problems getting along with the other kids. I hope the upcoming move to a more affordable part of town will be good for her."

The new school is less affluent and emphasizes the arts, whereas Lowell emphasizes leadership. (I think artists are leaders, but not the kind that Lowell is grooming the kids to become—CEO's, lawyers, scientists.)

## June 7, 2014

A quiet morning knit. Sunglasses and dog walked by twice on the other side of the street, ignoring me—or so I thought. I don't mind anymore now that I know that we are keeping tabs on each other in silence like Trappist monks. Suddenly, she walked up and asked about the fall-out of my encounter with the street sweeper yesterday.

"I don't think he even noticed that the line was caught," she said, and I agreed. "You were remarkably peaceful," she said.

"Yes, I surprised myself," I said. "I don't mind that the line broke and has to be rewoven. It gives it character."

"It's got history now," she said and laughed.

Under that huge hat, behind those dark sunglasses, is a sparkling intellect and sense of humor, I thought in amazement. If I had finished this project in one summer or even two, I would never have known that.

Increasingly, I think of these human connections that I'm forming as the real art. The physical act of knitting is more of an excuse to show up at the bench each day. The knitting is the frame, the structure or scaffold that holds the art. The emerging artwork is something I could never plan or control—bigger and better than anything I imagined. That is what makes it art, and that's why I show up and do the work.

June 8, 2014 No knit, out of town.

June 9, 2014

A dry leaf blown by a cool wind skipped down 16th Street today, paused at the knit line, then continued on its way. I've never really witnessed the blossoming and fading of a rhododendron until this year. First, an explosion of pinkness. Then the bush got the tarnished, yellowed look of Super8 film. And now, all the blossoms have fallen on the ground, leaving only brown stamens poking out like burnt noodles against the dark foliage.

"There she is—Miss America, she's our ideal," a voice sang out. I looked up to find Cynthia belting out the song, arms outstretched like Maria in *The Sound of Music*. Pete chimed in, both of them walking up the middle of the street in time to the music in a parade for an audience of one—me. Cynthia had on electric pink shorts as usual.

I asked, "How was your retreat?"

"Cynthia's prayers are super-charged now. She's become so holy, she glows in the dark," Pete teased. "Honey, let's go to bed now while it's still light out so I don't have to notice you glowing beside me," he continued while Cynthia chuckled with embarrassment.

Cynthia asked me, "And how are you doing?"

"I was down-in-the-mouth earlier," I blurted. "Yesterday I surrendered my dream of being a full-time artist. I worked so hard to put my art out in the world, watching my finances plunge,

174

and getting more bitter and anxious by the minute. I wasn't sure anymore if I was on the right path, or if maybe I was trying to force it. Then again, maybe I've been killing my dream by holding on too tightly because today, after letting go, I learned that two of my framed prints had sold in my show at the hospital. Delirious with the news, I made pesto pizza and had a glass of wine to toast risk, collaboration, art, love and God!"

Cynthia and Pete got an earful, but they looked genuinely happy for me.

A Latino family drove up in a car, stopping at the stop sign. Dad took his hands off the steering wheel and clapped loudly, exclaiming, "I'm so glad you're back!" His family looked stunned at the sudden outburst.

I rode home to a pink sunset, the last rays of light shining on a black cargo ship in the bay. A wobbly, not-quite-full moon in the sky.

## June 10, 2014

I pedaled to the bench in the rain today, but by the time I sat down, the rain had stopped. After the downpour, my sense of smell was keener. I enjoyed the smell of green things, and even the exhaust of passing cars.

My mind turned inward to contemplate two characters that have announced themselves to me recently: the Dutiful Daughter and the Ardent Lover. The Dutiful Daughter has a long to-do list. She's organized, responsible, efficient, time-focused, and goal-oriented. Her favorite words are should, plan, try harder. The Ardent Lover, on the other hand, is creative, passionate, and expansive. She makes time for the happy accidents and incidentals that come her way. Intuitive and nonlinear, she finds her identity and value from an internal place, rather than external achievement. But her ability to forget time makes her irresponsible, and days may go by without accomplishing anything of concrete value. At first, I wanted to get rid of the Dutiful Daughter, and just keep the Ardent Lover but I've realized I need the Dutiful Daughter to get anything done. I've employed her as a handmaiden to the Ardent Lover. When the

Dutiful Daughter dominates my life, I lean towards resentment, hopelessness and self-pity. I'm working so hard, where's my reward? I'm never satisfied with what is—the desired goal is always somewhere over the rainbow. With the Ardent Lover back at the helm, I live from a sense of abundance that just has to be shared.

Every artist, perhaps every human being, has to manage a menagerie of characters inside. Integration rather than excommunication as the way forward. How to get all these parts to sit down at the same bench and talk to each other?

## June 11, 2014

Today was a very busy day for the knitting bench. Roxie visited with her six adult dogs, two still on leash until they learn to follow her commands.

"Do you have plans to sell some of them?" I asked.

"No, they're family; they all sleep in my bed. I don't sleep very well sometimes," she added.

"You've got six puppies too, 12 total," I said.

"Yeah, I call them my 12 pack," Roxie joked.

Last night, I dreamt I was squishing fat green caterpillars that were devouring my vegetable garden. They wriggled madly as I stabbed them with my stick. Then, in my dream, I realized they would soon turn into one of my favorite kinds of butterflies, and I stopped jabbing them. After I woke up, I did a search on the internet for the caterpillar from my dream, and learned its butterfly name–spicebush swallowtail. Like my dream, it's easy to see other people and myself as mere caterpillars, and not recognize our true name. Sometimes my artwork-in-progress looks like an ugly grub, and I would be horrified if someone took a peek at it before it is ready. It's time to let go of the superficial judgments and shame, allowing a more expansive and creative process of unfolding.

## June 13, 2014

Ari and Luna emerged over the hill with their mom and

perched on the bench like birds coming to rest on a branch. Ari wore a green dress with white polka dots and orange tiger-print tights. The wacky combination made me laugh. Ari also had a plastic microphone but she refused to sing to me.

A tall college student jogged up wearing a headband to keep his curly blond hair out of his eyes. He told me to keep on keepin' on. He likes this kind of phraseology. Another time, he said, "See you when I see you."

After he left, Cynthia teased me, "So he's not shy after all. He's a bit young for you but maybe he could get you going!" (I had been complaining about constipation.)

Jerome passed on his way downtown to join the weekly gathering of protesters. He was doing a one-man protest with a sign that read, "Cars are Dangerous."

Prior to knitting I had been feeling at loose ends all day. Putting away the hose reel, I realized gratefully, this hour has knit me back into community.

## June 15, 2014

When I sat down to knit today, I could barely distinguish the outline of two boats floating on an invisible sea, but by the hour's end the fog had lifted. I'm tired of my thoughts, the endless voice-over of my mind expressing its opinion on everything. I want to be an empty bowl reflecting the sky.

## June 16, 2014

I confessed to Arnold about stealing his strawberries that grow by the side of his house, but he told me to also try eating some of the big, juicy ones growing on the roof of his shed in the back.

After a downpour this morning, the sun came out, and it felt like an entirely different day. The weather in Bellingham is bipolar.

Cynthia began pulling weeds around the bench, and Pete joined her in a massive weed-pulling campaign. Two girls came over the hill—the one with a hat from *The Cat in the Hat* pretended to walk the tightrope on my knit line while her friend in the fur mint hat begged her to walk normally. It was Crazy Hat day, part of the countdown to the end of the school year tomorrow. I will miss my free-spirited friends. Little girls are so unselfconscious and powerful.

I overheard a man telling his friend, "If you've wandered off the path, you can choose whether to get back on it after 500 yards or 5000 miles." They stopped when they saw me knitting, and asked about my project.

"This is my path," I told them.

The younger, bearded man works as a pastor at the university; the bald man was visiting from Thailand.

"A lot of people probably stop and talk to you. This is a ministry!" the younger man told me.

I thought that was pretty open-minded of him. His comment reminded me of Harvey's version of community service—throwing neighborhood parties. And, a former student of mine, who is a Minister of Color. During winter quarter he often arrived to class wearing brightly-colored duds; my favorite–an orange granny sweater with a chicken on the front.

Cynthia noted that since I had knit two hours today, I didn't need to come knit tomorrow—she wouldn't tell anyone.

I said, "That's not how it works."

As I was leaving, she said, "Sharing the wealth," and handed me a jar of strawberry jam made by the poet Luci Shaw.

I know it sounds silly, but the thought of eating strawberry jam made by a local poet somehow made the jam feel precious. I could almost imagine putting it on an altar.

Today's knit had come full circle—beginning and ending with strawberries. This confirms what I sensed last week—Don't focus on doing things, but on blossoming and ripening. Someone please tell me, how does a strawberry vine turn dirt into such sweetness? How do you make red, juicy fireworks of flavor for my tongue from mulch?

# 20

# Heartbreakthrough

June 17, 2014

I took my Scottish great-grandmother's bone needle to the bench today to mend the broken line. First, I cut the frayed ends off—a good five inches. Then I laid one end of the rope on the other and began stitching to join them. The moment felt sacred to me, like I was mending my broken heart. So many fractures made over the years now, I can't keep them straight! *Heart heals like good bone*, I kept saying to myself from a poem I thought I'd read somewhere. How did we come to imagine the heart as a bone? I wonder. It's curious. A broken tooth or bone is much easier to mend than a broken heart.

Cynthia brought a photo album of her beloved, deceased dad, so I put aside my surgery and looked at her book full of smiles, letters, love. She left, and I went back to work.

The results are not as pretty as I'd hoped—a bit lumpy and bumpy—but it feels strong. Some of the most difficult circumstances in my life have inspired my best artwork— heartbreakthrough into beauty. Just then, the sun split the dark clouds open and illuminated everything with brilliant light though it was about 7 p.m. I grabbed my camera to capture the transfigured landscape.

# 21

# Picnic at the Bench

June 18, 2014

Special guests were due to arrive from Canada today, so I decided to unwind the whole line in their honor. I only made it to 15th when my path was blocked by major construction work. I chatted with Mel, Karen's husband.

"All kinds of changes around here including your haircut," I said, and he blushed. The white mane that once flowed down his shoulders had turned into a snappy crew cut, his hair donated to Locks of Love.

"There's your next hose reel," he said pointing to the reel that held the huge yellow piping for the roadwork.

Climbing back up the hill, a white car drew up, with Herb, his wife Mary and son smiling out the window. Herb produced a green box like a xylophone case that unfolded into a picnic table with benches. A yellow tablecloth, white and blue porcelain plates, a baguette and a bottle of red wine made it look like we'd teleported to an outdoor café in Paris—but we sat behind the bench on the sidewalk. It was totally, wonderfully absurd, and I couldn't wipe the silly grin off my face.

The menu was magnificent: artichoke hearts, roasted bell

peppers, mozzarella balls and cherry tomatoes, salami, and prosciutto followed by organic strawberry yogurt and Mary's homemade brownies. We hid the bottle of wine to avoid getting an open bottle citation. We invited Arnold to join us for a glass of wine but he said he was too busy. Cynthia came and visited over a piece of cake.

We perched gingerly on our benches for fear that our collective weight would break them, but they held fast. Herb and Mary's son Paul was the exception—at over 200 lbs, he decided not to risk it, and sat in a deck chair. Tall, dark-haired Paul was smart and handsome but he had a girlfriend back in Eastern Canada. Mary peeked out at me from under her straw hat as we talked.

In his husky voice, Herb said, "Tenacity!" and encouraged me to keep on with my project. He was in his 80s, with curly grey hair combed back, bottle glasses, and a stocky build. Mary, 10 years his senior, sat like a queen, with delicate white hair and skin, and bold Lummi jewelry.

I felt bad about my lame, uninspired answers to Herb's questions like, "What do you think about as you knit?"

"My worries, people, money!" I said, but I was also glad because I didn't want him to put me on some kind of spiritual pedestal. I'm not a hero, just following orders.

I told them about the Lightcatcher exhibit, "Radical Repetition." Paul noted the use of repetition for powerful emphasis in Dr. Martin Luther King Jr.'s speeches. I talked about Gertrude Stein's poetry, and the importance of repetition in ritual. Mary surprised me as she recalled hearing a recording of the name of Jesus, repeated over and over, and how moving it was. I didn't think either of them was religious. Just then, the conversation was cut short by some kids walking towards us on the sidewalk.

I said, "A certain amount of naïveté is probably necessary for all commitments such as marriage—or this project. Had I known the knit would take three years, I would never have started."

"Funny you should mention marriage," Paul said. It was obviously on his mind, but he still wasn't convinced to marry his girlfriend. He offered to wind the knit line up the hill for me. I think he was pretty terrified by my knitting project—he kept talking in existential terms about being at the end of one's rope.

The sky was cloudy and grey, but it never rained on us. We got some nice pictures together on the bench, and then they drove off in the rental car. After their generous visit, I felt so encouraged I thought I could knit at least a mile now. Good timing, as usual, because I've been depressed lately, especially about my life as an artist, my inability to "make it" or move up the career ladder like other people, and my abysmal love life. All the usual petty stuff I find to occupy my mind, stealing my joy in life. I stayed another 45 minutes to finish this unusual hour of knitting, then walked home since my bike tire is still flat. I had had too much wine to drink and had to take a nap.

## June 19, 2014

I took my bike to the repair shop and got a new inner tube put in, then pedaled to the knitting bench. Jane and Arnold passed walking B.J. Jane has suddenly opened up to me, after three years of barely saying hello. I don't know why I am in her good books now, but it is really great! I'm becoming a neighborhood fixture, at long last. I picked up a big pile of dog-do left near the bench. I don't want any of my guests stepping in it.

## June 20, 2014

A cold and windy knit today. I knit in solitude until Pete came out with a steaming cup of decaf Earl Grey tea in a travel mug for me. He sat down on the other end of the bench, and told me about his childhood growing up as a military brat, always in transit from day one. When he was *in utero*, his mom took the train from Iowa to visit his dad who was on the East Coast awaiting active duty in Europe. His mom thought she was eight months pregnant, but she was actually full term—going into labor while visiting Pete's dad. After Pete was born, his dad begged the commanders to postpone his military duty, but they refused and Pete's dad departed for Europe. His mom rested a few days, put baby Pete in a laundry basket, boarded the train and returned to Iowa.

As a child, Pete remembered exploring castles with underground passageways in Germany, and going fishing with his dad on the weekend.

"When you move that much, you have very few relationships from your past to return to," Pete noted.

I could relate having grown up in Thailand, moving every two to four years each time my dad completed a translation project. The beauty of this knitting project is the sense of continuity it's given me. I find it so comforting, for example, to wave nearly every day to the UPS driver with her long brown ponytail and brown uniform. There isn't a need for words; we both recognize each other, smile and wave.

### June 21, 2014

Today was an absolutely glorious day to knit—the sky so blue, all the trees singing. I felt content to watch the crows hop about, and the white sailboats flitting on the bay. Arnold gave me a Jungian book about the psyche. Roxie continues her futile attempts to stop her dogs from barking at passersby. "Stop barking! Silence!" she yelled at them as Sunglasses and her shadowy dog walked by. I'm sure she feels badly about the racket, but those little dogs are hardwired to bark and there is nothing she can do about it.

### June 23, 2014

I had CATS written on both hands to remind myself to feed Marvin and Sandy's cats. Marvin strolled up the hill last week, stinky cigar in hand, to give me the key to their house. I put fresh kibble in the dishes for the hiding cats. Using a pancake flipper, I scooped out one large grey dumpling from the kitty litter box and threw it away.

When I got to the knitting bench, I noticed Carla's jeep door flung open, with groceries in the back seat. Carla's very ill, and no longer has the physical strength she once did. I debated whether to carry the bags up to the doorstep but decided not to meddle.  Soon, Carla came out again, and another neighbor offered to carry the groceries in for her.

Jerome stopped and said, "It's a beautiful day."

I asked him a question I've been dying to ask, "Why are you trying to get everyone to become a Seventh Day Adventist?"

He believes there will be dire consequences for everyone who breaks the command to keep the Sabbath on the seventh day, and he blames the Catholic church for changing the Sabbath to Sunday.

I tried to poke holes in his argument.  When I had run out of things to say, I looked up at him.  He stood with his arms hanging limply at his side like a misunderstood prophet or a sad clown, a look of pity and gentleness on his face.

"It's a beautiful day," he said again.

Thank God for safe, commonplace things to talk about like the weather!  A few cheers erupted from the house down the street.  Jerome said it was the World Cup, but that he wasn't into organized sports.

"Me neither," I said, "I just like disorganized sports."

He let out a short, hearty laugh, the first real laugh I've heard from him.

June 24, 2014

I took the bus because my bike got another flat yesterday.  Walking up the hill, I enjoyed crushing and inhaling the scent of lavender and rosemary, and the sunset-pink roses that smelled of apricots.

One of my favorite questions thus far: Are you knitting a hose warmer?

I looked across the street at my knit line, rolled up on the hose reel, and suddenly it struck me as a metaphor for my life.  Now that I'm no longer unrolling the line down the sidewalk, I have no idea how far I have to go until I reach the water.  Since I let go of my dream of being employed as a full-time artist, I no longer know if I'm making progress or even what progress would look like for me. I've renounced measurable achievements at the moment for something intangible like how honest a painting feels, or whether I'm taking risks with my work. I've traded external landmarks like sales or art shows for a focus on the inherent rightness of making art, and the inherent goodness of my life as it unfolds moment to moment. I wake up to a blank canvas every day, and improvise my life. I have to remind myself daily how lucky I am to be able to do this–to work two days a week at a job, so I can spend the rest of the time at my vocation.

Sometimes I have hope, but it's not a definable, quantifiable hope in a specific outcome like: if I achieve X, I will be happy. How lost I feel now compared to my purposeful, busy self of the past months. I didn't realize how much of my identity was derived from the story I was telling myself about my future. But conversely, taking my ripening seriously has meant finding myself again, accompanied by a certain angst that I lost my way under the guise of productivity and achievement. Somehow, I hope that even my struggles, especially my struggles, can bring encouragement to others doing those unpaid "unnecessary" things: writing poetry and gardening and visiting old people and meditating, and all the other infinitely important activities that make me glad to be human.

## June 25, 2014

Very quiet hour of knitting for the most part, although my mind was busy! A Native American family from North Dakota stopped briefly. The stocky dad was wearing a shirt with information about a powwow on the front, and the phrase, "You can talk the talk, but can you walk the walk?" on the back. He asked to take a picture of me from behind the bench, looking out past the hose reel and down on the Bellingham Bay.

Jerome stopped to say, "I could sure get used to this weather. When it's this sunny, you can even start to forget what the rainy days feel like." Sure enough, he pulled out a letter to give to me, placing it carefully under my cellphone so that it wouldn't blow away. I was afraid it might be a love letter, but it was his reply to my objections about his Seventh Day Adventist beliefs. I'm softening. I have even started to think he's right about keeping the Sabbath on Saturday. But I'm not going to become a Seventh Day Adventist. I need to make that clear to him because I'm starting to dread his visits.

The raspberries on Karen's vine have ripened. I gorged myself on them today after my knit. I'm thinking about making her a wooden sign that says "have a snack." After all that time spent coveting her raspberries, Karen told me recently that she purposely planted them by the sidewalk for passersby to enjoy.

## June 26, 2014

Just past 7 o'clock as I approached the bench on a glorious, sunny evening. Lina brought her electric cello and tinkered with it at the bench. Suddenly we saw a guy with a music case walking our way down 16th.

He said, "I've only been in Bellingham for two hours but I love it already, and I love the look of you knitting and playing music on the bench...would it be okay if I took your picture?"

He said it was for his wife back home near San Francisco, but I doubted it. Lina is gorgeous with her long blond hair and blue eyes, a man magnet. We said okay to the picture, then I asked to take his photo because he looked so hip in his yellow glasses and red hat, with the mandolino case dangling at his side. He had just arrived from California to visit Ben, my tea-drinking friend, who he hadn't seen in 10 years. I told him how to find Ben's door. In a few minutes the two guys came up to the bench to say hi. It was bittersweet for me to see Ben again. I have a little crush on him, but I doubt it's reciprocal.

When the guys left, Lina said, "There's more to your knitting project than just connecting to the sea. It's connecting us to other people in the neighborhood."

We waxed nostalgic about our childhood—rushing home from school to play with neighbor kids—hopscotch, pogo stick, paper dolls. Now we habitually hole up in our separate apartments, and don't talk to our neighbors. I gushed my gratitude yet again for how the knitting is bringing me into community. I knit 20 minutes into overtime, expecting Lina to leave but she didn't. We just sat savoring the sweet evening air together.

### June 27, 2014

I drove to the bench today and found another friend named Mary, a fellow artist, waiting for me.

She said, "You knitting this rope every day is pretty obsessive."

I laughed and thanked her for stating the obvious. I'm surprised no one else has said this to me in three years. Obsession goes with the territory of being an artist. Mary's obsession is picking up old bottle caps to string into snakes...she's been at it for years. We both feel slightly embarrassed about this need to return to the same thing over and over again. It's a short leap of one letter from *artistic* to *autistic* for a reason, I think.

We also talked about the artist's path as a spiritual calling. We must serve the visions that beg to be given form. It doesn't feel like an option to say no.

Mary compared an artist saying 'no' to a saint telling a heavenly apparition, "I'm sorry, I'm too busy right now–it would interrupt my routine."

I told Mary that making art is a form of divination for me; when I don't create, I lose access to a huge part of my psyche, my internal guidance system. Making art helps us both to make sense of life, to find meaning.

### June 28, 2014

I passed Jerome on the trail this morning as I walked to the knitting bench. I told him he was right—the Sabbath is Saturday, but that I wasn't planning to become a member of his church. And I asked him to stop trying to persuade me. It felt good and clean to get that off my chest. I want to stop being phony to please others.

Carla crossed the street to the bench, introduced her sister visiting from Michigan, and explained to her about my knitting project.

Her sister said, "I am part of a medieval reenactment group; my friend The Baroness knits tiny clothes for preemies—"

How practical, I thought. I should do that.

But then she said, "—who die in the hospital, for burial."

Some people would say that making clothes for dead babies is a waste of time and material. I say it's an act of love, of meaning, even art...Anthropologist Ellen Dissanayake, wrote that humans have a biological drive to "make special" which is also her definition of art. The Baroness is making special for grieving parents.

## June 29, 2014

I spent my hour at the bench smelling things. First, the roses outside Roxie's house showered me with sweetness. I didn't even have to put my nose into their creamy petals, the fragrance emanated two feet from the vines. I sat down to knit at the bench, and suddenly I smelled Christmas! Voices came from behind the bushes in the young doctor's front yard, then a cracking sound as a branch of a Douglas fir tree crashed onto the driveway. A man stood in the tree with a saw, thinning out branches, while the voices of a man and woman below shouted instructions to him. With each crash, the spicy, pungent scent increased. I hadn't seen the man in the tree until the tree limbs tumbled down, and then I only saw him because I was looking for him. A few moments later, I inhaled the smoky, sweet aroma of barbequed meat drifting on the breeze from God-knows-where. Maybe it was the clarity of the air or my nasal passages, but I have never had such an intensely pleasurable hour of spontaneous aromatherapy.

## June 30, 2014

A car drove down over the hill, then stopped abruptly and dangerously. It parked itself at a crooked angle on the top of the hill, and a woman got out of the car. She drew near to the bench.

"The view is beautiful, isn't it?" I asked her.

"Yes, I never get tired of looking at water," she said.

"Me too–it's kind of strange," I said.

"Not at all. It's always changing," she responded.

Today the water had lights in it. Yesterday, the surface held zigzags from the unseen movements of the wind scribbling its mysterious line drawings across its surface.

She said "At first glance, I thought you were spinning and that the hose reel held your roving."

I'd never heard the word 'roving' used this way before, *roving* is the long, carded strand of fiber that one uses to spin into yarn. I thought about my own roving: moving six times in two years, on the quest that began after I lost my job, spent six months in the monastery, and returned to Bellingham with a newfound freedom to pursue my calling as an artist.

Confession: I threw away the broken pieces of my first hose reel yesterday. Whatever poetry or reverence I felt has given way to my practical need for more storage space.

# The Fathers

July 1, 2014

As I walked towards Arnold's basement to fetch the hose reel I suddenly noticed a scene unfolding on the street corner. Pete, in a yellow cyclist vest, strode up to a little boy who cried silently as he pushed his bike alongside his mom and older brother.

"Did you have an accident?" Pete asked in a gentle voice.

His mom answered, "Yes," as the boy continued to cry.

Bending his six-foot tall frame in half to view the little boy's scraped knee, Pete said, "You look like a tough guy."

The little boy was now crying loudly.

"Stay on your bicycle. Try it again," Pete urged him.

The little boy continued up the hill, wailing as he went. I don't think Pete even knew that boy. As I sat down to knit, I said a silent thanks for what Pete had shown me about the Divine— strong, and also tender and encouraging.

A little while later, another dad approached wearing a baby in a front wrap, with a dog on a leash, and his little boy trailing behind him.

"Can I sit on the bench for a few minutes?" the boy asked his dad.

"You can sit on the bench for a few seconds," the dad replied.

The little boy, wearing pink clogs and a pirate ship shirt, clambered onto the bench. He was three years old, judging by his questions which came out like koans, difficult to answer. "How would a fire truck park across the road?" "Why is concrete hard?"

I asked his name. I think he meant to say, "Gareth" but it came out, "Gaweth." I asked him what his brother's name was.

"Gaweth," he said again.

Now I was very confused.

His dad explained patiently, "He doesn't have a brother. This is his sister, Eleanor."

I looked up at his baby sister suspended in the wrap, her round eyes fixed in an expression of perpetual astonishment at the world, her wispy hair floating in every direction.

Meanwhile, ants swarmed around the bench, a cause of great excitement for Gareth. The hot weather must be bringing them up out of the earth. Ants walked up the yarn like a tightrope, even getting knit into the line.

"Come on, Gareth, let's go have some pancakes," the dad said, and they trooped together down the hill.

As I walked home on South Bay Trail, another dad of sorts passed me pushing his pug in a dog stroller!

July 2, 2014

Exchanged a few words with Chuck the mailman and Arnold. Sunglasses said good morning and I could just make out the faint contours of her eyes behind her dark lenses. Lately, on my walks, I too have been afraid to make eye contact with passing strangers. Recognition of the mystery that we touch each other when our eyes meet, this contact, painful or pleasurable, always leaves a mark. The desire to respect another's solitude in conflict with the need to acknowledge the other's presence.

Alone with my thoughts on a very quiet knit this morning, I had a mental image of a girl with fire coming out of her ears and smoke rising from the top of her head, while tiny firemen like the Lilliputians in *Gulliver's Travels* climbed on ladders propped against her giant body, spraying water to douse the flames. Thus, it was strangely satisfying to see two fire trucks lumber silently by me as I walked away from the bench for the day.

### July 3, 2014

I finally got to ask Sunglasses her real name. She also revealed her job—teaching conflict resolution classes. She has had seven major dental procedures in one year, so she's taking it easy and walking her dog a lot.

### July 4, 2014

Tom told me he's glad he doesn't live in Michigan on Independence Day where people fire guns into the air.

"True story, I kid you not," he said. "A friend of mine was in the bathroom when a bullet came down through the roof and hit his toe."

I hadn't considered that a bullet must come down again after it's fired into the sky.

Cynthia and Pete came by with a candy crunch pie—I had hoped it was for me, but Cynthia had made it for Patty and her best friend of 50 years who is visiting her again.

### July 5, 2014

No knit today. I had to leave early for a wedding.

### July 6, 2014

Knit in a sun so hot it had me begging at a neighbor's door for a glass of water. Walked home through Boulevard Park, orbited by mosquitos. I slapped one with my hand. It burst, leaving a circle of blood on my palm like a stigmata.

## July 7, 2014

Knit in the setting sun today and the temperature was more tolerable. Caught the bus home at 9:56 p.m. I don't feel like explaining my project anymore. All I can say is that I need to do it; my explanations feel made up. Is this a cop out on my part?

Alice and Freddie visited me for a while. Alice's sick friend had drunk a cup of poison in an assisted suicide and died, surrounded by her mercy killer volunteers, an Episcopalian priest and her friends. It made me sad. Lately, I have been thinking a lot about life as a cup. America wants a steady diet of happy, but this leads to a superficial life that does not satisfy. *Let this cup pass from me, but not what I will but what you will.* Sometimes I am asked to drink suffering, and sometimes joy. I want to drink life down to the dregs. And I want a soul big enough to hold God.

## July 8, 2014

Lina came and sat with me a long time while the sun set. I've realized that she's a true friend in the making. After knitting here three years, I'm making some profound connections. People tell me their deepest secrets—the life-threatening illnesses, the boyfriend problems, the nightmares. I feel like a priest in a confessional sometimes. All I do is listen, and that is enough.

## July 9, 2014

Cynthia said a cheery good morning on her way to her spin class, a stationary cycling group at the gym. Jerome walked by going downtown, and later we passed each other on the trail as he trekked home. I am moved by the purity of his daily 10 mile walk. He does it just because. Not to impress anyone, not to write a blog or a book, not as art, not to train, not to raise awareness. He is existentially awesome without knowing it. I could never do that. Whenever I do anything I have to extrapolate meaning from it like juice squeezed from a grape. I have to turn my experiences into art. I try to imagine a life where I just live without needing to take this additional step of turning it into art. A lot of people do this, and I envy their simplicity. It sounded liberating to me at first, but, as I found out, I simply can't.

For six months, I sought to achieve this frame of mind at the monastery last year—ironing sheets and handkerchiefs, scrubbing mildew off bathroom tiles, making beds in the guest house, digging in the garden, picking up fallen branches, screwing lids on honey jars, and more. Apart from several moments of luminous tranquility, I grew increasingly depressed. I dragged myself out of bed each day, and realized I couldn't sustain it. The gift in all that misery was the clarity that I received. I'm an artist, not a Trappist nun, I realized, and later, one of the other sisters confirmed it when she received a vision of me wearing a flamboyant red hat and the words "Use yourself as your canvas" flashed across her mind.

I decided to stop trying to fit myself into someone else's shape, and to start using my personality—with all its quirks, strengths, and limitations—as my canvas. Sometimes you have to try living a life that is diametrically opposed to your current one, to find out who you are. Let go the part of yourself that you thought you couldn't live without. Squeeze yourself into someone else's shoes, and heave a sigh of relief when you step back into your own.

## July 11, 2014

Tom Wood parked his road bike and chatted with me at the bench. I said I was making an homage to him, a painting of a big tree made of flowers with giant butterflies and a hummingbird. (I worried that he might be mad at me for copying his idea, but he was not bothered by it at all.) He told me not to paint everything to a finished state, to "suggest" some things— that's where the poetry lies.

## July 12, 2014

Lina and I sat together on the bench for a long time, sharing our core, even tears.

## July 13, 2014

I perched on Arnold's rock wall, chatting on my phone. It

felt wrong to be physically near my bench, but mentally elsewhere, as people walked by that I knew. I had had a raw morning, crying over my abject failure to love the client I cared for last night, and feeling overwhelmed by the anger, exhaustion, and helplessness that arose in me.

The sun started setting. Tom's sprinkler caught the rays at just the right angle, turning water droplets to gold as they splashed against the house, falling like specks of fire down the window pane. Ben crested the hill. He'd heard my voice, and had come up to say hi. I said I'd be off the phone in 20 minutes and hoped he'd come back.

I sat down on the bench and started to knit, hoping against hope to see Ben again. After what felt like a very long time, he summited the hill with a clear pot of chrysanthemum tea and two white Japanese teacups. We sat watching a sunset that could only have been painted by someone tripping on psychedelics—a fiery orange, teal and saffron mess that was heart-wrenchingly beautiful. I wondered, Is this romantic? Nothing has been defined. It's unfolding in sweet silence, one petal at a time. I don't know yet what it is, the flower of friendship or something else.

After an awkward pause in the conversation, he said, "I watched the end of the World Cup."

At first I heard it as I watched The End of the World. My mind is always predicting what will come next—and is often wrong. This time, I was glad of it.

A tall man approached with a black poodle and introduced himself.

"Do you ever think about quitting?" Tall man asked.

"No, I'm too proud. There are too many people watching for me to fail."

"The pride is part of the journey too," he said.

I was grateful for his reminder that the journey holds everything, the light and the shadow.

I said, "The project is about thirst; it's called *For Longing*."

He abruptly changed the subject. Another guy approached wearing a beer-fest shirt—he's roommates with Lina and the young doctor.

The tall man asked him, "Are you old enough to be wearing that shirt?"

"Ouch," we all exclaimed in defense of our young friend.

Then the four of us lingered, held together by a magnetic force, our collective longing, perhaps. Despite the awkwardness, it was sweet as a draught of water in the desert. The street light came on and the sky was growing dark when I called it quits. Ben had locked himself out of his place. I stood with him while he knocked on Helena's door for the key.

"*Deja vu*," I told Helena when she opened the door. (Last time, she had been the one locked out.) She should make me an honorary housemate with my own key so I can bail them out when this happens again. Walked home at 10 p.m.

July 14, 2014

A family friend, Dr. John, chanced upon me knitting at the bench; he was housesitting nearby. He and I talked about the purity of making art that no one sees, like Emily Dickinson.

"Is a project like yours less pure because it's a performance of sorts?" he mused.

"There are different forms of art; I also make work in private," I said.

"I like to write poems but I only share them with a few close friends and family. I wonder if that is somehow a betrayal of the gift, if perhaps I am meant to share my gifts with the world?" Dr. John said.

"After I entered the monastery, I couldn't make art anymore. It was simply too painful to feel that no one would understand my language; besides I couldn't maintain a practice with just four hours a week allotted to my art. I felt that a part of me had died—at the time, I thought I had entered the monastery for life, that I would never again be able to go to an art museum or have a face-to-face conversation with another contemporary artist.

"Our modern culture seems to believe that if an artist stops making art, she will plug up an outlet so important that she will shrivel up and die. Perhaps an artist's work becomes richer if the artist stops making work for a time, if it's for the right reason," Dr. John said.

I was impressed by this doctor's ability to converse—to reflect, and then ask the right question, moving the conversation ever farther and deeper.

## July 16, 2014

I had forgotten my hat, so I held the handle of Arnold's giant two-tiered golfing umbrella between my pinched knees for shade. The umbrella itself took up half the bench, making me feel rather anti-social. A great calm had come over me since last night when my thoughts swooshed in spin cycle around my mind. I'd had wild horses in my veins, tossing and turning in my hot bed until dawn, when I finally fell asleep for a couple hours. How long until I realize that I can't think myself out of a mental tangle? The thing to do is to get quiet inside and create a space to receive something from Beyond.

Knitting on the bench in solitude today, that gift of clarity came to me. I realized my vexations were simply distractions, and the best action was simply to ignore them. They were not the ferocious, romping monsters I had believed, and they couldn't hold me back from my destiny unless I let them. The way forward is to say, Phooey on you!

Once I told the priest at Redwoods Monastery all the terrible things I was thinking in my head—and believe me, these thoughts were amplified by the silence of the monastery—he just laughed and said he struggled with the same things all the time. He told me I would still be wrestling with the same problems when I was 80, and not to let them get me down any longer. At first, I was depressed by this news, but then I felt liberated.

This was one of the greatest gifts of the monastery—baby steps toward the mastery of the mind. These monastics had struggled with their demons for 20, 40, 60 years, and in return, had learned compassion, freedom, and humor. One elderly sister said that she used to worry so much about perfection, but now she has put that aside to "go out to meet the other" with a smile or a kind word. When we stop focusing on our performance, we free up precious mental energy to become present to the people around us.

Cynthia lives out this freedom on a daily basis. Today, she popped down to the bench to say hello. She hasn't visited me for at least 3 weeks, and I've missed her so—even starting to take it personally though I didn't want to. Between her son's upcoming neck surgery and Carla's stem cell transplant, she has been preoccupied.

"Tell me what you want to drink and I'll get it to you in a jiffy," she said. She brought me out a Day-Glo green cup of ice water with a pink straw and a slice of lemon. "Pete's up there doing the housework, so I better go back in and give him some moral support," she said and left me feeling loved.

## July 18, 2014

The sun had set and the street light had come on when a woman parked her car and got out with a short-legged black dog. I thought, what a crazy time for a walk, but she had stopped specifically to talk to me. I recognized her face and tentatively said, "Sam?" It had been at least a year since we had last talked. She and her dog had just returned from kayaking in the sunset.

"I remember the day I first spoke to you," she confided. "At first, like everyone else, I thought you were crazy. But one day, after volunteering at the school, I decided to walk up the hill to the hospice where my mom lay dying. Several other moms who I barely knew including Rachel and Grace offered support by walking with me. Their presence that day was such a comfort. And seeing you knitting was very therapeutic," she said. "My mom died shortly afterwards."

"Do you remember us talking to you that day?" Sam asked me.

"Yes, I remember it well! It was the first time anyone spoke to me, after nine days of knitting," I said. That day was the tipping point when people stopped pretending they couldn't see me knitting a rope across the road.

Sam's story moved me. The first people to speak to me were a gathering of women, a sisterhood, who walked in support of their grieving friend whom they barely knew. Sam was sending her mom on a journey, and embarking on her own–and she was doing all of this good, hard work in community.

"You're doing good work," Sam told me.

"God works in mysterious ways," I said laughing, but I meant it. "This third year of knitting has been the most rewarding."

"Why? Because of the good weather?" she asked.

"No, because it took people a long time to warm up to me, but this year, I've actually made some good friends."

"Like me," she said. "I've been waving to you from the car all this time, and today, I finally decided to sit with you on the bench."

"Exactly," I said.

Sam gave me a hug and took her wet dog home.

## July 21, 2014

The sun is shining again after two days of clouds and rain. James came by with yellow in his eyebrows and under his fingernails from cooking cauliflower in turmeric.

"Wasn't that a great time last night at the block party?" James asked.

"Yeah, it was great," I lied.

"I really liked your roommate Ben," James said.

"Oh, there's been a misunderstanding—when Ben said he lived in "Christen's house" last night he meant my previous rental. I lived there, and after I moved out, Ben moved in," I said.

Last night, at the block party, I felt over-exposed and inauthentic. I was so self-conscious around Ben, I wasn't myself at all, and I felt that I had blown any chance I had with him. It was like a bad dream where I glance down and realize with a panic that I'm topless.

Later, Cynthia approached and said, "Wasn't that a wonderful time last night at the Block Party?" and I lied again.

Finally Pete drove up and asked me the same question.

This time I mustered the courage to blurt out, "I was in a bit of a funk last night but I'm glad everyone else enjoyed themselves."

And he said, "Well, God bless you!"

"Thanks, I need it!" I said.

Two lies, and a truth, I thought to myself. As Pete drove away, I found myself laughing.

## July 22, 2014

Cynthia stopped and said, "Carla is wrapping things up at her job in preparation for her surgery tomorrow. We're all in this together." Carla is one of Cynthia's best friends so she is very invested in helping her friend in every possible way.

A bee buzzed around me for a long time. "I'm not a flower, go away!" I told it in my heart, but the bee continued to inch closer and closer. I batted it away with the tip of my knitting needle but the bee became more determined. I jumped off the bench in a desperate attempt to get away, then realized how silly I was to let my fear of getting stung disrupt my knitting meditation. So I sat back down and tried to breathe, hoping the bee would decide not to crawl up my sleeve. It scoped out my red backpack and my shirt one last time and flew away. It's a ridiculous comparison, but I couldn't help thinking of the

Buddha steadfastly facing illusions under the Bodhi tree. And Christ's temptation in the wilderness.

As I wound the line up for the day, I saw a young man and woman sitting cross-legged on the sidewalk. It looked like they had plopped down on the pavement and spontaneously started meditating side by side. I thought maybe it was a new trend that I hadn't heard of...sidewalk sitting. But they said they were too lazy to walk down to Taylor Dock, and decided to enjoy the view of the bay from here instead.

## July 26, 2014

For the past week I've been wrestling with discontentment and sadness, though I keep telling myself: if I can't be happy today, I will never be happy in the future. The idea that if I had a boyfriend I'd be happy is an illusion—but I can't seem to shake it.

Happiness comes from within—it isn't based on one's circumstances. I learned that hard truth when I went to the most peaceful place on earth—Our Lady of the Redwoods—and brought my pain with me. One day I would experience unimaginable peace, and the next, a foul mood for no good reason. Pain comes from within as does happiness. That awareness has brought with it tremendous freedom—to stop running away from challenges and blaming other people, and start making the best of my life as it is. As a friend said to me recently, "You can't just pick out the cashews, you have to eat the whole trail mix."

It's liberating to settle into this imperfect and beautiful life I've been given, and so hard. Suffering is only unbearable when I project it into the indefinite future. At least that's what I tell myself. I am given the grace to get through it one minute at a time, like knitting a half-mile rope to the ocean one stitch at a time. Ah, but I will be happy when this particular season of suffering is over!!!!!!!

Carla, who had brain surgery last week, is back on her feet again.

July 29, 2014

Last night I knit by street light. My neighbor Dana who's a spokesperson for the local Democratic party stopped and advised me on the upcoming primary elections. I like her so much.

I wish Democrats didn't demonize Republicans, and vice versa. Having lived in so many circles, I've learned that there are great people hiding under every label you could think of—gay, pagan, Mormon, radical, conservative, Jew, feminist, evangelical, to name a few.

# PART FOUR

# LOVE LOVES TO LOVE

# 23

# Sweethearts at the Bench

July 31, 2014

Earlier this week, when I arrived at the intersection, the bench was occupied by two sweethearts who were reading a book of *New Yorker* comics together. I snapped a photo of them unawares. I didn't have the heart to ask them to move, so I sat on a low brick wall and knit there instead. A man told me in passing that I was the only person he had ever seen sitting on the bench until now. After half an hour, the couple got up and came over to me to introduce themselves. Then another young couple came and joined us. I was happy to realize that the magic of community isn't contingent on the location. It has happened so consistently at the bench, I had almost begun to ascribe talismanic powers to it!

This third year of knitting the message I consistently hear is "let go." I let go of the knit rope after it got tangled up in the street sweeper, and watched it rip in two. That required another relinquishment—a letting go of my desire for the rope to arrive at the ocean, whole and unbroken. Then I let go of my dream of becoming a full-time artist by the end of the year, a goal that was unreasonable and crazy-making. Now, I feel I'm being asked to let go of my dream of finding a partner. The vision of the young couple enjoying themselves on *my* bench was bitter, touching an ache for intimacy that was reawakened by my time in Holden

Village this winter. My desire has reached a fevered pitch recently, and that is the sign that it's time to let go yet again.

I told Cynthia about the struggles I've been having with letting go.

"Some people have a need to be in control more than others—I'm one of them," she said.

Ugh, it's true for me too. I never wanted to discover this controlling part of myself. Just when I think I've got the plot figured out, it takes a new twist, and I go nuts. I want the fairy tale ending and I want to know about it in advance—thank you very much—the prince will rescue Rapunzel, Ulysses will return for Penelope. Letting go this week has felt like dying. I've washed my heart with many tears, but it feels softer now as if several jagged stones have shaken loose.

I feel light, I feel hope, I feel joy.

## August 1, 2014

A woman walked by talking on the cellphone exclaiming, "O my gosh! O dear! O how ridiculous!"

Tom said thunderstorms were in the forecast and he was glad I had an umbrella. I had a hard time believing him since the sapphire sky above me looked so bright and clear, but the weather changes in a flash around here. Jerome stopped and bent down to say hi to me under the huge shade umbrella. He and I have settled into a pleasant, superficial exchange.

## August 2, 2014

A young man with tattoos asked me today what I was "building." His choice of language delighted me; he walked away laughing about my project. (Since starting this project, I have met more guys than I can count on both my fingers and toes, but it will take a very special man to find sex appeal in an eccentric woman knitter.)

Another woman asked me how much line I knit in one day. I told her, "an hour's worth!"

# 24

# Love Has No Why

August 4, 2014

Summer has started tilting toward autumn, I realized as I pushed my bike up the hill. Arnold's green ornamental maple has started turning red. I had unknowingly picked the perfect time to knit—coinciding with the sunset, a fiery ball in the sky etching a silver path on the water, a pale half-moon suspended opposite. Cool shadows spread themselves across my body as a man, woman, and two young daughters came up to me.

The dad said, "Now this question just begs to be answered."

When I told them about knitting to the water, the little girl said, "I can't believe you knit all that!" She stuck her tongue out and pretended to keel over in a faint.

"Isn't that inspiring?" Mom asked her.

"Just like your hair—I bet you didn't think about growing your hair, but it's really long," I said. Both girls had wavy chestnut hair that swayed about their waists.

The dad said, "Life's like that. It just grows and grows. When you start thinking about it, that's when it becomes tangled and complicated." He *namasted* me and they walked away.

My silent friend, cyclist *sans* cowbell, pedaled up to the stop sign, gasping for breath. I leapt off the bench, crossed the street and asked him, "What happened to your cowbell? Did it fall off? I really miss it!"

"It didn't have a point," he said.

"Does everything have to have a point? I'm still working on my pointless project over there," I said, pointing to my knitting needles lying on the bench.

He smiled, "I like seeing you there. Thanks for saying hi."

He had actually taken his earbuds out and removed his shades to talk to me. He had a craggy face, deep-set brown eyes, dripping with sweat. I could hear a heavy beat from his headset before he plugged his earbuds back in, and continued to the top of the hill where he would run up and down a flight of steps—all in the name of exercise.

A man and woman approached. "Why are you doing this?" the man asked.

"I can't explain it," I said.

"You felt compelled to?" he said.

"Yes, that's it," I said, relieved.

The common strand in so many of my conversations tonight was a desire for a verbal explanation. In the last few days, I have let go of the need to explain or justify things to others, and most importantly to myself, my hardest critic. Awareness that existence is meaningful enough, without the addition of a verbal construct. The presumption that I could give anything meaning through an idea in my head is absurd. Life exists, with or without me. As an artist, I have the good fortune of highlighting and embellishing it. Two friends recently encouraged me to stop trying to find my path or direction, and to trust instead that Love is the path. I'm still savoring this passage a friend sent me from Meister Eckhart where he speaks about living without a why:

*If anyone went on for a thousand years asking of life:*

*"Why are you living?" Life, if it could answer, would only say, "I live so that I may live." That is because life lives out of its own ground and springs from its own source, and so it lives without asking why it is itself living. He who lives in the goodness of his nature lives in God's love; and love has no why.*

Dana walked by talking on the phone. She returned and chatted with me as the sky turned pastel in the sunset's afterglow. She had spent a long day gluing pictures of Democratic candidates on boards. She reminded me that tomorrow evening the results would come out.

"We're all on the edge of our seats," she said.

I thought "not me!" and wondered if that was a symptom of political apathy. She looked as tired as I felt after a day of drudgery. I thanked Dana for sharing the charming story yesterday of the dog who's running against a prosecutor in the upcoming election. She asked if I'd ever like to dogsit for her, and we swapped phone numbers. I told her I charge $25 a day.

"That's too low," she said, "I'm going to pay you a lot more than that."

As she was about to leave, she stopped and said, "Thank you for knitting here. You really add to the neighborhood."

Her heartfelt words moved me. Somehow, the weariness had lifted from my shoulders while we talked.

I headed down the hill, popping by Marvin and Sandy's house to drop off the key after cat sitting for them last weekend. Their faces glowed from a weekend of contra dance with their daughters. A half hour of belly laughter and stories later, I got back on my bike and pedaled home with an overflowing heart.

# 25

# The Essential Wrinkle

August 4, 2014

I came upon some lovely gems in the book *Psyche Speaks* that Arnold loaned me, shifting my thoughts in a life-giving direction. Perhaps, the twists and turns in the plot of my life are what make it exquisite. Lockhart calls these unexpected movements, "wrinkles," which he contrasts with that which is completely flat and known. The word *explanation* came from two Latin words: *ex-* meaning "completely" and *planus* meaning "plain" and "flat." In short, superflat. When we explain something, we iron the wrinkles out, flatten, literally make plane. Which is, of course, exactly the opposite of our wish in telling a story: there the wrinkle is essential, a story without a wrinkle is not a story, it's a statement. A story pulls us into its twists, turns, folds. When a story unfolds completely I am at a loss, absent the tangle the story had drawn me into, longing for another. Jung says that the symbol is the best possible expression of something not yet fully known; the symbol enfleshed in poem or story reflects our lived experience of Reality better than a map or creed.

August 5, 2014 Missed my knit, lame excuse.

## August 8, 2014

Cynthia stopped by the bench with a heavy heart. Carla's cancer, rather than staying contained as we had hoped, is spreading. All plans on hold. Life screeches to a complete stop in these moments.

Cynthia sat down on the bench and we tried to pray. "Are you listening?!" she asked, looking up at the sky.

"I can't imagine the world without Carla Castellina," she said. "She's scared, Tom's scared, their kids are scared." I could feel the fear flowing down my legs and into the earth as she spoke. We sent out a prayer together for peace and healing, Cynthia's voice cracking with love and sorrow.

# 26

# Gush

August 9, 2014

Unbeknownst to me, a man named Rob had started following my knitting blog several weeks ago, tipped off by mutual friends of ours. He made a date to meet me at the bench, driving up from Bainbridge Island, a good two hour trek! I nervously donned my mascara, my biggest purple earrings and my zebra-striped shirtdress that morning. I never expected my blog to result in real flesh-and-blood relationships off-screen, and I didn't know what to expect. He sat on the bench beside me, asking me questions and sharing about himself while I stole shy sideways glances at him from under my hat. Toward the end of the knit, a man and a woman approached, each cradling a bowl of green figs the size of pears—I couldn't take my eyes off them. The woman asked if I wanted one. I said yes, but Rob said no.

"Take one for her—she likes them," my fig benefactor said.

"Cheers!" we said and clinked our figs together.

Freud would have gotten a lot of mileage out of that one, I thought. It was absolutely ridiculous and delightful. When I bit into my perfectly ripe fig, juice gushed all over my fingers. I was momentarily transfixed by my fig's slimy interior like a sea anemone or the mouth of an alien. None of these associations was appetizing, but that didn't prevent me from eating it with gusto. After Rob said goodbye, I put away my hose reel in a dream, my feet barely touching the ground.

## Undated, August 2014

Lina and her six year old step daughter came and sat on the bench. The six year old dusted my face and arms with a sprig of lavender "to ward off the mosquitos." Lina introduced me to a woman who is interested in joining our Red Tent Club that we just started, gathering once a month to help us seek solutions to our hormonal woes together.

"There's only one requirement for membership," I said. "You have to struggle with PMS."

I also met her yoga instructor who is giving Lina yoga classes in her home. He looked like he was made of rubber, bouncing up and down on his legs while he talked.

"I'm interested in a woman, and I'm thinking of contacting her on Facebook. Maybe I'll 'poke' her," he said.

"Why don't you talk to her in person?" I asked him.

"I don't see her anymore now that our yoga class has ended. She could have called me, but she didn't," he said.

Lina and I groaned.

"Ask Christen and I what we think about guys who make the first move," Lina said.

"Big points," I said.

Lina's boyfriend Tim suggested, "You could make a video of yourself singing and email it to her. How about singing 'I'm a man looking at you on my computer.'"

I couldn't stop laughing. When I finally caught my breath, I told the yoga instructor, "It doesn't really matter what you say to her, it's the gesture that counts." As he walked back to his car, I called after him, "We'll be rooting for you!"

# 27

# Comfort

August 12, 2014

Pete and Cynthia strode down the middle of 16th, holding hands.

"You two are so cute!" I said and they abruptly let their hands drop.

I noted their matching green and purple outfits.

"Yes," Pete said, "I wait until Cynthia gets dressed and then I get dressed. No contrasting colors—it's in the contract. And no polka dots!"

A smart couple with a French bulldog approached. They told us their dog Maggie is a rescue dog—a work in progress. Some of the time, she is sweet, and other times she is very unpredictable. At that moment, as if on cue, Maggie began vomiting yellow bile onto the road in front of the bench.

"Case in point," I chuckled.

Both the man and woman were dressed in black–she had on a striped shirt and stylish nerd glasses. Very French, a baguette tucked under an arm would complete the look.

They carried on, and another woman stopped and told us

about her 12 year old son who had had an allergic reaction to medicine, and was in a *rigor mortis* condition, unable to move after three months. Cynthia gave her a big hug, and she walked away feeling a little less burdened, I'm sure.

This morning, the word "comfort" presented itself to me when I woke up, so I flipped open my tattered *Webster's Dictionary*. A nearby word caught my eye.

Here are my top three definitions for *comforter*:

1. One that gives comfort.

2. The Holy Spirit.

3. A long, narrow, knitted woolen scarf or muffler.

I really couldn't believe that last one. Comfort comes from the Latin word *confortare*, to strengthen much, related to words like *fortify* and *fortitude*. I never associated comfort with strength before. When we give comfort to others, we're not providing something soft and ephemeral, we are building them up, reaching out like flying buttresses to hold up the walls of a Gothic cathedral. We all need comfort, and the problem with our culture right now is that we are so isolated from one another by technology we don't even know what the other is really going through, and thus are unable to provide each other this vital support.

Had Pete and Cynthia not lingered at the bench, this exchange would not have taken place. How do we create more spaces in our communities where people can be together long enough to arrive at this point of mutual vulnerability and healing presence?

It was dark when I quit my knit for the night. Pete emerged on the porch and offered to drive me home but I said no, almost calling him "Dad." Then Lina offered me a ride, but I was too stubborn. However, I felt very uncomfortable as I walked down the unlit and overgrown Garden Street, through a seedy college neighborhood, my imagination running wild as I clenched my cellphone ready to dial 9-1-1, and apologized to my guardian angel for making him work overtime again. Note to self: It's not staying light until 10:30 anymore, and it's time to adjust my knitting schedule.

## August 14, 2014

At the end of my knit, Cynthia gave me two cartons of soy milk, helped me wind up the line and hugged me goodbye. To my great surprise, she slipped into the pew beside me at church later that morning.

"Guilt," she said with a mischievous smile.

## August 16, 2014

"Just find some more blue sheep and you'll be doing great!"

"The OCD continues..."

I've had a quiet week of knitting but for a few comments from passersby. A lot has to do with the time of day—I've knit in the morning more often of late. I can't make the magic happen, I've learned, all I can do is show up. After weeks of blazing heat, it's rainy and overcast.

Pete and Cynthia took a break from yard work to join me on the bench. It felt good to rest in each others' shade, not saying very much, just being. Cynthia had on jeans with a hole in the knee, and a man's sweatshirt covered in paint. She handed me an empty berry carton, and told me to have at the blackberries in their backyard. My fridge overflows with applesauce and blackberries from the super-abundance of summer fruit I've gleaned.

After my knit, we walked down to Roxie's together to check out the puppies which are now at least two months old.

"This is Jack," Roxie told us, holding a rust-colored pup in her arms. "He's a breeder."

"How long until he gets to work?" Cynthia asked.

"When he's eight months old. Right now he doesn't even know how to lift his leg to pee," Roxie said. Roxie busies herself every day filling in the holes her dogs dig in her front yard. Round, smooth holes molded to the shape of a sleeping dog.

## August 19, 2014

Allen sat down and chatted with me for a long time today. Besides Jerome, he's the only guy I know whose number one hobby is walking. Allen works as a nursing assistant, and softly strums the ukulele while his client sleeps.

Recently, a dying client asked Allen point blank, "Isn't this job boring and depressing?"

But Allen said, "Someone was there when he drew his first breath on the first day of his life, and I feel honored that I get to be there at 2 a.m. when he draws his last."

Arrivals and departures, I mused as he continued up the hill wearing his hiking pack. Life is an airport but we pretend it's our permanent dwelling. Sitting on the bench knitting for my hour, I have thought about change a lot lately. So much upheaval and movement in the news this week with clashes between police and protesters in Ferguson, Missouri, it feels like the whole country is in an uproar.

How do I make my home on the edge of a fault line? Life calls forth trust, courage, and letting go from the depths of my being but it's not an easy process! The external changes in the world parallel a reshuffling taking place inside and around me— a sifting, cleansing and purging. Cleaning house frees up stuck energy, I think later this morning as I take out the stinky garbage and compost. What is disposable, and what isn't? What's core to my identity, and what is extraneous, a distraction, even an obstruction? It's challenging to write anything during this season of change.

## August 22, 2014

A concert at the bench today made of the sounds of modern life. Helicopter chop overhead. The gasp and bang of a nail gun down the street. Blue jay's *scree-scree.*

Two cyclists from Seattle pedaled up and said they'd chatted with me on their last visit in the spring. The woman carried her bike over my knit line. Tom came out his door and invited me to pick as many apples off their tree as I liked. Later Cynthia and I each filled a grocery bag full of luscious red apples. We rejected the ones with tiny worms poking their heads out their front wormholes at us—Cynthia kicked them into the alley in disgust.

Dana drove up and confirmed that I will be dogsitting for them on September 27th. I can't wait, especially because they are paying me well. I'm a little scared of their dog Sunny, however. She's a German Shepherd and hasn't warmed up to me yet while most dogs can't get enough of my love. Not a great omen.

## August 23, 2014

Knit to the plashing of the young doctor's fountain, and Johnny Cash in my head singing "Hold My Hand, Precious Lord." Arnold came by with B.J. whose tail was curled like a question mark. Arnold and B.J. stood in the middle of 16th for a long time while B.J. sniffed the air and tried to decide which way to walk.

"Sometimes we stand like this for 5 minutes," Arnold told me. He's a Qigong master, and has mastered the art of relaxation. He looked completely at ease standing there waiting for his ambivalent dog, whose puckered forehead added to the absurd effect. When a car drove up, Arnold finally, of necessity, took command, guiding B.J. off the road.

## August 25, 2014

Karen and Mel drove up in their green station wagon. I asked Karen how her recent retirement was going but the bright smiles on their faces were answer enough. In their 60s, they were lit up like honeymooners just back from Hawaii.

"I'm looking forward to Monday!" Karen said.

"Oh yeah, what's happening on Monday?" I asked.

"Nothing!" she said exultantly.

How strange to never have to face a work week again.

All week I have been thinking about my unguarded presence on the bench for one hour daily as a spiritual discipline. This knitting project helps me practice what I want to live in the rest of my life, and in my new relationship that's forming with Rob. I've been thinking about the kitschy statues of Jesus and Mary that you see sometimes in Catholic churches with their anatomically-correct hearts emblazoned on the front of their robes like juicy, red tomatoes. It's a picture of what I want to live–this radical open-heartedness come-what-may. Go easy on me, Life…

## September 4, 2014

I'm in a season of transformation, and again, words fail me! I missed 4 consecutive days of knitting this past week visiting Rob. I finally knit today. Bonding with Dana's German Shepherd, Sunny, went well—she did not bite my fingers off.

## September 5, 2014

I started my knit at 7 a.m. today.

"You're here bright and early! Are you planning to finish your project today or something?" Roxie asked.

I just laughed. Cynthia, freshly back from her Spin class at the Y, sat on the wet bench with me. She spread a page of newspaper ads for me to sit on while I debriefed her about my lovely weekend with Rob. Then she updated me on Carla. She had gotten the results from the scans, and her tumor had shrunk by a third. She's devastated—having hoped for news that the tumor would have completely disappeared.

"She had her own calendar, expectations of when it would happen," Cynthia said.

Letting go of the stories we tell ourselves about the future is probably the hardest form of relinquishment. I'm terrible at it. All I can do is notice when I'm drifting into fantasyland, and jerk myself back to reality again. It requires a tremendous effort of will not to borrow happiness from an imagined future. But I don't think true happiness is possible without a concentrated effort to remain present which Walker Percy says is like threading the eye of a needle. When I let go of my dreams for the future, my hands become open to the bounty of the present. In the monastery, they called this attitude towards life, "accepting what is given." A certain pliability in response to life's movements is essential. *Fiat mihi.* Be it unto me according to thy will.

# 28

# Mary

September 6, 2014

My artist friend Mary was sitting cross-legged on the bench when I arrived. We listened to the birds whistling and tweeting from a nearby tree. Conversation flowed in typical nonlinear artist fashion. Mary asked how my art is going.

I told her, "I'm maintaining—I've reached a point where I need to take a break from painting to create a work space instead."

"Like sharpening a knife," she said. "You can chop with a dull knife while getting diminishing returns, or you can take a break, sharpen your knife, and resume chopping with much more efficiency."

She wants to make a holy card of me knitting at the bench. Patron saint of bus stops and benches. I find this very amusing. She was worried that it might come off as irreverent, but I love the idea of picking local personalities and ascribing random things to them.

I asked her about her connection to Catholicism because she references it in her art; I assumed she grew up Catholic and had abandoned it in her adulthood but no, she is just intrigued by it. One rainy day when she couldn't get her car to start, she said a

*Hail Mary*, and promised to become Catholic if the car started running. It did. She hasn't become Catholic, and it's haunted her ever since. Her husband told her it would have been a lot easier to call a tow truck! Talking to my friend Mary is like enjoying an unobstructed view of the bay—present, transparent, real.

## September 8, 2014

Both Sunglasses and Tom gave me a cheery good morning within seconds of each other. I thought to myself, this is what neighborhood feels like. I like being the safe person for neighbors to greet every morning. Cynthia came and sat with me on the bench, proudly displaying three eagle pins on her hot pink fleece, one for each of her sons who had completed Eagle Scouts.

"It's practically unheard of to have three sons all complete their Eagle Scouts," she told me a few weeks back.

We hugged goodbye, and she crossed the street to help Carla, entering the front door without knocking.

I've been thinking about Time again and my habit of projecting worries into the future and spoiling the present. I am inspired by this quote by Therese of Lisieux:

> *You are quite wrong to think of sorrows that the future may bring; it is, as it were, intermeddling with Divine Providence. We who run in the Way of Love must never torment ourselves about anything. If I did not suffer minute by minute, it would be impossible for me to be patient; but I see only the present moment, I forget the past and I take good care not to anticipate the future.*

I rode my bike home along the boardwalk of Taylor Dock, heart soaring, light glancing off the surface of the water that rippled over neon eelgrass.

## September 9, 2014

On my way to the bench, I was bent over taking pictures of pine needles like Chinese calligraphy on the sidewalk when a woman approached wearing a Coca Cola shirt.

"The world is so beautiful–sometimes I wish I could take pictures all the time, but I don't have a camera with me, and you do!" she effused.

I sat down to knit, feeling holier than the pope. Suddenly, I got something stuck in my nose and started sneezing. My nose ran, and a tiny seed husk came out, and I was cured of all smugness. I would much rather stay humble (close to the ground) than be humiliated. Humble from humus = earth.

My internal DJ started out the hour with "Just as I am Without One Plea" followed by "Electric Slide." This DJ has eclectic tastes ranging from Appalachian hymns to 90's butt rock. With such a noisy mind, who needs an iPod?

The wind played with my hair, blowing it sideways across my face. I listened to the roaring of trees behind me like a gale blowing on the ocean. The silvery rustling of poplar leaves. No sound from the Doug firs or the doctor's fountain.

Tom said hi, and exchanged a flat "how are you?" with me. It's the kind of rote exchange that leaves me thirsty for more. I'm not sure if he wants that, or if he is capable of it now that his wife Carla is so sick. Sometimes you can disrupt the script by inserting surprise, the unexpected honesty. Today, I don't want to push it.

# 29

# Void and Fullness

September 10, 2014

*Grace fills empty spaces but it can only enter where there is a void to receive it, and it is grace itself which makes this void.*

*Always, beyond the particular object whatever it may be, we have to fix our will on the void—to will the void. For the good which we can neither picture nor define is a void for us. But this void is fuller than all fullnesses.* ~Simone Weil, from *Gravity and Grace*

I sat down to knit and the emptiness that had dogged me all day came over me. I tried to accept the Void as gift, reminding myself that hunger anticipates satisfaction. I was partly successful, but not completely. Part of me wanted to squelch the emptiness at all costs, was willing to use an act of violence to suppress it, to blame someone, anyone. It is painful to feel powerless, to feel that I am acted upon, rather than an actor, but sometimes the Void just sweeps me clean and there is nothing I can do except sit on my hands and wait it out. Very few people stopped by to distract me from the gnawing inside, which made it worse.

That said, I am starting to fear the emptiness less, to see it as a desire that will be fulfilled at least some of the time. Recently,

I desired a loveseat, and a loveseat in mint condition appeared next to a dumpster and an old cowboy offered to deliver it to my apartment in his U-Haul. Then Rob appeared to sit in my loveseat with me. I wanted cactuses for my apartment, and an old man with whiskey breath on the elevator offered to bring some by, and he did. Acceptance of a divine timeframe is key— I'm hungry now and I'm okay. Refusal to take matters into my own hands (addiction). To weep, to hunger, to fail, to be hated and poor is to create a vacuum for grace to erupt like a geyser from the hollow in the rock of my heart. Nature abhors a vacuum. No sooner does a clearing appear after a forest fire, then wildflowers spring up.

Can I trust this principle in my life, in my friends' lives, in the world? So much suffering, so many voids.

Yesterday, I awoke from a nap to Love sweeping through my veins like a flash flood in the desert. Apart from the operation of grace in my life, I'd be ready to drink my Kool Aid and rest in peace.

But I know for a fact that grace happens–
- Woman who was raped, now happily married.
- Roommate who was labeled infertile, mother of two babies.
- Friend addicted to porn and psychedelics recovers.

I get giddy thinking about it because these wounds, these voids, these aches are all potential sites for the impossible to happen–and it is happening. "Blessed are those who hunger and thirst for righteousness, for they will be filled," Jesus said. The main question is, do I believe?

## September 11, 2014

*... I mean Negative Capability, that is when a man is capable of being in uncertainties, Mysteries, doubts, without any irritable reaching after fact & reason ...* ~John Keats

"It's a full-time job just holding onto my hat and this umbrella," I told Tom Wood and his friend out on a stroll. A strong wind blew, white caps flecking the surface of the bay.

"You need an assistant to hold the umbrella for you. Maybe you could get a student to do an art internship with you," Tom said.

"Conceptual Art Internship. Duties include: holding umbrella," I said laughing.

"There seems to be only one bench on all of South Hill," he remarked. Tom had tried to find the bench the other day but he was on the wrong street.

"There's actually another bench lower down on 16th along the same bus route," I said.

"Oh, does the bus still run?" he asked.

"No," I said.

"So now the bench just exists for you," he said and, "When's your expected completion date?"

"I don't know—that's part of the project," I said.

"So when you are done with the project, you can retire from knitting every day?" he said.

After they left, I sat clenching the umbrella handle between my legs to protect myself from the glaring sun. But the wind kept trying to yank the umbrella out of my grip. *When the wind takes me, it takes you to,* Great Lake Swimmers song in my head today. Tiny seeds scattered in the wind. I love the wind! A reminder that everything is alive, even the air.

"So you don't listen to music while you knit?" a woman asked.

"No, I like to listen to the sounds of modern day life," I said. Today's sounds included a stump grinder. I was disappointed that I didn't notice when it stopped, only when it started. The mind adjusts itself to noise to make it more tolerable.

A woman with a large fluffy white dog walked wordlessly by.

I finished dog sitting Sunny for Dana today. After barking sharply several times last night, Sunny settled down and slept

231

peacefully. When she licked my hand in the morning, I knew I had won her over. She even let me stroke her ears, but only for a few seconds. I took a photo of Sunny smiling in front of a grand Victorian mansion that looked like a haunted house.

## September 15, 2014

The line now stretches down to 10th St. Hurrah! I had fun stretching the line down six blocks with Rob's generous help. Will it reach the ocean by the end of this year's knitting season?

## September 16-21. No knit.

# 30

# Sunset

September 22, 2014

Late night knit from 7 to 8 p.m., full of striped mosquitoes that dive-bombed me repeatedly like kamikazes. Cynthia and Pete rushed over to me at the bench.

"Did you tell us you were going on vacation?" Cynthia asked.

I had plum forgotten. I didn't think that my absence of five days would make a difference to anyone.

"We were worried that you were sick, holed up in your apartment and needing nourishment," Cynthia said.

I told her about my coastal backpacking trip with my sister and aunt, followed by a wonderful weekend with Rob. Pete and Cynthia carefully unwound the knit line across the street for me and I filled with gratitude. I have been going slowly all day–almost didn't make it to knit but I'm glad I did because it was so people abundant.

The setting sun spilled golden sunlight through a horizontal slit in the clouds, diffusing downwards in a soft rectangle of light on the water like a panel from a Rothko painting. I showed Cynthia my new eye cream and she started rubbing it around her eyes.

"It's age-defying cream," she said. "I'll be five years old by the end of this hour of knitting!"

James meandered over, wearing a bright yellow "I Love The Ducks" shirt. "The age that I am inside me is much younger than my body," James said. "The older I get, the more able I am to stick with something for a long time."

Turning to me, Cynthia said, "You must be really old because you've been working on this project for the last three years."

Pete sat on the end of the bench, giving pats to all the dogs that walked by with their owners.

"Come over here and let me pet you!" he called out to a dog with long, stringy hair in its eyes.

The dog yapped at him.

"Or come over here and bite me," Pete said and tousled the dog's fur.

A young man walked by carrying his dog whose useless leash hung from around its neck.

"Why is it that everyone carries their dog past the bench?" Pete said loudly enough for him to hear.

"My dog refuses to leave the house so I carry him. Later I'll put him down and he'll get his exercise by running home," the owner explained.

"We see a lot of people dog-carrying instead of dog-walking," Pete said.

The dog in arms, Oscar, started growling at the fire hydrant in Tom's front yard. "For whatever reason, he hates it," the owner said.

"Perhaps the shape suggests a midget in a red shirt with little arms jutting out on either side," I mused.

"Look, Christen, the sky is turning pink!" Cynthia said.

"Good job, God!"

"Sometimes I see something so beautiful, it stops me in my tracks. Like that lady across the street," James said pointing to the woman who had been standing on the crest of the hill for several moments, not moving, her back to us. "She looks like she's writing a poem inspired by the sunset," James said.

"Or maybe she's just catatonic," I suggested.

Cynthia and Pete turned in for the night, while James started down the hill, in pursuit of the sunset.

Suddenly Alice and her friend crested the hill, and crossed the street to sit on the bench with me. Her friend described a psychiatric treatment called EMDR which involves activating both sides of the brain through eye movement. It's a highly effective modality even though scientists don't fully understand why it works. And here's the kicker: knitting is a form of EMDR! A friend of hers had had her leg amputated due to cancer, and whenever the pain of her phantom limb became too strong, her husband would grab her knitting needles and she'd knit until the pain subsided.

"How's *your* mind?" Alice asked me.

"Great," I said. "Since knitting, my short-term memory has improved, my mind feels clearer, and I'm able to relax and be in the moment."

James returned from his walk, and the sky grew dark as the three of us lingered at the bench.

Alice told us about her mother. "She was only happy anticipating the future, or remembering the past, the present was always shit, shit, shit."

James said softly, "Did your mom have a potty mouth?"

"No, I do!" Alice laughed. "My mother taught me so much," she said

"—about what not to do!" her friend finished her sentence. They offered me raspberries freshly picked from Alice's garden, then headed home. James wound up the line for

235

me.  I had been carried through the entire hour of knitting by my friends.

# 31

# When You Possess Love

September 23, 2014

Today is officially the first day of fall. It's absurd to assign a calendar date to the start of a season. Fall really started about two weeks ago, but now we are free to say "Happy Autumn!" and drink steaming cups of apple cider. I had a quiet knit but for Steve's leaf blower, lawn mower, and rattling chariot contraption. Arnold's maple has skipped the intermediary phases this year and gone straight to a dingy brown. I saw Carla wearing a knit red cap over her head (bald from chemotherapy) enjoying the foxgloves in her yard. She expressed gratitude that she could walk around again.

The sky couldn't make up its mind whether to rain–a few drops started down just as Cynthia crossed the street cradling a laptop.

"I hope I don't get electrocuted!" she said. She was wearing her signature hot-pink workout clothes that I have come to love.

Before I was fully awake this morning, Love washed over me like a tide come in. Breathing in and out. But as soon as I got up, my fears attacked me, an army of leeches. My paternal grandpa was just hospitalized with a numbness in his arm. Mortality makes me tremble, a sense of helplessness like driving a car downhill on ice. I don't fear my own death–I'm afraid of losing the people I love. And yet, this thought found me earlier this morning, *When you possess Love, you possess all things. Do not be afraid.*

From a nearby tree, the squeaky, whistling birds filled the air with song between the droning of the leaf blower. Chuck the mailman walked by smiling. Yellow snapdragons burst out of a lawn. I was glad to knit, to watch people come and go, the ordinariness of daily life rooting me, paradoxically, in the Eternal.

## September 24, 2014

Halfway through my knit, Cynthia approached in a sage-green cardigan, her hands cradling a travel mug of tea and a dunker wrapped in a napkin.

"Top of the morning to you!" she said. "Here's something to take the edge off."

It was a cold, rainy day and the bench was shiny and wet. I gushed gratitude from inside my stiff yellow raincoat.

"Don't thank me—it was all Pete's idea but he couldn't find his shoes..." She said she has The Boys in the Hoods praying for our sick neighbor Carla, and the prayers are working. I coined The Boys in the Hoods for our Trappist friends at Guadalupe Monastery in Oregon. I asked if she and Pete still had plans to go on retreat there this October. She said it was on the back burner, depending on how Carla was doing. I said I might be interested in going, though I have mixed feelings about taking time away from Rob. She reminded me to hold on to the activities and interests that nourish me.

"Tend your garden," I mused. "I used to think I was a full-blown monastic, but now I've realized that I just have a little monk inside me."

She said, "I think everyone has a monk inside them but not everyone wants to acknowledge it."

I nodded in agreement, "Yes my novice director at the monastery used to say that your capacity for solitude and your capacity for relationship spring from one and the same place. You have to accept yourself in order to love another person. And to accept yourself, you have to face yourself, and to face yourself, you have to enter your solitude, and to enter your solitude you must face your deepest wounds. Your solitude is a wild and scary place, but also one of great healing, the wilderness where you encounter God. And that's your meditation for the day," I concluded sheepishly.

I can be such a windbag sometimes. Cynthia just smiled at me with a look of bemused tolerance. I love her so.

I finished my knit under a grey sky as soft as angora wool.

# 32

# The Element of Surprise

September 25, 2014

"I thought you were just knitting while you waited for the bus, but apparently—" glancing at the hose reel full of knit rope, "—it is your life! Wow!" a man on a bicycle said as he crested the hill.

"What you are doing is very specialized," the natural gas inspector told me as he crossed the street.

I love the element of surprise in life and art. Public spaces like street corners and sidewalks lend themselves best to the *frisson* that art seeks to provide. The person who walks into a gallery or museum, on the other hand, enters with a baggage cart full of expectations. I paid $20 to enter, it better be good! I've waited my whole life to see the Mona Lisa, I better like it. In such a setup, the work of art has very little chance to deliver the goods. Especially since most museum goers spend less than 30 seconds in front of each painting, and I am sorry to admit I often fall into this camp! A typical museum is simply too much to take in, too many rooms packed too full, too many labels to read. The fact that I have ever had a moving encounter with a work of art in this set up is miraculous. The artist of the street, on the other hand, has a much better chance to provide the passerby with a real, life-giving encounter. Rather than the fixed terms constructed by the museum, the person on the street is interrupted by art in a free exchange where anything is possible.

## September 26, 2014

Knitting in the rain is a divisive activity. People either avoided me today as a scary, insane person or they came up and raved about how "dedicated" I was. Near the end of the hour, Cynthia emerged with a towel and a hat.

"You silly girl! Here, dry your hair off!"

## September 29, 2014

*Joy is the overflowing consciousness of reality.* ~Simone Weil

# 33

# A Long Obedience in the Same Direction

September 30, 2014

Arnold handed me a key and asked me to start locking the basement to "keep everyone happy." I think he means his wife. There have been several burglaries in the neighborhood including some by the Bicycle Thief who rides a bicycle to a house, steals a few things, then hops on the absent owner's bicycle, abandoning his own bike as a calling card of sorts.

Jerome approached and told me he likes to eat everything except head cheese and instant mashed potatoes. I don't like the sound of head cheese.

Yesterday Lina and Tim drove up beaming. Yes, our Red Tent Club was very short-lived. Lina is expecting a baby, and they just got engaged. Lina held up her ring for me to admire.

Tim said, "I'm happy to see you back knitting, it renews my faith in the Universe."

I said, "That's all it takes?"

Tim just looked at me with his solemn grey eyes.

The sun shone, the water sang deep blues. The birds busted

their sides chirping. And I felt officially ready to be done.

Forget process and meditation and mindfulness, I just want to get to the bay. I want to start some big, juicy paintings and dance around splashing paint with wild abandon. I am tired of sitting on a hard bench in one position. I knit an extra hour or so, hoping the overtime will speed my progress. It probably won't. This project has a timeline of its own. Anyway, it makes me *feel* like I'm making progress. I am dog sitting Sunny again this week just up the street so it is very convenient to knit, knit, knit.

So, I ask myself, what am I learning? I am learning to wait patiently. Waiting is hope-filled suffering. More is accomplished through waiting for God than years of muscular effort. Waiting is one of the most powerful forces in the world. The great work of the world is accomplished by waiting. I feel that the true work in my case is not a hose-reel full of knitting but rather the transformation of hearts, the circle of communion that has formed around an abandoned bus stop.

## October 2, 2014

The white Roto-Rooter van drove by several times with "Away Go Troubles Down the Drain" emblazoned on the side of the vehicle. I loved the grins on the driver and passenger's faces. Two women drove up, parked and peppered me with questions. Sisters. The brunette was visiting from L.A. to give her blonde sister moral support after a surgery. What a great way to turn a negative into a positive. They were both very upbeat, snapping photos of me knitting.

"This is so Miranda July," the brunette told me.

I was joined on the bench by Allen who is starting his six month and two week program to get in shape before his 3000 mile hike. He has already ordered four pairs of tennis shoes for the trail. Allen confessed to drinking too much beer and eating too many chips with hummus in the past few months.

Rubbing his belly, he said, "After about age 50, a man gives up on his body. After all, the childbearing years are over. Why bother?"

With the weather improving, my spirits have lifted. I'm willing to go the distance once more. After all, I can't fail at this artwork as long as I don't give up. It isn't a demanding project. It requires no skill–just grit. Show up and do the work. Unlike a painting or a sculpture whose completion may require incredible problem-solving skills or insight to complete, I just have to knit from A to B. The shortest distance between two points.

## October 4, 2014

My artist friend Mary visited me again. I knit into overtime, enjoying our conversation so much. My muscles started to ache so Mary knit a few rows for me to the drone of Cynthia's lawn mower in the background. I didn't know what to do with my free hands, so I twirled yarn around my fingers.

## October 5, 2014 No Knit

## October 6, 2014

I knit to the setting sun, pink and orange clouds glowing like coals. James approached and introduced Chris, a barefoot runner who smelled pungent with sweat. James asked, "Is your work influenced by Buddhism?"

I said, "I'm interested in the universal use of repetition in ritual practice like saying the rosary or observing the breath."

"Repetition induces a state of calm. It's like shelling peanuts," James said.

Our startled faces belied the need for more an explanation.

"It's so much easier to talk when your hands and part of your mind are occupied. Walking is repetitive. My favorite vacation ever was walking the Camino de Santiago in Spain, a medieval pilgrimage in honor of St. James," James said.

"Is it Catholic?" Chris asked.

"Yes, but I didn't do it as a Catholic," James said.

"Could an atheist do it?" Chris wanted to know.

"Sure, sure," James continued. "I walked the pathways with

my adventuresome daughter—that's what made it so wonderful."

Walking as meditation, peregrination, practice.

I walked to the bench today because I wanted the extra time to reflect on my life. But by the time my knit ended, it was dark. I used Cynthia's bathroom and when she offered to drive me home, I didn't refuse.

# 34

# Trust as a Pair of Feet

October 8, 2014

The sky was muffled by fog, the horizon a vague strip of
blue. I tucked a wool blanket over my knees, fuzzy cloud cover
for me. I had a magical knit, after several days spent feeling
frustrated with the timeline of this project. First, Josh and
Thomas approached, lavender in hand. Josh had a sprig stuffed
through a buttonhole in the middle of his chest.

"We are stealing lavender from the neighbors...want
some?" Thomas handed me a sprig of lavender and I stuck it
behind my ear. The artist-collaborators and partners,
recently back from Bellagio Artist Residency in Italy, told me
tempting tales of bedspreads turned down each night, chefs in
white coats serving gourmet feasts, and renowned scholars and
artists to rub shoulders with every day.

I jumped off the bench to hug them goodbye, and Thomas
gave me a kiss on the cheek (he's from Montreal). The exchange
left me warm and happy.

Carla crossed the street with a fancy black and floral beaded
purse for me to borrow for an upcoming gala with Rob.

Later Cynthia swung by the bench and told me, "The purse
is from her mother-in-law and she's only used it once in 30

years." She said Carla is having a major surgery done next Monday which will hopefully put her on the path to full recovery. In the meantime, she's having repairs done on her home—I've seen plumbers, painters, and gas men buzzing around her property for the past three weeks. She's a force of nature, even now.

I grabbed my camera in time to snap a photo of the plumbing truck with "Any Size Job" on the hood. That's my motto too. I want to be a YES person—whenever an opportunity presents itself, say yes. I missed so many experiences in the past, including a housesitting gig in Rome, because I feared the unknown.

Lina's boyfriend, Tim came and sat with me on the bench and told me again that he and Lina have decided to get married and keep the baby. He is unemployed, Lina just got laid off of her massage job, and they don't know where they will live. To make matters worse, he has a felony on his record for the possession of marijuana (before it was legalized in Washington State) and no one will hire him. It all sounded rather hopeless and overwhelming to me, but I didn't say anything.

"You just have to have faith and do your best," Tim said. He showed me a sketchbook full of plans for his new business selling microbe rich garden soil. He is a picture of the kind of trust that I long for. Trust as a pair of feet to walk into the unknown, even impossible future.

October 13, 2014

I pushed my bike up the street as a fierce wind buffeted my body. I sat down to knit as the grey clouds multiplied overhead, then began dumping rain. Bring it on, I thought and the word "undaunted" came to me: courageously resolute especially in the face of danger or difficulty, not discouraged. I thought about the Spanish scientist of the soul, St. Ignatius, whose advice was to face adversity with a lot of bravado like a parent's no-nonsense attitude to a child who is throwing a tantrum. The rain stopped, and I thought, That was it?

Cynthia perched on the far end of the bench beside my

crumpled raincoat. She called out to Sunglasses, "You look naked without your hat!"

I started winding a skein of blue yarn into a ball, wondering if this is the last skein in the project. I'm knitting faster, my fingers moving themselves now, every cell in my body straining for the water.

## October 14, 2014

"I just can't do it—I just can't drive over your knitting," a woman called out from her grey station wagon.

"People do it all the time. It's part of the project," I say.

"I still can't do it. I'm going to drive down a different street instead."

"Bless your heart," I say.

A mom stopped with two young daughters, one wearing tiny pink glasses and a shirt with a hedgehog in a teacup, the other, a floral print.

"Did you want to show the lady something?" the mom prompted the daughter who looked five years old.

"Stitches," she said, lifting her chin to reveal a bristling row of black threads.

"Ow, how did you get those?" I said.

"I fell flat on my face."

"Did you trip over something?" I asked.

"No, I fell off a swing."

"Look at her knitting needles," the mom said. "They look a lot like the needles the doctor used to stitch your chin, only they're much bigger."

## October 18 – 19 No Knit

# 35

# Downpour

October 20, 2014

*If your interest is to hold onto time, then you will regard it as
something slipping away that's being lost. But if your interest is
transformation, growth and change—wanting to ride the wave as
it's cresting—then there is no problem. You are immersed within
the flow of time, and you are dripping wet!* ~Bill Viola, artist

I was horrified to see a chunky old television and a black TV
table dumped in front of the bench when I arrived to knit. I sat
down beside my blank-screened friend, wanting so much to turn
it into a parable about the benefits of detaching oneself. (There
is nothing quieter than an unplugged TV.) I began knitting under
tumultuous clouds. Pete came and sat on the bench for a while.

A woman walked by and asked, "What will you do when the
line reaches the water?"

Pete chimed in, "We'll have a ribbon-cutting ceremony!"

One woman wanted to know why I was knitting a rope to the
bay, and Pete ad-libbed, "She's afraid of the water, but she's
always wanted to swim so she's knitting a rope to tether herself
so that we can pull her up if she gets in too deep."

It was very handy to have Pete around to field questions for me. The woman wasn't sure whether to believe Pete or not, and she moved on.

A lot of people have started saying they think I've already reached the water. I think I should check my progress soon.

Pete informed me that Cynthia has gone to Seattle to tend Carla for the next week or so.

"They're both strong women, so they would probably start killing each other if she stayed two weeks," Pete said.

Lina's step daughter approached with a coloring book and a case of rainbow markers.

"Are you the Coloring Fairy?" Pete asked. She turned and headed home since the dark clouds didn't bode well for coloring outdoors.

Pete got the truck and loaded the TV and table into the back. All of a sudden, it started to rain buckets. Pete ducked into the back seat of the truck and closed the door to wait it out. He cracked his truck door open to photograph me knitting in the downpour before retreating again.

I laughed and hooted with the sheer intensity of it. My shoes got drenched but thankfully my Frogg Toggs kept the rest of me dry. As each drop of rain hit the road, it bounced upwards making a crown briefly before another took its place. The entire surface of the road danced with liquid crowns. Water gushed merrily into the grate near my feet; the knit line turned into a dam holding pine needles and maple leaves. I thought, Dear God, let me live before I die. And yes, in that moment, I felt very much alive, abundantly so. It all lasted less than 5 minutes but was such fun. The rain dwindled to a few specks here and there, though the gutters still churned with excess water. Pete emerged chuckling from his refuge in the back of the truck and offered me a ride home when I finished the hour.

I ended up bicycling instead, my eyes washed clean by the rain. Golden leaves reflected mirror-like in the clean streets. The air was pregnant with the malty smell of wet leaves.

October 22, 2014

I desperately want to have a celebration with dear friends near and far at the conclusion of this project. I haven't checked if the line has reached the water yet—I might do it today—and I'm a bit nervous to find out. I love the idea of jumping into the wild, blue sea together. I have a vision of all the guests and neighbors passing the ball of knitting down the hill, fire brigade style while I sit demurely knitting at the bench. When the line reaches the water, word of the arrival would be passed up from person to person all the way up to me. Making a journey without taking a step. A giant human spinal cord running up the hill. Connections made visible. And then after a polar bear swim, I picture glitter, pom poms, funny hats, noisemakers like crackers and such, something bubbly, and lots of yummy food.

Last night, I dreamt I was in the deep end of a swimming pool, when suddenly a little girl about three feet tall jumped into the water. I moved closer, worried that she might drown. In a few moments, she hit bottom, then sprang to the surface of the water, a huge grin on her face. Dear God, let me live before I die, indeed.

# 36

# Telling Time

October 24, 2014

*There is a time for everything, and a season for every activity
under the heavens.* ~Ecclesiastes 3, NIV Bible

I braced myself for the moment of truth. Today I would find
out whether the knit to the sea would end this year, or resume
next spring. Strong winds had blown autumn leaves against
Arnold's gate, creating a leaf sculpture that stood up by itself
after I opened the gate and tiptoed through. I have been storing
the knit line in the back under an eave since Arnold mentioned it
gave off a damp odor. The line was wet and dirty from the
recent rain as I started unwinding it down the hill.

I crossed a busy street, careful to pull the line only when cars
weren't going over it. The line was much skinnier in the first
year of the project. The lean years and the fat years, I
mused. And it really feels true. My life has become so much
more abundant in the things that matter since my return from
Redwoods Monastery—meaningful work, self-acceptance,
friendship, love. I started down the steps watching my supply of
knit line and hoping it would take me to the end of the
dock. Shortly after I started down the boardwalk, it petered out.

To my surprise, I wasn't devastated. I snapped a photograph

and began rewinding the line thinking, That settles it, I'm in for another month or more of knitting next year. Spring is an inspiring time to celebrate, and it's when the project began.

Full circle. In my end is my beginning. All I need for my deepest happiness will be given, and in good time. The main question that I must ask myself then is, what time is it right now? How do I respond to the circumstances that I face in this moment? I must become a skillful interpreter of the times, a dancer, rather than a passive spectator. So I sit here, breathing deeply after a cup of green tea, happy in the awareness that it will soon be time to let the knitting needles rest for a while.

# 37

# Compassion and Compulsion

October 28, 2014

I awoke this morning thinking about compassion. I thought
of the people I know who are struggling amidst difficult
circumstances—the couple waiting to find out if their housing
bid went through, the young man grieving his broken heart, the
old man surrendering his driver's license and independence in
one fell swoop. It's not easy being human, subject to ten
thousand things beyond our control. My struggle
with attachment and compulsion is pure gift, cracking my heart
open to compassion. I do not think it is possible to become holy
or enlightened in isolation from my neighbor. We
arrive *together* or we do not arrive at all.

Compassion comes from two Latin words *passio* and com
which mean "suffer with." And the person I must first learn to
suffer with, to love, is my self—not the perfect, idealized version
but the cracked and chipped self, the only self I've got. I reached
a low point last Friday—I must have checked my email at least
15 times that afternoon, so desperate for someone, anyone, to
acknowledge my existence. Can I have compassion for my
lonely, ashamed, email-addicted self?

Henri Nouwen writes that the compulsive self is the false
self who looks outwards for what can only be found within, in

the Divine. Inner solitude is not a vacation from the stresses of life, but a place of encounter with our demons—our nothingness, our helplessness—an encounter that opens us to God, in ongoing, fiery transformation.

And so I climb back onto the abandoned bench of my heart to encounter the only One who can make me whole, the Love that fills my emptiness to overflowing.

# PART FIVE

# CONNECTIONS MADE VISIBLE

# 38

# Chaosmos

Winter brought new beginnings and challenges. In November, two days after my birthday, I temporarily trashed my studio apartment to create a painting niche in my living room. The prioritization of my art practice precipitated change, even chaos before it was re-assimilated into a new order. Making space for love, for creativity, is serious business. Sometimes it feels like the whole universe conspires to distract me...the random phone call from the acquaintance just as I sit down to draw...the sudden arrival of laziness, headache or fatigue...the coworker who calls in sick on my one full day to paint...the compost bucket orbited by fruit flies. Everything a siren song away from what I am here to do: Make. Art. Now. To deal with the distractions, I created an art-making schedule that was realistic. Unlike old schedules that were dead on arrival because they were not sustainable, this one gave me room to be human, to care for myself. I start painting at 10 a.m., after a relaxing morning spent journaling, sipping tea, and eating a healthy breakfast.

May 1, 2015

Transitions–how I hate them–and this transition back to the bench was no exception. Actually, *Transition* is too mild—how about *gauntlet* or *obstacle course,* I thought chuckling. Yesterday I went to the yarn store and met a gaping hole on the shelf where my blue yarn used to sit. I got a horrible feeling of a pit in my stomach when the store associate checked the distribution center only to find that they too were out of "ocean" blue yarn. The idea of introducing a new color this late in the project was unthinkable. My intrepid store clerk decided to check if someone had stashed the yarn in an unexpected place and found six skeins of it atop an aisle. I bought three pounds just for my peace of mind–that should last me to the end of the project.

Today, I arrived at 16th and Taylor eager to resume knitting but when I checked under the eaves where I had left my hose reel at Arnold and Jane's house it was gone. I pounded on Arnold and Jane's front door for a long time, but no one answered. Berating myself for not alerting them to my 2015 start date, I worried, what if they took off for Europe or India? It was very plausible. I checked Arnold's meditation shed in the backyard to see if, by chance, he had stowed it there. The knitting certainly has lots of positive energy, I thought only half-joking, but it wasn't there.

At a complete loss, I decided to sit on the bench and just meditate. This certainly wasn't how I had envisioned my first day back. A few minutes later, Jane popped out their front door and hugged me. She and Arnold hadn't heard me banging on their front door, and they weren't listening for it because no one uses the front door. Arnold emerged next with B.J. for their morning walk. He looked flustered when Jane told him I needed my hose reel.

"Put those down, you'll need both hands," Arnold said, so I left my backpack and purse and obediently trailed him down the path that winds around the house past the strawberry patch. He shoved opened a heavy brown door to what looked like a wine cellar or prison cell, and hoisted himself down into a tiny cobwebbed room. It was dark and cramped but I spotted my hose reel in the shadows where he had stowed it for safe keeping over the winter months. He lifted the hose reel up to me and I hauled it up and out. Gazing adoringly down at the hose reel full of ocean-blue yarn, relief flooded me. Moments later, I sat down to knit.

Roxie pulled up, her petite self dwarfed by her green truck.

"It's good to have you back," she said.

Pete strode towards me, arms outspread to give me a "16th and Taylor welcome." Jerome approached and said, "Hi Christen. This certainly is nice weather we're having." He didn't stick around because Cynthia made a beeline to the bench in her fluorescent-pink shorts, gave me a hug and sat down to visit.

"Welcome home," she said and I breathed a sigh of sweet relief.

## May 2, 2015

I listened to the crow tsk-tsk-ing in a tree nearby, and the sea gulls laughing and wailing as they soared on the cool morning breeze. The sun crested the hill behind me at 9:18 a.m., caressed my shoulders with warmth, then hid behind clouds. A car disappeared over the hill, groaning as the driver pulled into reverse and backed precariously up through the intersection (the best compliment ever.) A woman emerged from the truck, her knee in a Velcro wrap, and asked what I was doing and if she could take a picture for Facebook. I told her, this is my fourth year knitting here.

And she said, "Bless your heart," in a British accent.

Much has changed. A new brick building has replaced the concrete playground. Karen and Mel the neighbors who grew free raspberries for passersby have moved away. They tore up the raspberry canes before they left, leaving them by the road with a "free" sign. Karen gave two ivory china teacups to me, left over from the garage sale before she went. Yet, so much remains comfortingly the same. I return to the exact same spot every year. I can imagine coming home to this crooked bench every year for the rest of my life.

## May 3, 2015 - Missed my knit for a trip out of town

# 39

# FunkyTown

May 4, 2015

As I sat down to knit, I noticed an upcycled school bus with fierce eyes, teeth, and FUNKYTOWN spray-painted on the front...a strange new addition to this posh neighborhood.

"I know this is an art project–but it's really about bringing the neighborhood together," James said, stopping to chat in a moss-green Panama hat. His dog Cody died so he's walking his friend's poodle Barkley now who's the same breed as Cody, but peach instead of grey.

"Are you warm enough?" Cynthia asked me.

"Not quite," I said.

A nippy wind blew through the neighborhood this morning. I forgot how cold it is to knit in the shade before the sun tops the hill but I am trying to stick to a strict morning schedule in my last year of knitting at the bench.

Grace and Rachel, the women who accompanied me in the first days of this project, approached with two new walking recruits. I asked them how many years they've been walking together and they said, "Four years—it's cheaper than therapy." The four of them crossed the road just out of earshot and finished their "therapy," untangling each other's knots with active listening and brainstorming. Their daily ritual of walking together is a gift to wake up to each morning, a living sign of community.

## May 5, 2015

I wore my Frogg Toggs but the rain quit by the time I sat down to knit. Several work trucks went by; my favorite had a plastic iguana strapped on the back bumper and two Hispanic men who stared blankly out at me as they passed. I'm sure they were wondering what would compel a woman to sit on a bench and knit a rope across the street.

I met someone who confessed to struggling with debilitating anxiety attacks. Her honesty gave me permission to open up about the multifaceted funk I've been in recently—anxiety, hopelessness, crying for no known reason. I've felt out of control, and exhausted with my attempts to recover, ashamed at knowing that I am surrounded with beauty and love, yet I can't snap myself out of my funk. It steadied me to speak to her, comparing notes on what we are doing to find our footing again. It almost made these past few weeks worthwhile. There is something about affliction that makes me ashamed, makes me want to hide. How wonderfully strange to do the opposite, and to comfort another through my affliction—a paradox.

The FunkyTown bus has moved on; I hope it's a good omen.

## May 6, 2015

A white truck with Barron Air Ducts painted on the side was parked in front of Cynthia and Pete's home.

"Are you having your air ducts cleaned?" I asked Cynthia as she deadheaded the dandelions.

"You are psychic," she said dryly.

I arrived bundled in two coats today–only 51 degrees but it felt much cooler. Two crows argued with a seagull on the green roof opposite the bench.

A woman with long, curly brown hair pulled up with her

daughter in the seat beside her and asked, "And what is it that you are doing?" She had a low voice and I thought she might be angry.

I told her about my project, and she said, "That's the best thing I've seen in weeks," and drove away smiling. A while later, she came back and asked to take my picture. "This is the kind of thing that makes life fun," she said, walking around in her knee-high brown boots and snapping pictures.

I gave her my business card with a drawing of a knitter on it and *connections made visible* written across the top.

"This is you?" she said. "I have your knitter card in the door of my car...Connection's Made," she called over her shoulder as she left.

I thought, I'm sitting here with cramps and a wan smile plastered on my face and I just made someone's day. Not bad. I grew up thinking that I had to be strong and happy all the time or the world would fall apart. It is liberating to realize that it's not the end of the world to go into a funk for a couple weeks, or just a day. It's even okay to admit it publicly. My computer didn't go up in flames, my teeth didn't fall out. My boyfriend still loves me. Of all the things that could go wrong, nothing did. I even made a friend yesterday. Maybe being an artist and baring my soul to the world isn't so bad after all. The FunkyTown Bus is back but I'm not feeling superstitious anymore. After all, my funk was just PMS on overdrive.

## May 7, 2015

*Stop leaving and you will arrive. Stop searching and you will see. Stop running away and you will be found.* ~ Lao Tzu

# 40

# Showing Up

May 8, 2015

Today I snapped pictures of wisteria as I hiked up the hill to the bench. Wisteria drooped from the eaves of houses, crept over trellises and windows like a monster plant from a B-grade horror movie, but its purple blossoms were straight out of *Anne of Green Gables*. Spring is such a girly girl. Who knew that Nature has her own inner Disney princess that she flaunts once a year? It's not in good taste, and rubs the minimalist in me the wrong way and I love it.

Most of the hour I sat and listened to the robins. I learned recently that songbirds have special singing cells that regenerate each spring, and then die back down the rest of the year. It wasn't my imagination that they get extra loud and exuberant in the spring, as if they clipped microphones to their feathered breasts.

Jerome stopped to say that he had to decide between taking a nap or going to stand on a street corner with a sign to warn people about the End of the World. "I decided to take a nap," he confessed.

"You are really funny," I told him and he looked pleasantly surprised.

After Jerome left, James pulled up on a Portland road

bike. He was going to a Codger Walk. A Codger Walk, according to James, is a gathering of retired men who walk together.

"There are codgers, and there are codgerettes. We walk for an hour, and then we sit and drink coffee for an hour and a half." Changing the subject, he told me about the Japanese concept of a living treasure.

"For example, the Grand Canyon is America's living treasure. And you are our living treasure here on South Hill," he concluded. I was touched and a bit embarrassed by this comparison between the Grand Canyon and me.

I said, "I think we're all living treasures in our own funny way. *Ichi-go ichi-e*—It's a Japanese phrase that means 'one time, one meeting.'"

The phrase is associated with the Japanese tea ceremony. The host and the participants honor each other's presence, demonstrating their gratitude with courtesies like bowing and using gentle, humble speech. Realizing that each encounter is a gift that will never recur encourages us to treat others with reverence.

## May 11, 2015

The hardest part of my day is often the moment when I sit down at the computer without a clue what I'm going to write, and write anyway. I show up. That is the secret to being a creative person. It isn't always the magical, intoxicating, inspirational life that you might imagine. The second hardest part of my day is getting myself to the bench for my hour of knitting. Today, I arrived sometime after noon, more than two hours later than I intended. After I get over my procrastination hurdle, the rest of the day chugs along nicely. It's not that I don't love writing and making art. I do! It's just that making art–like anything else worthwhile–takes courage and faith. It requires absolute honesty and conviction. Sometimes, I don't want to take the plunge. I want to wallow in a warm bathtub–inhaling bergamot bath salts, sipping rose tea and *think* about doing brave things instead.

# Neighborhood Happens

May 12, 2015

Most of the hour at the bench was uneventful.  Suddenly
Mike sat down on the bench with me after his morning walk and
coffee and Mollie joined us.  She had on an Alaska sweatshirt
which immediately sparked a wonderful exchange.  The Alaskan
waitresses who plunk your plate down, a lit cigarette between
their fingers.  Alaska, like a theme park, with tourists flying
hither and yon in helicopters and small planes.  The hype.  The
excellent beer.  The fishing.  The names of towns: Homer,
Talkeetna...

Mollie said one time she and friends were driving towards
town and it snowed so hard that the road closed behind them.  A
strong wind blew trees across the road, and the snow fell so thick
they couldn't see where they were going, much less know if they
were still on track.  They thought they were going to die yet they
still inched forward in their car.  Finally, a pair of tail lights
appeared in front of them and they followed the lights.  Arriving
to town, they befriended the driver, an employee of *National
Geographic*, whose tail-lights had led them to safety.  For the
next few days of the blizzard they hunkered down in the snowy
town with nothing to do but feast and tell stories and celebrate
their survival.  I sat quietly knitting as they talked, not having

anything to add yet joyfully reveling in yet another encounter at the bench.

## May 14, 2015

Today, a brief appearance of Carla who is recovering nicely from chemotherapy, her curly new hair in a stylish pixie cut.

My mind has been busy with unrelenting worry this week.

# 42

# Contractions

May 15, 2015

I've a new insight into my worries. I've been in a relationship with Rob now for nine months. I'm in deeper than I've ever been. It feels dangerous to reveal my faults, fears, desires, and eccentricities to another person to whom I have no guaranteed, permanent bond. It's crazy to spend so much time with someone who could disappear from my life at any time. Emotional intimacy is a two-edged sword, wonderful when we're together and doing well, but terrifying when we're apart or struggling.

It requires trust to believe that he, who is a biologically separate being, is still there. Is still *here* rather, loving me as much as I love him even when we're physically apart. (He's in Seattle most of the time while I live in Bellingham.) Like prayer, making and maintaining a connection with the other, is both exhilarating and scary. A passage from the familiar to the unknown. Even though I am deeply attracted to the unknown of committed love, shimmering golden around the edges, it's a reality that I cannot enter without shedding my identity as an independent, self-contained woman.

I think I'm having contractions. My heart enlarges to love, then like a muscle, tightens into a knot of fear. The relationship is quite possibly being born, emerging into a new closeness and commitment, its contours and solidity becoming more definite, more permanent. But like the islands in the bay socked in with fog today, we are a mystery, veiling and revealing parts of ourselves to the other over time. Expand–Contract– Expand. Inhale, Exhale. Open, Close. Nature is made up of these contradictory impulses, processes, movements. Seeing the fear as part of a larger, natural movement helps me to stop resisting it. No one judges a mother for having labor pains. Framing my fear as contractions helps me be more hopeful and less hard on myself. Fear is not my ultimate destination; love is—though what shape it takes is still in the making.

## May 17, 2015

I missed my knit on the bench, arriving back in Bellingham after 10 p.m. Alas, it's becoming habitual for me to skip my Sunday knit. Oh well. I'm not a perfectionist anymore. Perfectionism makes everyone and myself unacceptable to me, a miserable way to live. The most I can count on are a few perfect moments–the leaves on Arnold's tree a luminous green, backlit by the morning sun, or the black irises in the backyard like regal Victorian ladies in quivering purple peplums. Then again, there is something better than perfect. It's two imperfect people loving and accepting each other exactly the way they are. That kind of love changes everything.

## May 18, 2015

The sun is shining, the buttercups have opened and there's cottonwood fluff drifting on the breeze. Today I arrived only 15 minutes late. Jerome stopped en route to buying a hand-operated horn to drive away off-leash dogs.

"I'm looking forward to Heaven because I'm pretty sure there won't be any aggressive dogs or rap music up there," he said, and added, "I only have two problems to deal with in life— people behind the wheel and off-leash dogs."

I thought, that sounds pretty good to me, but then I don't walk all day every day. I saw the Ladies Walking Club who asked me to please post a sign announcing "the unveiling" when the rope is unwound to the bay.

"I forget what cause you're knitting for," a man said as he loaded Cynthia's black garbage bags full of grass clippings into the back of his truck.

"It's an art project," I told him.

"Just an art project?" he said.

"Just an art project," I said softly.

## May 19, 2015

"There's Yarn Lady!" a little girl announced to her mom on seeing me out knitting on the bench. "She's yarned a lot."

"Knit," her mom corrected her.

Last night, I had a dream that a hand was planting seeds inside me, a harbinger of new growth. I have been making changes lately; tiny tweaks to my life yield dramatic results. I bought my first bus pass since getting my car, and I've been driving less. It's a trade-off: more time in community, exercise and savings, but less speed. I'm becoming more aware of my own deeply rooted patterns, perhaps what I've avoided by focusing on others' faults. I wish I could say it's a joyful, maturation process for me, but every part of me resists the positive and inevitable changes that are happening. The hardest thing to let go of is my illusion of self-sufficiency. I always thought that to find my way in life I just needed to try really, really hard. I am learning the great truth of interdependency—I am not meant to make this journey in my own strength but rather with others, intertwined like a strong cord.

# Stop the Glorification of Busy

May 20, 2015

A saw whined in the distance. A man with a cough got out of his work truck. Clouds hung low over the sea blurring the horizon into sky. I wore my red sweater zipped up to my neck because the sun hadn't penetrated the clouds and I was cold. Grace puffed up the hill, alone.

"How are you?" I asked.

"I'm dying," she said, "but I'm still going to continue up the hill and do the stairs on the other side."

"You don't have your friends to distract you today," I noted.

"Tell me about it," she said. "I have this to motivate me," she pointed to the extra pounds around her waist. "I know every body is beautiful, big and small but my husband recently lost 30 pounds and he's smaller than me now in the photographs and I don't like it," she said.

"I'm rooting for you," I told her.

"And I'm rooting for your knitting," she said as she continued to the stairs.

Shortly after she left, Grace's walking partner, the new recruit with round spectacles, strolled up, her scruffy toy terrier on a leash, its skinny back legs flicking grass onto invisible business. I told her Grace had walked up the hill, and she said how useful it is that I am here knitting.

Later she returned and said, "I have to go do my job now."

"Where do you work?" I asked.

"I have two jobs," she said.

"You must be really busy," I said.

She said, "I try not to look at it that way. I read a slogan recently that I liked: Stop the Glorification of Busy."

As someone who has devoted years of my life to useless tasks like knitting this rope to the bay or painting portraits that no one buys, I like this slogan very much. Yet, I so easily lose myself in keeping busy and money-making schemes. Why? Because it makes me feel important and successful. My addictive feedback loop is to accomplish goals and get noticed. Too, it's really hard to take my work seriously if I don't get paid. I have a friend who writes four hours a day on a book, and has labored at it for the last 10 years. Her devotion feels like a miracle to me. Recently I heard of two artists who made a pact to pay each other $20 per hour spent in the studio. When asked to do something that conflicts with their studio time, they can honestly say that they have to go to work. At the end of the month they don't owe each other any money so long as both of them have maintained their end of the agreement.

The problem with art is that it requires more time and expense to create than anyone but the very wealthy can afford. Once I kept a timesheet of how much time I poured into my art but it just made me bitter, so I quit. The impetus to make art arises from a different economy, an older one back before time equaled money, before assembly lines. Time as life energy. Time as gift. Time as mystery. Time as devotion.

Whenever I start marching to the world's busy beat, there is a gentle voice that asks me why? I want to do work that has meaning in time and eternity, even if it doesn't pay off my grad school loans. To keep my heart clear and uncluttered so I can hear the inner voice that guides me like a line running through each day to the end of my life. I give myself permission to "waste" time, to cultivate a life of integrity and peace. And I also give myself permission to keep the "real" job, and the paid work that helps me pay the bills. It's a delicate balancing act, like the boy who zipped past me on a bicycle, his arms raised off the handle bars, spread open like wings.

# Waste Not Thine Hour

May 21, 2015

As I knit, I often fantasize about a rowboat to go with the knit line when it's complete and on display in a museum. Today the rowboat was made of sugar-cubes, glistening white and delicate in the middle of a yarn "sea." I conjured the wall text saying *the sugar boat symbolizes the sweetness and impermanence of life.* How short human existence is–the duration of a sugar cube dissolving in a cup of coffee, or an eye opening and closing. Compared to the life span of stars, geologic time, what am I? Although it might seem morbid, I think about my death almost every day. The awareness of my death motivates me like nothing else. I feel a sense of urgency knowing that just as my life had a very specific beginning when I emerged crying from between my mother's legs so too my life will have a definite endpoint. WASTE NOT THINE HOUR runs the length of a historic building in Bellingham, exemplifying a kind of moralizing that's out of fashion, yet still rings true. I'm not afraid of dying as much as I'm afraid of running out of time to make everything that needs to be made. I am pregnant with paintings, sculptures, a book, jewelry. Potentiality. A foaming ferment of life just waiting to emerge.

Given my sugar cube rowboat vision today, I was sad but

not surprised when Cynthia came to the bench and said that Carla had discovered another tumor two weeks ago and is resuming chemotherapy today. I had sensed something was amiss–Pete and Cynthia, usually so gregarious, have been holed up in their home, only emerging to mow the lawn or drive away.

"It's hard for all of us," Cynthia said as she crossed the street to pick up Carla and Tom's recycling bins and put them away. She is one in a million.

We all want Carla to pull through, want to hear her laughter floating on the breeze from her dinner parties in the summer time. I barely know her—she is very private, and all I get are glimpses of her taking in the newspaper or driving to work in her black jeep, yet I want her to get well, to take that trip to Sicily with her love, and to enjoy as much life as she has given to others.

## May 24, 2015

Today I talked with the mother of two children who come to visit Fairhaven every summer. They move each year between military bases, right now they are stationed in Korea. I asked the mom how she does it—uprooting and starting over again and again. She said she has come to enjoy the fresh start, the sense of adventure. The military community is exceptionally supportive—they're all trying to survive. When a new family moves to the base, everyone pitches in to provide bedding or dishes while the family waits for their boxes to arrive.

"You don't have time to decide whether or not someone is your type, whether or not you like someone. Since none of us have family close by, we have to become that to one another. Our loneliness is a greater bond than any difference that might separate us," she explained.

## May 25, 2015

Sky like white-out this quiet Memorial Day morning. The rain came on gradually. A few spots here and there dotted my pants. Pretty soon, I started to feel soggy so I put on my Frogg Toggs. During my tedious knit, I thought about boredom and fear. I have a friend who tries to do something she is afraid of every month–trout fishing, crabbing, memoir writing, cycling across Europe, and more. She is a YES person—when asked to try something new, she almost always says yes. She sparkles with life, and has the energy of three people put together. Even though I like adventure, I enjoy it in small doses. Too many new challenges, and I wobble like an elephant on a unicycle. Then again, when I restrict my life to only what makes me comfortable, it makes for terribly dull dinner conversation.

Given how simple and routinized my life has become–one might say *staid* if feeling uncharitable–it strikes me as strange that one of my fears of commitment is boredom. As someone who has moved constantly, the thought of settling down in one place with Rob for the rest of my life is, well, *unnerving.* I'm scared of running out of things to talk about. (My YES friend prefers to call it a "companionable silence.") I'm afraid that the person who once captivated me, might become a part of the furniture, or that I might become wallpaper to him.

Most of all, I fear my own emptiness. The thought of being lonely and married feels worse to me than being lonely and single, two mirrors reflecting each other. My mother once claimed she is never lonely in married life, but I think I will always be lonely on some level—there is this huge silence inside that I cannot put words to, as mute and vast as a snowy mountain or a whale in the deep though I'm not sure it's that grand. Sometimes I think it's just a hollow vase (made in China) in the space I call my heart. I'm reminded of poet Rilke's definition of marriage as "two solitudes touching." It never seemed very satisfactory to me. Despite this solitude that I cannot fully share, I do so love the thought of growing old beside my love like two redwood trees, roots knotted together for strength.

## May 26, 2015

At 9:10 a.m. a street sweeper whirred down the street heading straight towards the bench, its circular bristle broom scrubbing, washing and vacuuming the street. I gathered up my knit line and crossed the street until it had safely passed, glad that the line didn't get tangled up or torn in two this time. *GIVE BLOOD TODAY* said a sandwich board on the corner of 16th and Taylor put out no doubt by Carla who is the director of the local blood donor program. I glimpsed her walking on the arm of a younger woman to a car, her head wrapped in a flowery turban, and wondered if she was headed to Seattle for another round of chemo. She rarely talks to me anymore; it's probably more energy than she can muster to make small talk with the neighborhood knitter.

## May 27, 2015

Cold and overcast again. The Ladies Walking Club passed going uphill in orange, hot-pink and papaya workout clothes with tiny dogs on tethers. Morning knits are quieter than afternoon knits. I miss Cynthia and Pete who are too preoccupied with their morning routine to visit much. At the tail end of the hour Mollie joined me on the bench. We ate the organic strawberries she brought to share.

She has started crocheted camouflaged things including a black-and-yellow striped cozy for the guard rail on a ferry. I like the idea of invisible art—it runs counter to everything most artists (including myself) strive for—to get noticed, to stand out, etc. Mollie's goal is the opposite, a kind of extreme self-effacement like a praying mantis or a moth that blends into its environment, disturbing no one, yet vigilant and alive. She channels her excess creative energy into advancing the cause of other artists…helping them get shows, doing fundraisers to buy local art for women's shelters, teaching homeless people how to make jewelry from recycled materials. She received the Mayor's Award for the Arts this year but, of course, Mollie never told me.

## May 28, 2015

"Do you mind if I ask you what you're making?"

"I'm knitting a stream down to the bay."

"Oh…Ok…" (nervous laugh)

## May 29, 2015

I took a picture of one of the big fluffy neighborhood peonies that exploded like popcorn out of a tiny, tight bud.

Roasty toasty on the bench. 78 degrees and it's not even officially summer yet. The sun is coming up earlier each day. I'm going to have a burn line on my neck if the sunshine continues. Today Grace and Rachel stopped to visit, motioning to a truck driver to drive over the knit line.

"That shows how much they respect your knitting," they told me as the driver finally decided to drive over the rope, a large grin on his face.

No profound thoughts today. Quite the contrary. I thought about underwear instead. I had on a retro brown pair edged with lace that always gives me wedgies. I *know* wedgies will happen and I still wear them. The point is to discreetly remove the wedgie without anyone else noticing. It's a real art. I overheard the walkers discussing tiny underwear for joggers that wicks sweat away. And then a bit later, they started discussing leggings, "I wouldn't wear them to the office...Leggings are not pants, just as a bra is not a shirt."

This weekend, I plan to unroll the knit line and see how far it goes. Who knows, it might actually reach the water. Grace and Rachel said there are two high tides and two low tides every day. I am definitely going to aim for high tide, less far for the knit line to travel before it touches the water.

## May 31, 2015

Resistance is *fertile*. Sometimes my mind makes wonderful slips giving rise to a fresh awareness. Resistance slows me down, brings me back to the blessed and, at times, frustrating here and now...It's been almost four years since I started knitting this rope to the ocean. You would think by now I would settle down and enjoy the journey instead of fantasizing about the after party.

Today Rob and I decided to measure the rope's progress, to "unfurl" it all the way, as Rob put it. As we unwound the line together, I pointed out the thicker segment where I had stitched the line back together after it got wrenched apart in the swirling innards of the ill-fated street sweeper. My excitement built steadily as we continued downhill and the hose reel still looked full as if it would never run out. Even after we had unwound the line to the start of the boardwalk, it looked like there was ample rope to take us down to the water. We passed several people who inquired about our strange activity including one man who drove away laughing uncontrollably, while my Rob kept exclaiming, "You've done a LOT of knitting!"

I couldn't believe it when the line stopped two-thirds of the way down the boardwalk. It was a real letdown. I've given it my *all* this month, hoping to complete the project before I teach an art class at the end of June. But, like every artwork, this project has its own mysterious timeline. And I am usually "done" way before the work is. How do I stay present after I've reached the point where I am all done, when I've already given my all? How do I increase my capacity for discomfort? I think it's realizing that while I'm alive I am never done. For me, to live is to grow and fail and celebrate and love and lose and grieve and bruise and get back up on the bench and keep knitting.

Rob and I took turns rolling the line back onto the hose reel and up the hill like a deranged cowgirl and ranger. It was like a metaphor for relationship—pacing ourselves, trying to stay in sync with each other, communicating, getting tangled and untangled, cheering each other on, sweating and laughing. The longer I am in this relationship with Rob, the more it feels like a miracle to have made it this far. I am filled with awe when I think of couples who have made it 20, 40, 60 years together.

Later that evening, Cynthia called my cell phone to ask me about the status of the rope and whether it had reached the water. I guess she couldn't contain her curiosity long enough to wait until tomorrow morning. Yep, I'll be back on the bench for God knows how long.

# 45

# Subtidal

June 1, 2015

My artist friend Mary was sitting cross-legged on the bench wearing a labyrinth pendant when I arrived. This time, we exchanged stories of our childhood. My adopted Thai sister's heart began failing while I navigated puberty and endured bullies at Centralia Middle School. Every morning, my sister refused to eat more than a few bites, despite my dad's attempts to tempt her with bacon, a rare treat for a family of our size. She was skinny from the day my parents adopted her, like a poster child for malnutrition with a huge smile that lit up her brown face—we assumed all she needed was some fattening up, unaware that she was born with a congenital heart defect. Now her heart was quitting on her and she was even skinnier than usual. One day she died sitting on the toilet propped up by my dad.

The next two years were a blur as we moved back to Thailand and tried to go on with our lives. Then my mom got a phone call on her birthday from a nurse who was taking care of a baby abandoned by a teenage mom with HIV. She wanted to know if my parents would take him in. My mom said yes through a waterfall of tears. My parents named him Moses, or "Mo" as we called him, in hopes that like his biblical namesake he would escape Pharoah (AIDS), floating on a basket incognito through the reeds. For a year or more we hoped against hope, watching his antibody count swing up and down, and falling in love with our chubby baby brother. But by the time he was three, he had full-blown AIDS. Helplessly, I watched him turn into a walking skeleton, his body emaciated by diarrhea, his skin erupting in skin sores. Meanwhile, my mom had given birth to my youngest brother, Nate. I kept trying harder and harder to take care of my parents and siblings and get straight A's in school, meanwhile hating myself for feeling depressed and angry. It was a psychic burden that felt too heavy for my family and me, and it nearly broke us.

So much has changed for the better in my outlook since then. Yet nothing is ever the same after you've survived an ordeal of this magnitude. The world's suffering had penetrated our home and our hearts. I go about my life in the midst of affluence, but I can't completely forget that on the other side of the cardboard of my consciousness, there are people enduring more than I can imagine. I don't know how to hold the suffering that exists in the world and the pleasure that is mine without feeling a tinge of unease, even guilt. I don't know how to hold the awareness that at any moment, more tragedy could erupt in my life.

June 2, 2015

Misty rain this morning. The raindrops have transformed flowers and leaves into crystalline wonders, decked out in pearls and lace. I couldn't help snapping a few pictures on my hike up the hill. Grace gave me a ride the rest of the way in her Lexus. "We'll all have dewy faces," she said waving goodbye.

I yearn for her innocence, for grace, my heart still raw from sharing about my childhood with Mary yesterday.

Pete crossed the street with a plate full of goodies for Carla, picking up her newspaper en route to the front door. I asked him what he made for breakfast.

"Bran muffins! But I didn't make them, Cynthia did. I'm just the delivery boy," he called back at me. Later as Cynthia and Pete drive away in their tiny blue car I caught a glimpse of them smiling and waving through foggy windows.

# 46

# Peace Warrior

June 3, 2015

I forgot my bus pass today but the driver mercifully gave me a free ride, my backpack bulging with a new ball of yarn and a pair of lightweight, modern knitting needles. At about half the length, they don't have the visual impact of my heavy granny needles, but my forearms are tired and I want to pick up speed for the final stretch.

Everyone has been asking about my progress lately.

Ann, the tiny retired psychology prof who walks to Western every day approached. I assumed she was a type-A workaholic—because what other retiree would go to the library every day, pouring hours of her retirement into an academic paper?

"I'm writing my last chapter in a book of over 500 pages. You know the Truth and Reconciliation work that they've done in Canada with the natives who were abused at the boarding schools? It's like that but it's with the native people in Eastern Washington. It all began when I was a professor at WWU, and I was asked to give a presentation in Eastern Washington on Family Violence to the people from the reservation. My talk went into overtime because more and more people kept coming to the microphone to share. I found out that a Jesuit priest had sexually abused them. I didn't know what to do. I came back to Bellingham. I was distraught; I just couldn't put it out of my mind. So I called a Jesuit friend and asked him what to do. And he told me to file a complaint. So I did, and I got testimony from the victims. They settled out of court. I know that most Jesuits do good work in the community; it's just a minority that make the rest of them look bad. Then they all get painted with the same brushstroke. But until the Jesuit Order comes forward and condemns these acts as wrong, they will all continue to bear the shame."

I sat thinking, wow, she's gutsy. I know Ann–she is a faithful Catholic who attends mass every day.

"Chris, it's like this. If I punched you in the face and gave you a bloody nose, and then walked away and never did it again, there would still be a barrier between us. In order for that barrier to come down, I'd have to admit that I did something wrong, and say I was sorry. This is what's happened to these people but on a much bigger scale. The priest who committed these horrific acts continues to deny it. He lives like a king–albeit under house arrest–at a nearby Catholic university where he gets all his meals, medical and dental care. I've talked to the victims–some of them have gone on to lead happy lives, but others are horribly wounded. I think about them and pray for them every day. I *know* them."

I gazed into her eyes and saw the depth of her identification with these people who were not a statistic, but friends. I saw the fire of love and justice that drives her up that hill every day. I saw a warrior disguised as a five-foot-tall granny.

## June 4, 2015

As I walked down the hill and along the waterfront, my eye caught sight of orange flags in rows marking the rocky coast.

A woman in gumboots smiled up at me and said, "Today is going to be one of the lowest tides of the year–at negative 1.1 feet–so we're waiting around to see what will be revealed…We'll probably see some crabs, eel grass, sculpins, midshipman fish. Midshipman females lay their eggs in the sand—"

"No, they don't, they lay their eggs on the underside of rocks," her white-haired male colleague interrupted.

"He should be the one telling you the story, he's the expert," she said smiling, "Tell her what they sound like."

"They hum. They sound like a barbershop quartet."

I found this hard to believe so I researched the midshipman fish, and discovered that they have been known to sing loudly enough to awaken people sleeping on houseboats. The males sing, the females grunt. The singing of the male releases a hormone in the female that induces her to lay her eggs in the male's rock nest. Even more fascinating, there are three genders of midshipman fish each with their own reproductive behavior. Type I males sing using muscles in their swimming bladder to woo females, whereas Type II males have larger reproductive organs. Type II males, look more like females so they are able to sneak incognito into the female's nests and fertilize the eggs, in a behavior called cuckoldry or satellite-spawning. Type II males and females don't sing for long, whereas Type I fish serenade on and on.

June 5, 2015

Rachel and Grace warned me that my neck was getting burnt by the sun, so I covered it with my sweater.

"We look out for each other," they said.

I sat listening to the crows and an electric saw in the distance for most of the hour.

I have spent the week surprised at the rawness that has opened up inside me since the memory of my siblings' deaths returned in full force. There's something about this bench, this hour of knitting meditation that works on me, opening up the places in my subconscious where I haven't yet let go.

Subtidal, I keep telling myself. It's as if my psyche had been sitting in a tub with water and bubble bath up to her armpits, and suddenly the tub has drained, revealing everything, especially those parts that I kept carefully concealed from myself...my anger, insecurity, doubt.

I tell myself—the subtidal zone contains the most vibrant life, it teems with sea creatures—some of them poisonous but also the Dr. Seuss fish that hum. These deep places of the heart give rise to rage and fear but also creativity and love. I'm choosing to adopt the compassionate curiosity of a scientist who peers into the depths, who wonders at the movements there and notices life and growth.

I tried to pray earlier this morning, to force faith and feelings of trust. It didn't work. People who try to explain the suffering of small children or the random accidents that happen in the language of faith make me nauseous. I can't stomach it.

Later, I go to Adoration, an inexplicable thing that Catholics do, and I am flooded with love. A Love that wants to push its way into all my pores, my lungs, my belly. I'm breathing and drinking love, love, love. I'm sitting in a waterfall that keeps pouring over me, and I don't want to move but I finally do after about two hours. So the question for me isn't whether I believe in Love, in God. I know, experientially in my body, that God exists the way I know sunshine or the pavement under my feet. The question is whether I believe in a God who is loving and competent. Or is God loving and just really, really bad at running the Universe? Maybe falling asleep at the wheel from time to time—say during a flash flood, or when my baby brother dies of AIDS?

Big breath. I don't get any answers, I just get power-hosed with more love. I don't think there's an answer that could satisfy me, make the heartache go away. But I know that I don't want to play God, to try to control everything in an effort to avoid more heartache and loss. And this is what I hear: Trust is a process just like spring is a process. Don't try to trust Me all at once for everything. Just trust Me with what's in front of you, one step at a time. Don't be hard on yourself. Faith is not unwavering trust, it's being present and honest and staying in the relationship with the questions unanswered and the heartache. Our relationship is not going to end just because you're upset. It spans years of highs and lows.

And this is what I know: I am held by Love. I can doubt all I want but I can't doubt this ocean of Love where I live and move and breathe. I can play God, and try to control everything (a surefire path to misery), or I can surrender to that which I do not understand, a love and wisdom that's far beyond me. Those are my choices, at the moment.

And I can't help it, can't help but love a Universe that gives rise to fish that hum and knits to the sea. I just can't suppress this wild joy that bubbles up in what's left of my tattered little heart, despite everything.

## June 7, 2015

I didn't knit, but my dad invited me over to talk about what I shared last week on my blog about the losses sustained in my teen years. I was really nervous, not knowing what he would say. He shared openly and honestly, even tearing up a little, in his response to what I had written. I don't recall this happening before. Vulnerability begets vulnerability.

Earlier this week, Josh and Thomas headed up the hill on their daily walk.

"How is it that your outfits match completely—except for your shoelaces?" I asked, taking stock of their matching horn-rimmed sunglasses, black shirts and shorts, and crew cuts.

"Well, after 30 years, it's no secret, we shop together," one of them told me.

"How do you stay together 30 years?" I asked, my curiosity getting the better of me.

"It just happens," Thomas said.

"It just happens? What do you mean, it just happens." I couldn't believe my ears.

Josh stroked Thomas's chest, "Honey, it feels just like yesterday, doesn't it? The spark is still there." A pause. "Lavender helps. Do you want some lavender?" Josh offered me a piece.

"It seems early for lavender—early June—I don't know the lavender schedule," Josh said. I took a piece of lavender and inhaled the spicy scent.

"How long have you been knitting?" Thomas asked.

"Almost four years."

"See?" Thomas said. "It's a metaphor. It just happens."

I laughed, getting his point.

"Work, it's all work," Josh said as they continued up the hill.

June 8, 2015

I stumbled out the door clutching a piece of toast slathered with almond butter and honey. The honey dripped all the way to the bus stop; a drop landed on my flip-flop near my big toe. A sticky sensation ensued with each step. Got off at 14th and State and walked up the hill past sprinklers that filled the air with white specks of light in the morning sun. Quiet knit with my sprint knitting needles while birds trilled in nearby trees. The walking ladies passed several times on 16th, taking a break from the steep uphill route up Taylor Street while temperatures soar into the high 80's.

Towards the end of my knit, Josh and Thomas appeared.

"Here's a lavender pick-me-up," Josh said, handing me a new sprig. They had been debating what to do with their summer. Josh wanted to stay home and do yoga.

"I know it sounds hippie dippie but I think doing yoga every day helps me on every level. I just want to stay put, do yoga, read junk novels, make a new body of work, and maybe find a new reading for my fall class," he said.

Meanwhile they've been offered an expenses-paid trip to South Korea to attend their art opening, and a summer artist residency in Santa Fe.

"Summer is limited," Josh said.

"Yeah, it creates this sense of pressure," I replied.

294

"Last summer we were gone the entire time...we arrived back in town at 4 a.m., I taught my first class at 10 a.m. I was a zombie. I mean, I just read from my syllabus like a script. I felt really bad for my students," Josh said, the more loquacious of the two.

"What are you doing this summer? I suppose you are finishing this knitting project?" he asked.

"Yeah, it's my tether." I said.

"It's your leash!" Thomas said.

They thanked me for my free mini-therapy session and continued up the hill.

"You're like a bartender!" Josh called back over his shoulder.

## June 11, 2015

"You must have calluses on your fingers by now from all that knitting!" two guys in a truck loaded with orange tubes stopped to say.

A cool breeze blew off the water, and I drank in deep gusts of fresh morning air.

A construction worker got out of a truck, unfolded a tripod stand, then opened an orange sign that said ROAD WORK AHEAD. I could hear the beep, beep, beep of the front loader as it backed up looking like a giant yellow cricket.

I've spent the last couple of days with my inner critic, berating myself for being anxious, and taking out my insecurity on Rob by controlling and criticizing him. Then I wallow in shame and hopelessness. Love always enfolds me, but I block the awareness by being hard on myself and others.

Where does that leave me? I'm sure I can find a way to be hard on myself for being hard on myself! Feeling stuck, I question, why even bother? Maybe I'm just a flop at relationships. I started reading a book called *The Mindful Path to Self-Compassion: Freeing Yourself from Destructive Thoughts and Emotions*. It's given me tools that are helping. Last night I decided to try a tool from the book—acceptance. I have had chronic insomnia for the last four months or so, a pattern that has become dreary in its predictability. I set up a bedside table with some books and a rosary on it and told myself that when I woke up at 3:30 a.m., I would simply think about God and read. Instead, I got a full night's rest and awoke feeling invigorated.

June 12-14 No knit. Mini vacation before classes start.

June 15, 2015

I sat down to knit in the June sunshine.

Cynthia joined me early on saying, "I need to give you an update on Carla. She just started hospice care. She's sleeping most of the time now, but the good news is she's not in pain."

"Why did they give her such a heavy dose of pain meds— wouldn't it be better if she could say her goodbyes instead of sleeping?" I asked.

"It's her brain tumor that's causing her to sleep now. She stopped walking last Friday," Cynthia said. Cynthia had already said her goodbyes to Carla last week before Carla went to sleep.

"The whole thing is surreal," Cynthia's face was peaceful but sad, her eyes watering slightly.

I said, "You've been a really good friend to Carla,"

"Carla was a good friend to me—and everyone," Cynthia said.

Dying at 66 seems so young, just one year older than my mom. I can't believe I saw Carla just a week ago walking to her car, her new crop of hair fluttering lightly in the breeze. Now her sons and daughters-in-law have driven up to be with their mom in her final hours on earth. The whole time that I knit, people kept arriving with small gifts in hand to pay their respects.

I felt strange knitting and watching as people came and went. The wacky tone of my knitting performance felt out of key with the gravity of what was taking place nearby.

"She's doing her work now," Cynthia told me, and I wondered what kind of internal work she could do while fast asleep. She had completed her project for the Red Cross before succumbing to the tumor but she hadn't made it to Sicily with her husband Tom as they'd hoped.

# 47

# Stripped

June 17, 2015

I sat knitting opposite our dying neighbor's house. I really need to get her some flowers and write her a card, I thought. I wanted to thank her for the kindness she showed me. Before I left for the monastery, she and her husband threw an art show of my work in their home, and raised over $400.

Cynthia sat down on the bench beside me and said looking across the street toward Carla's home, "She's gone to heaven. She died yesterday surrounded by her family. I'm just glad she's out of that body and at peace. It's the rest of us that are sad and grieving, not her."

I sat quietly, letting this knowledge sink in. It was hard to comprehend that the woman I watched step into her jeep last week was no longer here. "I was just thinking about buying her some flowers," I said. "Now it's too late. Maybe I could give them to her family."

Cynthia said, "Why don't you buy yourself flowers instead?" She radiated a quiet peace. She had fought hard for her friend's life, and having lost the battle, she has mysteriously accepted it. Now she's supporting the living, potholder in hand from the tray of muffins she delivered to her grieving neighbor and his children.

A friend pulled up in her car, parking illegally in front of the fire hydrant. She came and hugged Cynthia, speaking softly about the funeral arrangements, wiping tears from her eyes. Then placing a gift on the front porch, she left.

An untimely death is not the ending that I had desired for Carla. How do I hold her death? *In my end is my beginning,* T.S. Eliot penned in his epic poem, *The Four Quartets*. Has Carla made a fresh start in a new form beyond space and time? I sit quietly in the warm sunshine, and listen to the robin's cascading song.

# 48

# The Space We Occupy

June 18, 2015

Another sunny day at the bench though rain is in the
forecast. Cynthia and Pete drove off scrunched into their tiny
blue car together. A short male jogger asked me what I was
doing, and exclaimed, "That's beautiful! Phenomenal!
Fantastic!" in rapid succession. I love people who (ab)use
superlatives. Mollie slowed her truck to tell about the upcoming
block party that she's organizing and the art garage sale Roxie is
hosting in early August. I asked if she had heard the news that
Carla died, and she hadn't. "She and I danced together. That's
what I'll remember," Mollie said. She added, "Life is precious."

One of the bereaved sons with the handsome Italian features
from his late mother came outside to let his tiny dog stretch its
legs in the yard. We said hi but didn't bring up his recent
loss. The truth is I'm just a witness, a bystander, to their
grief. While Carla was alive, I struggled to accept her
reserve. She kept a polite rapport between us, greeting me en
route to her car or the mailbox but rarely lingered beyond a few
seconds to visit. Perhaps my daily appearance across from her
house felt like an invasion of privacy. Or perhaps her life was
full of people already; the heart has its limits. I am strangely
grateful for her aloofness now, for sparing me great grief this

time around. My grief feels secondhand—I feel for the family, for Cynthia and Pete and the people who grieve her absence.

Recently, I went to a Sufjan Stevens concert, and he talked about death all evening. Not exactly the feel-good fare that I'd expected. He said each one of us occupies a space—both psychic and physical—the death of someone we love makes us aware of that space. And yet, when someone dies, they still occupy a space inside of us. In some sense, they are always a part of us even if their physical body no longer remains with us.

Occupying space has been on my mind for some time. After I was sexually abused at the age of twelve, I withdrew into the recesses of myself perhaps out of shame and a need to protect myself. I can see it in the rigidity of body in old family photos; the frozen smile. I shouldered all the blame for anything that went wrong around me, and like many women, I kept making myself smaller and smaller. I was that forgotten chair shoved against the wall, the masterpiece lost under a pile of sketches, the teapot gathering fuzz behind the microwave. I abandoned myself. As I've blossomed into my thirties, something has shifted. I've realized I'm no more broken than anyone else; playing small doesn't make the world a better place. If I wait until I've got my act together to show up for life, I never will. I'm taking myself both less seriously and more seriously, bringing a little joy and color to another's day. I'm occupying my space—inhabiting this world in all its fullness.

## June 19, 2015

A helicopter thundered past me, coming and going. The shadow of a crow crisscrossed overhead. A plump jogger passed bidding me a cheerful good morning. The Happy Trails Dog Hiking Services Van drove by, windows tinted for the dogs' privacy, I guess. Three motor boats zipped over the bay, leaving frothy wakes like erasure marks.

I met a little boy named Jack with keen green eyes, wearing a robot T-shirt and walking with his coffee-toting Dad. Jack sat on the bench and asked his dad where the bird poop went.

"The rain probably washed it away," Dad said.

"No, I flicked the poop off the bench," I said.

"Honey, if we walk by the bench enough times, we'll probably see some more bird poop," Dad said consolingly.

Note: I debated whether to write about the large bird dropping when it appeared about a week ago where I usually sit on the bench, but I excluded it from my journal, not knowing it was going to play an important part in the narrative development. You never can tell. Having taken care of the more important question of the bird poop, the boy turned his attention to me.

"Daddy, what is she making?" Jack started every question with a rising "Daddy?"

"Sweetie, why don't you ask her?" Dad said. And when he heard my answer, the Dad said, "Can you believe it? She's knitting this rope all the way to the water!"

"YEAH!" Jack said without skipping a beat.

"She's knitting down, down, down, all the way to the water," Dad kept saying all the way up the hill.

Jerome stopped to say he's going to start wearing his summer hat today, and he's sure his relentless badgering of City Council is soon going to pay off in a dog leash law. His beard has started growing back, scruffy and red.

## June 21, 2015

A young woman emerged from Tom's house, iPod in hand, and started jogging briskly downhill. Several crows dive-bombed her. The poor girl covered her head with her arms and quickened her pace out of their territory while the crows continued cawing long after she had gone. Testy. Maybe they are guarding a nearby nest.

The door opened again, and Carla's son and his wife came out and sat on the front doorstep. "A bunny!" she said, and pointed near Cynthia's car. The brown rabbit loped into view as I craned my neck around.

This week I submitted a proposal of my knitting installation with rowboat to the Lightcatcher Museum. My stomach churned as I turned it in, I was so excited and nervous. Now that the Chair has stepped down, I have been asked to teach drawing at the university again. I hope to tuck in my hour of knitting before classes start at 10:00 a.m. I've been thinking about artists as connection makers. How do I impart this to my students? It's easy to teach techniques, and undoubtedly techniques are important as a foundation. It is much more mysterious how to nurture the conviction, the attitudes and the practices that will sustain them over the long haul. Perhaps we discover these for ourselves? Or learn them by osmosis.

# 49

# Belle Shalom

June 22, 2015

Belle Shalom introduced herself, a short grey-haired woman wearing a neon-orange T-shirt and a teal sweater, the colors vibrating together. Belle had driven by on other days but today she decided to stop and chat. She started firing off questions the minute she parked her car on Cynthia's gravel lot.

"Do a lot of people ask to take your picture, and does that bother you?" She asked to take my picture, and went back to get her camera from her car. She started fiddling about with the camera buttons, and finally got it to work but the photos turned out dark, backlit by the sun. Also, she had trouble fitting the entire scene into one image.

"I guess it's like a joke: you had to be there," she said, which I think is a brilliant way to explain why experiencing a work of art in person is far better than looking at a reproduction. We finally got an okay picture when I craned my neck around to face the morning sun.

She said, "You are very persevering. Or maybe the word is *tenacious*."

I was grateful for the compliment; I'd been feeling ragged around the edges.

Belle continued, "Sometimes with a work of art you aren't sure if it's about the artist's ego—maybe they're hiding a deeper meaning from you—but I don't care; all that matters to me is if I'm attracted to it. If I like it, that's enough. I don't want to be an artist, I just want to learn to sketch. I've got terrible spatial perception. I just want to be able to go on my daily walk, and draw the difference between a duck and a bird."

I gave her my card, and told her to look me up for art lessons.

On one of her walks she had recently come across a tree with a bicycle in it, and was hoping to get a photo of it.

"I want to know how the bike got there, if it was stolen, or what. I bet you two bits it won't be there today because I'm never on the dime," she said.

I relished her quaint expressions; her quick, curious mind and spunk.

"You're so open and inviting," she said to me.

"Connecting with people is part of the art," I said.

After she left, I sat savoring her name, truly feeling that I had received *belle shalom*, or beautiful peace, in that exchange.

# 50

# Hygge

June 23, 2015

Yesterday, I was befriended by a young man out walking
a dog. I didn't notice his accent at first. He came here several
years ago as an exchange student from Denmark and stayed with
a host family on South Hill. Now he's back, walking their dog
and escorting their daughters to their second-to-last day of
school. He sat on the bench for a long time yesterday, gazing out
at the blue bay. He plans to swim in it every day.

When I wondered out loud how he could stand the chilly
temperature, he said, "We're Vikings, you know, we're used to
the cold."

He had classic Nordic features, blond and blue-eyed, wiry
build. He loves Bellingham and feels that Pacific Northwesterners
are spiritual, connected to each other and the earth. Today he
dropped off his host sister and then sat on the bench again. He
said that the bench has become a landmark for him since we
talked yesterday, helping him navigate his way home instead of
getting lost in his jet-lagged state which he likened to walking
underwater. He taught me a new Danish word *hygge* pronounced
"hooga" which roughly means "cozy," but it encompasses many
things from a feeling of well-being to friendship, candlelit warmth
and contentment with your surroundings. I felt honored when he

said that sitting on the bench was *hygge*.

He had completed high school which goes up to 13th or 14th grade there, and had enlisted in the military. He remained on duty an extra four months serving as guard to the Queen of Denmark. Now he's working in a sheet metal factory where he saved enough money to come here for a month. He showed me a scar that ran down this thigh to just above his knee. A huge piece of sheet metal had slipped out of his grasp, just missed the "family jewels" and grazed his thigh instead. He could have easily broken a bone, and felt lucky to have avoided a worse injury. He's more cautious now.

He told me about Danish culture. The legal drinking age is 16, while the driving age is 18. This allows young people to learn their limits and moderate their drinking before they start driving. They also get paid to attend university. Even though he thinks it's a good idea, some young people abuse this privilege by living with their parents and spending their stipends on alcohol instead of educational expenses. He wants to attend university and hopes to become an EMT or a nurse, saving lives as his line of work instead of a soul-sucking sales job. He only lasted a few shifts as a telemarketer—he literally felt pain in his chest, the work was so meaningless to him.

A monster truck roared by, floating high on jacked-up tires. "He's compensating for something," the Dane said, "We should be using our energy looking for solutions. Tires are made from oil, and those huge tires are a waste."

I asked if they used solar panels in Denmark but he said it's too dark there so they harness the wind instead. After my knit, I walked uphill for my first day back teaching at the university, hoping I could bring some *hygge* to my new students.

June 24, 2015

I was half an hour late to knit at the bench today, but the timing was perfect as a car pulled up and two men got out and came over. Unbelievable! It was Jacob, an internationally-known Swedish artist who just installed a sculpture in Bellingham, and his friend Pablo, an art dealer from Seattle. Despite

308

their credentials, they were friendly and down-to-earth, and invited me to come paint an abstract sign board for the upcoming parade on Saturday, a collective art work entitled *Demonstration*.

I was surprised at how taken Pablo was with my knitting project. He gave me a lot of great input, and it's given me a much better sense of the direction to take my work. He advised me to scrap the idea of making a knit "sea" and rowboat after I finish the project, and just display the hose reel which he felt was strong enough on its own. He said many beautiful things about my project, words which assured me that he understood the spirit of my work.

Later that afternoon I made two paintings with latex paint in about 40 minutes—one purple and strawberry, one black and red—with Jacob and Pablo. I hope to participate in *Demonstration* this Saturday. This chance won't come again.

### June 25, 2015

I unwound the line to see if it had arrived at the bay; many people have told me recently, "Surely you've reached the water by now." The thought that perhaps the line has already arrived and I'm just wasting time has dogged me. Strange that I still worry about wasting time—the whole endeavor is a waste of time, from a practical point of view. As I unwound the line down the hill, almost everyone wanted to know my purpose, as if knitting to the sea is not reason enough. I like the story of the climber who when asked why he summited mountains, said, "Because I can."

Once again, I fully expected the line to reach the water. But when the rope was fully unwound, it merely extended to the end of the boardwalk. An additional floating dock extends straight off the end of the boardwalk, and the line will run down it to the water eventually, perhaps in a month or so. If you didn't know better, you would think that I was purposely extending this project for the sake of my art career! It certainly has been amazing to meet people through this unlikely work of mine.

I encountered an elegant older woman with black glasses and an electric-pink shirt out walking her dog and her husband. I smiled at her and said hi as I reeled the knit line up the sidewalk. Her husband stepped forward, bending over to take a closer look at the line, and she said, "Stay out of it! Stay out of it!" She spoke to him as if he were a dog about to stick his nose in some roadkill. There is something powerful and transgressive about artistic expression, bordering on magic, that terrifies some people, I thought, smiling and feeling witchy.

## June 26, 2015

It's been a whirlwind of a week. I've started getting up at 5:45, to make it to knit before class every Tuesday and Thursday. I take a while to get going in the morning so I need the buffer. I'm being stretched beyond my personal limits, between knitting, blogging, teaching and caregiving on the weekends. Somehow I continue…pure grace. As if that wasn't enough, we're having a record heatwave—2015 is set to be the hottest year in history. Even at 8:30 a.m., the bench is already warm.

After weeks of Tom opening and closing his front door without a word exchanged between us—our old chitchat seems inappropriate now—I finally found the gesture to express my sadness at the loss of his wife.

"I want to give you a hug," I said, jumping off the bench. I gave him a slow, heartfelt hug, and he said, "Thank you," in a low voice.

We were both moved, and nothing more needed to be said. I sat back down and bent over my knitting, feeling shy, as he drove away.

# 51

# Missing the Bus

June 27, 2015

Despite the forecast of record heat on Saturday, I was
determined to take part in Jacob's collective artwork,
*Demonstration*. When I arrived at our meeting place in front of
the museum, Jacob greeted me in his striped shirt, torn jeans and
tousled hair. (He has been wearing a different striped shirt every
day for 15 years now as an ongoing performance work.)

He said, "You are smart—you need a dumb painting to
carry," as he handpicked a very crudely painted board mounted
on a stick for me. Our ragtag group of adults, children, and dogs
marched down the streets of Bellingham holding colorful
abstract paintings. It was a moving art gallery, animated by
human bodies. We walked past the Farmer's Market as
locals paused to wonder and wave. How lovely to celebrate
together, to demonstrate something positive without the use of
force or the need to convince anyone of anything. I felt like I
was floating down a river, seeing my town afresh each time I
glanced over my shoulder at the vibrant paintings bobbing up and
down the street behind me. Several participants ducked out of
the procession after the first half hour, but I was determined to
stick it out until the end. By the middle of the walk, the heat had
become intolerable. I had long finished my bottle of water, and

was parched, sweating profusely and in need of a bathroom. Meanwhile, the ugly wooden painting I was carrying on my stick kept getting heavier and heavier. In the scorching sun, we wound our way down into the dusty grounds of the abandoned toilet paper factory for a photo op. As we started back towards the museum, I walked with Pablo who had on a posh straw hat to shield his bald head, a large camera swinging from his neck. Our conversation turned towards the future of the knitting project as a work of art after I finish my knit to the bay.

Out of the blue, he offered to introduce me to a museum curator who had driven up from Seattle to take part in Demonstration. Before I'd collected my thoughts, he introduced me to a petite woman with brown hair and a penetrating gaze who began peppering me with questions, zeroing in on what my knitting project was about. I tried to answer her as intelligently as possible, distracted as I was by the heat, and my bursting bladder. I could tell that when I spoke about the social and relational aspects of the work she became intrigued. She said, "I have time this afternoon to visit the hose reel."

I was caught off guard, and on autopilot I said, "I have to catch a bus to visit my boyfriend in Seattle, but perhaps we could schedule a different time?"

Then we parted ways. It wasn't until I reached the bus station on the other side of town that I realized what I had done. I called Rob and in a wan voice said, "I just told a museum curator that I couldn't show her my hose reel because I had to catch a bus."

Rob said, "Oh Christen!" Then he tried his best to comfort me but I was inconsolable, shaken out of my pleasant daydream and into a pit of despair. I had just missed the Bus that I have been waiting for all these years—the dream of showing my work to a museum curator and maybe even exhibiting it—for the sake of a ten-dollar bus ticket. Had I been thinking straight, I would have skipped the bus ride and driven myself down to Seattle in my car after showing off the hose reel—maybe I could have even carpooled with the museum curator. How could I have been so stupid? I have never been good at thinking on my feet, but this really took the cake.

My thoughts whiplashed me as I tried to come to grips with what had just happened. At least there's poetry in it, I told myself mournfully. I mean, all these years, I've been knitting at a former bus stop. And if the Bus comes one time, there's bound to be another one, right? But this is Bellingham, a sleepy little town and an opportunity like this may never come again.

I thought about my students' fear of failure, how I forced them to draw with pen instead of charcoal last week so they couldn't erase their mistakes, whispered in one student's ear, "Sometimes it takes courage to allow yourself to fail." I don't want to live in hesitation and self-doubt, so busy erasing my mistakes that I have no time left to create the future. You can't make art—let alone, truly live—without risking failure every single day. That said, this failure smarted like rubbing alcohol smeared on my eyes. It wasn't embarrassment so much as disappointment and grief. To have my dream come so close and then slip through my fingertips. I knew without a doubt that I'd blown it. Big time.

June 29, 2015

A sky full of clouds. I have never been so happy to see clouds in my life.

Arnold crested the hill, towed by his dog B.J.

"You're braving the hill today, eh?" I said.

"Ask him," Arnold said, looking down at B.J.

I said, "I'm considering painting the bench blue after the knit is complete."

"You better use a stain, because if you use regular paint it will look like shit," Arnold said in his raspy voice. He's always dependably blunt.

"Right now it's ugly, but at least it's uniformly ugly…and you know, I'm not going to maintain it, and neither are they," he gestured in the direction of Cynthia and Pete's house. Then Arnold said, "Good Morning and Goodbye."

I am using color therapy today, wearing lots of patterns: plaid, polka dots and stripes to cheer me up. I'm grateful to be an artist whether or not I get my 15 minutes of fame. There is joy in the process, right?

# 52

# Buried

June 30, 2015

"I have something important to tell you," Cynthia
said, which means she is going to talk about Carla. She
continued, "They rearranged the furniture in her living room.
You remember where the long couch was? They put her hospice
bed there so she could look out the window at the water."

I said, "That's how I want to go, looking out on the ocean."

Cynthia started to tear up. "Carla propped your guardian
angel icon on the grand piano so she could contemplate it
from bed. And the icon is still there," Cynthia said. "She didn't
want anything to do with religion, but she sure loved that angel."

Carla had bought the angel icon at my art sale before I left
for Our Lady of the Redwoods Monastery. In the icon, the
guardian angel cradles a baby in one arm. The medievals
symbolized the soul as a baby in swaddling clothes, or a
shroud—depending on how you look at it. (My favorite
depictions of Mary's Dormition depict her spirit emerging from
her body as a tiny baby wrapped in white that is borne
heavenward by angels.)

I asked about the funeral service and Cynthia said it was a
green burial. They wrapped her body in silk and laid it in the

ground, covered with flowers. Each of the guests was given a flower to drop on top of her body if they wanted. There were three piles of dirt and shovels nearby for guests to bury her.

I said, "I love the honesty and simplicity of it; I didn't know it was legal to bury a body without a casket."

Cynthia noted how well it suited Carla with her love of composting. "And in three months, they're going to plant an oak tree where she was buried," Cynthia said, in closing.

# 53

# Cosmic Compost

July 1, 2015

Since my conversation with Cynthia, I can't stop thinking about compost, scat, decay. In nature there is no such thing as waste or garbage. I feel disgust at all the pounds of my trash that's loaded on a train to go to a landfill where it will sit for several centuries. As a trash-producing human, I am an anomaly in the universe and it makes me want to change. To be the bird that gathers discarded dog hair to line her nest. Or a barnacle that builds a fortress on a sunken ship. Or a bacteria culture that breaks down cow manure into fertilizer yielding up a harvest of juicy tomatoes. Perhaps this morning is a start in that direction because I did something bizarre before my knit—I packaged up my feces in a container to give to a friend suffering from chronic indigestion to try a fecal transplant, hoping that the happy flora of my digestive tract would bring healing. (Editorial Note: It didn't).

I'm reminded of the shock-artist Piero Manzoni who made Merda d'artista (Artist's Shit) by filling 90 tin cans with feces, labeled in English, French, German and Italian. His father, who owned a cannery, had reportedly told his son, "Your work is shit," which perhaps inspired the piece. Manzoni eventually sold one of these cans for 30 grams of 18-carat gold. The pricing of his excrement on par with gold evokes the tradition of artist as alchemist, and the alchemist's grand quest to turn shit into gold.

Nature is the Alchemist, par excellence. Without the alchemy of decay there would be no food, no life on this planet. Once again, it's time to rethink my relationship to the shit in my life. My recent attempts to patch things up with the curator via email and a phone call have come up empty. No number of taxi cabs could ever help me catch up to that bus. I've walked around with an ache in my chest for the past few days, weeping bitterly, in the knowledge that I came within inches of realizing a lifelong dream, and then lost it through my own carelessness.

If nothing else, this devastating experience has made me more human, because most people suffer from shame in one form or another. It's this terrible sense of not being enough that causes so many of us to hide our true selves. My fateful encounter with the curator has forced me to face my shame head on. I had buried it so far down in the bowels of my psyche I couldn't access it consciously. However, the shame was there, leaking out in more insidious forms like bile. I went to Confession recently and told the priest about my struggles with faultfinding, contempt, envy.

To my surprise, he answered, "All of these things are coming from the same inner wound, the fear that you are not good enough," he said gently. "If you tend that shame, these other symptoms will get much smaller."

So, I am getting in touch with my shame—I'm even canning and offering it to the world in this journal entry. If we could all accept ourselves exactly as we are, I wonder what would happen. Pure gold, I reckon. Nothing is wasted—the failures, the embarrassments, the losses, the negative thoughts—all perfect ingredients in the cosmic compost pile.

July 3, 2015

This week each day's photo of the bay looks almost identical to the last day's picture. In four summers of knitting, I have never seen so many blue skies in a row. It's as if time has stopped, but of course it hasn't. Most changes are imperceptible to the eye which is a rather coarse tool, registering only quick movements. It requires time-lapse photography to really see the imperceptible–the arc of time, the growth and change that continue *ad infinitum*. It's striking that humans are the only animals to have developed this ability to record these changes. Cameras, diaries, newspapers. Remembering is an obsession of ours. But I think it is a healthy obsession–within limits. I can't imagine life without memory. To wake up every day with no recollection of the past or how I got here would be a life afloat on a very vast sea indeed. Recording this project in word and image has instilled in me a deeper awareness of time and a reassuring sense of continuity.

July 5, 2015

A sweet overcast morning with a little breeze. I heard Roxie's dogs barking up a storm, and later Roxie headed down the hill calling out to me, "Good Morning Christen." An ordinary hour colored by the awareness that my brother's wife was in labor with their second child while I sat knitting.

July 6, 2015

A grey-haired woman said, gazing at the hose reel, "That's quite a picture of how our small actions accumulate over time. I have enjoyed watching your progress—I feel like I know you— at least a bit."

In many ways, the residents of South Hill are more aware of me than I am of them, especially the people that drive by in their cars. I catch a blurred impression of their faces if I'm lucky, but they see me sitting here on the bench every day.

Roxie strolled towards the bench in a lace blouse, her hair grown long and lovely. She praised the hose reel overflowing with knit yarn.

"It's kind of crazy," I said.

"Good crazy," Roxie qualified. "What are you going to do with it once you finish?"

I said, "I am hoping to display it in a museum."

"We'll put that energy out in the universe," Roxie said.

"Say a prayer for me," I said as she walked away.

"I'll say more than one prayer for you," Roxie called back over her shoulder.

Cynthia came down to street level with a Tupperware full of compost in hand—banana peels splayed like octopus legs. She asked how my weekend alone went. Rob and I agreed to take a weekend apart after the intensity of the last one—Rob had just moved into a new apartment, and I had all but fallen apart over the missed connection with the curator. She sat down with me on the bench, laughing and waving hesitant drivers over the knit line. She said she feels Carla is still present with us.

"I hear her laughing from time to time and catch glimpses of her sitting in the branches of a tree in her big black skirt."

I think it's kind of spooky, but Cynthia finds Carla's continued presence reassuring.

## July 7, 2015

I arrived at the bench to the sound of a jackhammer, and a neon-orange construction sign. It was fun to watch the spectacle of cars navigating the semi-obstructed road just south of me. The orange and white neon cones. The dump truck's erections. The neighbors chatting with the flaggers. An entertaining diversion while I knit. The sky has been hazy for the past three days due to a fire that ravaged five acres of land on Portage Island. I've appreciated the slight cloud cover; the cooler weather makes me feel perky again.

Cynthia crossed the street clutching a carton of orange juice wrapped in a pink bathroom mat. I didn't ask for an explanation, preferring to revel in the surreal moment. This morning I wrestled with whether to do my early morning knit before teaching and finally decided to knit afterwards instead. I told Cynthia I felt bad about slacking off on my morning discipline.

She said, "Knitting for an hour a day is discipline

enough." She had just spent time with Carla's mother—the poor woman has lost both of her daughters. Thank God she has Cynthia.

The Dane approached with Sulia, a beautiful Hispanic woman with green streaks in her hair. He said he had tried to visit me but I wasn't there at my usual time. Sulia had big, sensitive eyes tinged with sadness.

When I told her about my knitting endeavor she said, "That's quite romantic." While we were talking, a neighbor pulled up in her new car, straddling the knit line like a bridge over a stream rather than squashing it under her tires. Then Jane and Arnold came by with B.J. on a tether.

"Say hello to Christen, B.J.," Jane said.

Sulia said with wonder in her voice, "You know everyone!"

"Four years," I told her, "I've been knitting here for four years."

## July 9, 2015

Pete, Tom, and Camellia's dad, Karl, approached the bench and hung out. I served as the knitter-facilitator in the background while they talked about the recent barbeque that they'd attended (a bit of a bust although the food was good). An SUV pulled up, and two neighbor kids, Camellia and Emmett, jumped out to show us fists full of crow feathers and pine cones from their recent expedition.

I've been thinking about discipline lately and my tendency to overdo it. I've got a certain militaristic fervor that is handy in small doses but can quench the Spirit when I push myself too hard or become rigid. So it was good to knit at 4:45 p.m. yesterday instead of forcing myself to knit at 8:30 a.m. Structure and commitment are life-enhancing, but without freedom they soon become stifling to me. A friend of mine equated it with a dream she had of dancing around ancient stone pillars. To thrive, we need both—stability and movement, structure and change.

## July 10, 2015

"What happened to our sunshine?" Pete moaned.

"Hey, no complaining!" I said. I am so relieved at the return of cooler days even if it means overcast skies. I have anxiously read each record-breaking weather report with global warming on my mind all summer.

"Surely you are done by now?" Jane called from her Volvo.

"No. The floating dock is longer than I thought. I still have to knit down the gang-plank to the floating dock." When you are knitting your path, each leg of the journey feels eternal.

A mom with her small son and daughter came hiking up the hill. "Cherries!" the kids yelled in unison. The boy made a sour face when he bit into the unripe plum. The kids looked over at me and wondered what I was doing, so I told them I was knitting a rope to the water. As they continued walking up the hill, I could hear them discussing my project in soft tones. They paused halfway up the hill and stood staring down at me some more. In that moment I knew the project was worth it, all three-and-a-half years of it, regardless of whether the hose reel finds its way into a museum someday. The knowledge that a little girl and boy will grow up with the memory of a woman who knit a half-mile line to the bay is enough for me. Memories are a kind of wealth, a deposit inside a person that remain long after an event has passed.

## July 13, 2015

Construction work has now moved farther uphill. It rained last night and the air smells of wet earth and green things. I sat down for my usual knit, and Cynthia and Pete came to swap stories with me about their weekend. Harvey the filmmaker joined us and asked to interview Cynthia and Pete on the bench. It was powerful to listen to my neighbors' take on the project.

Pete said with a grin, "Christen's like a silent Pied Piper, attracting all kinds of people to the bench, primarily drivers of Volvos."

Cynthia said her day felt complete when she saw me doing my hour of knitting. We all agreed that we've become family and will keep in touch even after the knitting ends. Then Cynthia and Pete left to strip the paint off the front porch.

I've been waiting a long time for the line to reach the bay and it is almost there. Is it okay to get excited now that the consummation of this project is near? I'm a passionate person, but life's hard knocks have taught me to channel passion into patience and not get attached to outcomes beyond my control. That which I desire cannot be achieved overnight, but I now believe I will arrive. How does one hold both the passion and the patience at the same time? I would rather not live in the bittersweet tension of longing, but that's a cop out—and I know it. There are no shortcuts.

## July 15, 2015

*I can't get rid of italics tonight so I'm just going to roll with it. Today I received an email with a picture attached of Cynthia and me sitting on the bench taken by a visiting artist who called out to us "Permission to pass?" I'm so glad he captured this picture of me with my lovely neighbor—a memory I will savor for years to come.*

*I've had an urgency about showing up for my knit on time. In the past week or so, I've missed two visits simply by not coming to the bench at my scheduled time. (People counting on me to show up? It's a wonderful and strange awareness.) Today I forgot to set my alarm and slept in. I decided to drive to the bench and arrived 10 minutes shy of 8:30. So glad I hustled, because my artist friend Mary came strolling towards me as soon as I arrived.*

*"Need some help?" she asked gazing down at the yarn tangled around the hose reel due to my carelessness last night. It took Mary five minutes to undo what would have taken me an entire hour. She gently loosened the mess, gave it a few wiggles and it came free of the wheel in one piece. Another reminder that I am not meant to make this journey alone. Help appears when I need it. Friends listen and cheer me on. I am incredibly blessed.*

*Mary and I talked about some of the challenges we each face. She wants to change her perspective of the situation and view it in a positive light instead of running away. Quantum physics—your perspective changes your reality. I used to think that was a bunch of New Age baloney, but I've realized there's truth in it. I think we're all contributing to the great river of Reality by our attitudes and perspectives—when one of us shifts our reality for the better, we set in motion the possibility for others to shift theirs as well.*

# 54

# Karma and Maya

July 16, 2015

   I wasn't sure it was smart to attempt unrolling the line tonight because I'd woken up from a nap groggy and out of sorts with an upset stomach. However I dragged myself to the bench anyway. When I arrived, something felt different. Suddenly, I intuited that Cynthia had stripped the bench along with their porch. I texted her, Wow, the bench looks gorgeous! She had stripped the bench of all its mold and mildew, restoring it to its original goodness. The bench felt satiny and smooth and oh-so-inviting.

   But today I wasn't planning to knit, I reminded myself. It was time to measure my progress instead. It was after 8 p.m., the temperature warm but tolerable for the work ahead. The sun was about to set over the glistening water. As I unwound the line down the hill, I stopped to gaze enraptured at the light shining through the ruby petals of a hollyhock's towering spire. The unwinding went smoothly and soon I had reached the dock. People with tiny dogs, moms pushing strollers, silver-haired couples and teenagers sporting tans were out *en masse* on this perfect evening, peppering me with questions. A lovely older couple attached themselves to me, saying they had watched my progress over the years and were excited to witness this moment. The rope kept unwinding–I dared not anticipate whether it would reach the water. Finally I was on the floating dock abuzz with people catching crabs. A small Asian boy playing with a wire crab cage smiled in our general direction, and a young man and woman sipping drinks and sitting on plastic tubs at the far end of the dock made small talk with me.

"I thought it was a very long crabbing rope!" the guy told me regarding my line. "Today's the opening day of crab season."

I could see that the knit rope more than reached the end of the dock, though I decided not to dip the end of the rope in the water until the final celebration. The older gentleman high-fived me and everyone smiled. I felt radiant. The golden light of the setting sun gilded all of us as we posed for a few happy snapshots.

Suddenly a family with twin girls approached and started talking excitedly about the project.

"We just followed the yellow brick road, and there you were," Mom said referring to the blue line that they had followed from the bench down to the dock. The two girls attend Lowell Elementary, and have watched my project from afar over the past three-and-a-half years. One of the girls, Maya, started snapping photos of me on her brand new SLR camera, while the other girl, Dharma, asked if she could crank the handle of the hose reel for me. The mom asked to carry my heavy purse, and the Dad helped carry the hose reel up the steps. Before I knew it, Dharma and Maya had pushed the hose reel and wound it to the top of the hill, their muscles straining, their faces proud at their accomplishment.

Dharma kept saying, "I just love to help people!" The truth is stranger than fiction sometimes; I kept asking myself, am I dreaming? Are Dharma—the essential nature of the Universe—and Maya—the illusion of passing things—really helping me wind my hose reel up the hill? If I hadn't snapped a picture of the twin girls cranking the hose reel, I would be tempted to think I had conjured the entire evening.

The sun continued to set, and as Maya snapped pictures on

326

her hulking camera, the mom said to me, "The sun is setting on your knitting, as my daughter's photography has just begun."

It was a spectacular sunset, a sort of neapolitan ice cream swirl that kept gathering more intensity in orange, purple and pink.

"That sunset is crazy!" I said.

And Dharma chimed in, "Crazy beautiful!"

I felt suspended in time–present and grounded, yet euphoric. We kept exclaiming how happy we felt to have shared this experience.

"It's 9:45 p.m.," Mom said, "Way past your bedtime girls, but this was a special occasion."

Dharma and Maya gave me sweet hugs, and Mom handed me back my purse, and we parted ways.

Yesterday was my last day of knitting at the bench, and I had no idea. It had felt like any other day yet somehow the bench had known. Her task complete, she had been reborn. Stripped down to her essence, that spare bench shone, its contours now soft and inviting. Painting or decorating it now felt as superfluous as my fantasy of displaying a rowboat alongside my hose reel. I don't need to do mental calisthenics to make my art or myself better, more worthy, I realized. I felt caressed by peace as I breathed in the deep knowing that I am enough.

# 55

Dear Reader,

The long labor of knitting is done, yes, but the artwork is nowhere near finished. Now I need you to complete the work—your presence, your imagination, and your magical powers of memory. I need you to witness the moment when the knit line finally touches the salty brine; when the bench and the bay are united for a brief moment in time. As you recall, I purposely held off that moment of consummation because I wanted you to be there. I am not sure you realize this, but I don't consider the knitting the "art." At the very most, I see it as only half of the equation—you and the neighbors of South Hill are the other necessary half. The work is as much about the connections that we have knit together over these rich years as it is about the blue knit rope. Without you, I'd just have a large pile of cord.

I've shared an intense, soul-searching journey with you all these years, and now I would love to hear yours, and at the very least, say thank you. Knowing that you were listening gave me the courage to open up to whole new levels of insight and honesty. Though most of the time you've been silent, I have sensed your faith in the value of this project, my writing, me. I've never considered myself a writer, but because you readers showed up, I wrote.

I've put August 1st from 6-8 p.m. down in my calendar as a tentative date for the celebration.

Much love and gratitude,

Christen

# 56

# Sixth Principle of Gestalt Theory

July 20, 2015

I've burnt two pots in the last 24 hours. The house reeks of the black beans that I left on medium high for four stinkin' hours while I was at the neighborhood block party. It took Comet, a scrubber and a metal spatula to scrape off those charcoaled remains. Upon further reflection, I've concluded that I haven't made peace with the end of my daily knitting practice, and much more, the sudden loss of regular contact with the people that I've come to love.

Yesterday I went to Mollie's Hawaii-themed block party. Mollie had each guest pick a Hawaiian word from the dictionary to write on a name tag.

I overheard Cynthia explaining the word she picked, "It's Hawaiian for long, fast, narrow boat or—" her eyes sparkled mischievously "—a tall, well-proportioned woman."

I picked my word randomly again this year, flipping the dictionary open and dropping my finger on a word with my eyes closed. My word was *hemo hemo* for "loosening" or "take off." How appropriate for the last stages of this project! In a sense, I am casting my stitches off now, loosening my grip, and opening up to what lies ahead. But what if the art was primarily composed of relationships rather than paint, yarn or film? What then? As an artist, I'm accustomed to signing a painting and setting it aside. Art as social practice is different, and I am at a loss for how to wrap up this work, because the art is not an object but a process and a place and a series of unscripted interactions with neighbors who have brought such fullness into my life.

I was thirsty so I wandered over to the beverage table to down cups of ice water and juice when suddenly a lanky man with pheasant feathers jutting out of his cap asked me about my knitting project. I explained that it was done.

He leaned forward intently, his grey eyes glittering, and asked, "But are *you* done?"

"The knitting is done, but the project is not done, and neither am I," I said.

"Closure. It's the Sixth Principle of Gestalt Theory," he said. "I'll give you an example. What is the logo of the World Wildlife Federation?"

"That's easy, it's a panda," I replied.

"No, it's not. It's just blobs of black paint. Your mind connects the black blobs and interprets them as a panda. That's closure—when you connect the dots and make meaning out of them."

"I like that interpretation of closure as connection very much," I said. "I was feeling sad about the end of the project. I couldn't even bring myself to type the words *Closing Reception*."

"You were thinking of closure as finality, as death. But that's not what this kind of closure entails. Your closure will result in other people's openings," he said, and as I thanked him he made a little bow and left the gathering. He returned later without the pheasant feathers in his cap and I could detect none of his previous mystery that bordered on divinity. He had given me a profound gift, a new way of seeing the work that I must do to bring this project to completion. It is about making connections, distilling the meaning of this life-changing experience into words and images and placing it in a new context for people to encounter. I don't know yet what that will look like—whether a book, photographs or some kind of museum installation. But one thing I trust is that as I share this experience with others, it will spawn new ideas, artworks and social experiments for the increased well-being of our communities.

# All is Full of Love

August 1, 2015

We set up camp on Tom's front lawn, across from the bench. I had no idea how many people to expect, so my dear friends and Rob helped me put out 24 chairs, two blankets on the grass, and two tables for the potluck. Guests started arriving around 6 p.m., and I was suddenly surrounded by hugging, smiling friends, family, neighbors and their dogs including B.J. and Freddie. My nephew even showed up wearing a bright blue shirt in honor of the knit line.

At around 7 p.m. I climbed onto the ice chest to get everyone's attention.

"Thank you for these transformative years in your neighborhood," I said. "Tonight you are going to unwind the line instead of me because you are the Art."

Everyone began clapping spontaneously. I demonstrated how to unwind the line, and then passed the hose reel off to the first volunteer. The neighbors, including children and dogs, as well as my friends and family, grabbed onto the blue rope behind the hose reel and we began walking the half mile together down to the dock. It was as if the line had sprung to life and was flowing down the street, connecting us all. At first I walked holding on to the knit line, later I held the leash of my neighbor's dog, and watched in awe as the moment I had dreamt of for so long unfolded before my eyes better than anything I had imagined.

Rob did traffic control duties, stopping cars on busy 11th Street until we all crossed in safety while my dad kept an eye on the tension of the line. As we passed the fancy condos near the bay, a group of people on the third floor balcony let out a loud cheer.

Soon we had made it down to the boardwalk, neighbors taking turns unwinding the hose reel as we went.

I turned to Rob and invited him to put the end of the rope in the water with me, but he insisted, "You did the work. This is your moment."

I gently untied the end of the line from the hose reel and dropped it into the bay where it lay floating on the water like a limp blue worm. Sort of anticlimactic, I thought. Suddenly, the dock rocked and we heard a huge splash. My dad had stripped to his shorts and was swimming vigorously, pulling the line with him. He swam into the path of dancing light made by the setting sun, while I called to him, "There's more! There's more!" I had way overshot the distance with my knitting, but it felt abundant and right. Someone started yelling, hip hip hooray, and we all joined in, Hip hip hooray, HIP HIP HOORAY until my dad had swum the line out a good 50 feet from the end of the floating dock. We started laughing and applauding so vigorously that the floating dock began lurching precariously with all our bodies on it. For a second, I imagined the dock coming untethered and floating away with us like penguins on an iceberg—and me having foregone the expensive event insurance and permitting. Thankfully, everyone made it safely off the dock. As we slowly made our way up the steep hill, taking turns winding the hose reel back up, Rob kissed my cheek and we walked hand in hand together, our hearts brimming.

Then Rob got his turn with the hose reel, and sprinted uphill with it the rest of the way. When we arrived back to the bench at the top of the hill, we had all worked up a great appetite, and began filling our plates from the table that overflowed with fresh berries, watermelon, figs, salad, tamales, casseroles, pie and chocolate cake.

One of the neighbors, Premila, who had barely interacted with me over the years said how inspiring it was to watch me knit. "Everyone has to find their own path of unfolding but that I hope to find a similar project to undertake," she said.

"Stay open and let the inspiration find you," I counseled. "When I started the project, I had no idea that this would come of it."

A man in a straw hat said his pastor had worked my knitting project into a sermon so he had decided to come this evening and experience it for himself. (Another connection made. The older gentleman who had watched me unwind the line to the water on July 16 was pastor of the church where Cynthia and Pete attend.)

We ate until we were stuffed, lingering in the golden glow of each other's faces as the setting sun turned the sky a brilliant shade of pink, filling me with a longing sweeter than I could ever hold.

# KNITTING LOG

**May 1 – October 31, 2012**
Knit 104 days
Missed 49 days


**July 1, 2013-November 2, 2013**
Knit 125 days
Missed 0 days


**May 1, 2014-October 28, 2014**
Knit 174 days
Missed 7 days


**May 1, 2015-July 16, 2015**
Knit 75 days
missed 2 days

---

**TOTAL: 478 hours of knitting at the bench***


*This tally does not include the extra hours that I knit in
addition to my one hour a day minimum.

# ACKNOWLEDGMENTS

Family, friends and neighbors, thank you for making the knitting project what it is. Miles, thank you for reading my book three times and believing in me. Your friendship means the world. Dad, thanks for proofreading and formatting my book. The thought of printing this book before your interventions is downright terrifying! Elizabeth, thank you for taking *Skein* seriously and making it stronger through your feedback. You are a dear friend. My faithful blog readers (including the Luminous Awareness Group), thanks for making the journey with me. I am indebted to Brendan and Adam at Village Books for helping me navigate the world of indie publishing. Vanessa, thank you for letting me turn a magic moment on the bench into the cover of *Skein*! Judy, heartfelt thanks for your wonderful design sense, encouragement and flexibility. Janelle, you captured the final moments of "For Longing" with your stunning photographs. Here's to many more kombucha sessions. Cheryl, you gave me the courage to write my first book. Thank you for the wonderful photoshoot!

Grandpa, thank you for your steadfast love. Dear friends of the heart, I love you. Tim, interning with you was a turning point for me as an artist. Thank you for showing me the nobility of all, especially people with disabilities. Malissa and Peter, my teachers, a profound bow to you. Thank you, fabulous art students! Sr. Celeste, deep gratitude for your longstanding friendship, creativity and wisdom born of experience. Sharron, great gratitude for your faith in me, countless independent studies and office visits, and the gift of being your TA.

Sherrie, you are an incredible life coach. Thank you for helping launch me as an artist. Lynne, I am indebted to you for your healing gifts. My friends at Our Lady of the Redwoods, I will always think of you as my second family. Great gratitude for the profound kindness of friends from Sacred Heart and Assumption. Linda, here's to many more "Allelujahs!" Thank you for your attentive listening.

John, I'm still moved by your generosity. Zack, thank you for starting me on my path. Presence is grace! Herb, you make me proud to be a Canadian.

Renee, thanks for giving the hose reel its debut at Social Fabric. Elli and Lauren, thank you for being Finals Week Fairy Godmothers with me. Here's to many more collaborations! Shannon and Summer, thanks for putting your incredible talents to work on the Poem Booth Project! Long/Cockcroft/McDaniel Family, thank you for your hospitality and love.

Wow, so many people to thank and this is only a small beginning.

Thank you Love.

# Book Study Guide

1.  At the start of her project, Christen is not sure if her work is art or a yarnbombing project gone awry. What do you think?

2.  The word 'stripped' comes up several times in this book. How does Christen's use of the word shift by the book's end?

3.  In her chapter, "Missing the Bus," Mattix writes about the painful experience of coming close to realizing her dream which she loses through her carelessness. Have you ever had a similar experience of loss or disappointment? How did you respond?

4.  Resistance is fertile. How have you experienced resistance to becoming your best self? What purpose does resistance serve in your life?

5.  On July 10, 2014, Mattix talks about two very different parts of her personality: "The Ardent Lover" and "The Dutiful Daughter." Name a few parts of your psyche. How do you make space for them? Which parts are dominant? Which are more passive or shy?

6.  Mattix names several strategies for meeting her neighbors. What strategies have worked for you?

7.  Have you ever followed up on a wacky whim? What happened?

8.  Mattix describes her growing intimacy with place in the years she spends at the bench. When and where have you experienced an intimate connection to place? How has that place changed over the years?

9.  Throughout this book, Mattix records many conversations. Is there one in particular that resonates with you? Why?

10. Commitments can be scary. Like Christen, have you ever made a commitment and then wondered at your naïveté? Are you grateful for your naïveté or do you regret it? What keeps you committed? How do you renew your commitment?

11. Your closure will result in other's openings. What has opened in you as a result of reading *Skein*?

12. What are some of the hurdles that Mattix must overcome on her journey towards becoming an artist? What are some hurdles you have overcome on your journey to becoming your true self?

13. A thread that runs through this story is an acceptance of reality as it is. How is that acceptance revealed?

14. In Chapter 27 *Comfort*, Christen writes of our need to create spaces for vulnerable, face-to-face exchanges. Where do those spaces currently exist in your community? How might you create more or better opportunities for authentic connection?

15. One of the major themes of the book is slowing down to savor the present moment. What practices do you use to bring you into the present moment?

16. Christen tries on monastic life before reclaiming her identity as an artist. Have you ever tried on a lifestyle or identity that was totally different than what you were doing? What did you learn from it?

17. "Let me live before I die!" Christen exclaims. When

have you felt radiantly alive? When have you realized that you were sleepwalking through life? What would make you feel more alive, more of the time?

18. A sense of absurdity and mystery runs through the book. Are you satisfied with how Christen makes peace with it? How did you deal with an incomprehensible event in your life?

19. In "Void and Fullness", Christen writes about pain or emptiness that has been healed or fulfilled over time. Can you point to experiences of wounding or loss that have been transformed in your life and the lives of those you love?

Photo by Cheryl Stritzel McCarthy

**Christen Mattix** is a community-based writer and artist living in Bellingham. She received an MFA from the San Francisco Art Institute in Painting and a BFA in Drawing from Western Washington University. Christen's poems have been published in *Psalter & Lyre* and *Clover, A Literary Rag*. Her visual art has been shown at The Whatcom Museum, SAM Gallery and more. *Skein* is Christen's first book.

**christenmattix.com**

# PERMISSIONS